Technology, Education—Connections
The TEC Series

Series Editor: Marcia C. Linn.
Advisory Board: Robert Bjork, Chris Dede, BatSheva Eylon,
Carol Lee, Jim Minstrell, Mitch Resnick.

Data-Driven School Improvement:
Linking Data and Learning
ELLEN B. MANDINACH AND MARGARET HONEY, EDITORS

Electric Worlds in the Classroom:
Teaching and Learning with Role-Based Computer Games
BRIAN M. SLATOR AND ASSOCIATES

Meaningful Learning Using Technology:
What Educators Need to Know and Do
ELIZABETH A. ASHBURN AND ROBERT E. FLODEN, EDITORS

Using Technology Wisely:
The Keys to Success in Schools
HAROLD WENGLINSKY

Data-Driven School Improvement

LINKING DATA AND LEARNING

EDITED BY

Ellen B. Mandinach
Margaret Honey

Developed in association with the
Center for Children and Technology,
Education Development Center, Inc.

Teachers College
Columbia University
New York and London

Published by Teachers College Press, 1234 Amsterdam Avenue, NewYork, NY 10027

Copyright © 2008 by Teachers College, Columbia University

Library of Congress Cataloging-in-Publication Data

Data-driven school improvement : Linking data and learning / edited by Ellen B. Mandinach and Margaret Honey ; developed in association with the Center for Children and Technology, Education Development Center, Inc.
    p. cm. — (Technology, education-connections, the TEC series)
    Includes bibliographical references and index.
    ISBN 978-0-8077-4856-5 (pbk. : alk. paper)
    1. Education—United States—Data processing—Congresses. 2. Educational tests and measurements—United States—Congresses. 3. School improvement programs—United States—Congresses. 4. School management and organization—United States—Decision making—Congresses. I. Mandinach, Ellen Beth. II. Honey, Margaret. III. Center for Children and Technology (Education Development Center)
    LB1028.43.D367 2008
    371.2'070285—dc22

                                                                2007048833

ISBN 978-0-8077-4856-5 (paper)

Printed on acid-free paper
Manufactured in the United States of America

15   14   13   12   11   10   09   08   8   7   6   5   4   3   2   1

To our colleagues
at the Center for Children and Technology,
whose creativity and insight
are always a source of inspiration

Contents

CHAPTER 1

Data-Driven Decision Making:
An Introduction

Ellen B. Mandinach & Margaret Honey

In the wake of the accountability mandates that are an integral part of the No Child Left Behind Act of 2001 (NCLB), not only are school districts being held accountable for improving the academic performance of all students, but educators are being asked to use assessment data to guide a wide array of decision making. The assumption is that by looking at test results over time, school leaders can determine how and where to invest resources to improve performance, and teachers can target instructional practices to meet the needs of each and every student. Such "data-driven" practices have captured the imagination of the education policy community, prompting U.S. Secretary of Education Margaret Spellings (2005) to say:

> Information is the key to holding schools accountable for improved performance every year among every student group. Data is our best management tool. I often say that what gets measured, gets done. Once we know the contours of the problem, and who is affected, we can put forward a solution. Teachers can adjust lesson plans. Administrators can evaluate curricula. Data can inform decision making. Thanks to No Child Left Behind, we're no longer flying blind.

In fact, data-driven decision making is by no means new. Teachers have used a wide range of data sources—from in-class assignments to pop quizzes and homework—to make judgments about their students' understandings. Many of us reading this volume probably can recall experiences where we were "invited" to visit a teacher for extra help—invitations based on our teacher's analysis of where we needed to improve and strengthen our knowledge base. School administrators routinely have used data to make managerial and operational decisions, including how many teachers to hire, how many textbooks to purchase, and what changes to make to school facilities in response to population growth or other factors.

What is new, however, is that data are now inextricably coupled with accountability. As the Secretary states, "Information is the key to holding schools accountable . . . ," and it is this coupling that gives the phrase "data-driven decision making" a kind of urgency that did not exist prior to NCLB. But for data and assessments to be usable for either accountability or instruction, certain characteristics must align them to practice. Nichols and Berliner (2007) and Petrides (2006) distinguish between assessments *of* learning and assessments *for* learning, the former providing data on what and how much students have learned and the latter providing data to help improve teaching and student learning. As Stecher and Hamilton (2006) note, features of state assessments used for accountability limit the assessments' utility for data-driven decision making, thereby presenting a conflict of data use for accountability as opposed to for informing instructional practice. According to the Education Commission of the States (2000), data from assessments should have appropriate fit, utility, quality, validity, reliability, and feasibility for effective use. Ikemoto and Marsh (2007) also outline several factors that impact data-driven decision making, including accessibility, timeliness, perceived validity, staff capacity and support, and organizational leadership and culture.

Educators at all levels, from the schoolhouse to the state house, routinely are being asked to use data to inform practice. Teachers are expected to attend to both formative and summative measures, classroom-based and high-stakes assessments, and all manner of other data in between. Principals are required to deal with individual, classroom, and schoolwide data for instructional and administrative purposes. Superintendents and other central office administrators use data to inform decisions about resource allocation, and in some cases to evaluate teachers' job performance and allocate bonuses and incentive pay (Earl & Katz, 2006; Knapp, Copland, & Swinnerton, 2007). The stakes have become increasingly high as schools and districts strive to attain adequate yearly progress.

With increased accountability, practitioners are now expected to acquire the necessary skills and knowledge to be effective data users and decision makers. In the accountability-driven model of education, the need to use data will likely intensify in years to come. Thus there is growing interest in ensuring that educators are adequately supported to use data to bring about substantive and lasting improvements in student learning.

A number of changes are taking place to increase the effectiveness of data-driven decision making. Technology applications are making it possible to collect and examine a wide range of data sources with increased ease and efficiency (Bertfield & Merrill, chapter 11; Crawford, Schlager, Penuel, & Toyama, chapter 7; Hupert, Heinze, Gunn, & Stewart, chapter 8; Long, Rivas, Light, & Mandinach, chapter 12; Thorpe & Honey, chapter 9; Wayman, Conoly, Gasko, & Stringfield, chapter 10; Wayman, Stringfield,

& Yakimowski, 2004). Having tools that respond to users' needs is a first step toward effective data use. Another requirement is building educators' knowledge about the assessments from which the data derive (Confrey & Makar, 2005; Fullan, 2000; Long et al., chapter 12; Mandinach, Honey, Light, Heinze, & Rivas, 2005; Webb, 2002). As Moss, Girard, and Haniford (2006) note:

> Professionals working in different contexts have different decisions to make, different sources of evidence, different resources for interpreting the available evidence, and different administrative constraints on practice. Educational assessment should be able to support these professionals in developing interpretations, decisions, and actions that enhance students' learning. (p. 109)

Few educators receive formal training in the principles of assessment, data use, or statistics. The good news is that there are growing numbers of professional development programs and resources designed to build educators' understanding of different aspects of data-driven decision making (Bernhardt, 2003a, 2003b; Creighton, 2006; Education Commission of the States, 2000; Love, 2002; Love, Stiles, Mundry, & DiRanna, in press; Picciano, 2005) and a proliferation of books that provide guidance to administrators and teachers about data use (Boudett, City, & Murnane, 2005; Depka, 2006; Earl & Katz, 2006; Holcomb, 2004). Such programs represent promising steps in helping educators build additional capacity in the use of data, but few programs have yet to be rigorously tested to determine the relationship between data-informed practices and increased student learning.

The acquisition of technology tools that easily and efficiently support users' needs, a robust and cohesive technological infrastructure, and targeted professional development go a long way in establishing the use of data throughout a school system. In addition, there is the need to create a coherent, explicit vision of how data should and can be used. The vision, in conjunction with the technology and professional infrastructure, helps to create a culture in which data are fundamental, integrated, and expected components of practice.

Firestone and Louis (1999) explored the characteristics of schools as cultures. More recently, Firestone and Gonzalez (2007) examined the integration of data cultures into school cultures and school improvement processes. The authors distinguish between accountability cultures and organizational learning cultures. Accountability cultures take a short-term perspective and focus on test scores, whereas organizational learning cultures take a long-term perspective and emphasize the improvement of student learning. The two cultures are further distinguished by an accountability culture's focus on using data to identify problems and monitor compliance with mandates.

In contrast, organizational learning cultures use data to identify and diagnose problems, with the objective of improving instruction.

Data-driven decision making is receiving significant attention from the research, practice, development, and policy communities. Two special issues of educational journals recently have been devoted to data-driven decision making (Wayman, 2005, 2006). As noted above, professional development programs are proliferating. University-, school-, and industry-based developers are creating technology solutions to facilitate data-driven decision making by administrators and teachers (e.g., Grow Network, 2007; Wayman et al., 2004; Wireless Generation, 2007). Policymakers also recognize the growing importance of data-driven decision making. The Institute of Education Sciences in the U.S. Department of Education is devoting substantial resources to the creation of statewide, longitudinal data systems (Whitehurst, 2006). The Data Quality Campaign (2006a, 2006b; Berry, Fuller, & Reeves, 2007; Laird, 2006; L'Orange, 2007) has been created to provide support and resources to states as they work to develop their longitudinal data systems and outlines the 10 key elements needed for such systems (see also www.DataQualityCampaign.org). The U.S. Department of Education also has commissioned a study of data systems and decision making, as part of the National Technology Activities initiative, to examine the kinds of systems available to educators and their prevalence, support for such systems, usage patterns, and influences on instruction (Means & Padilla, 2006).

Our approach to understanding data-driven decision making has taken a somewhat different tack. In the fall of 2005, the EDC Center for Children and Technology (CCT) convened a 3-day conference, "Improving Achievement Through Linking Data and Learning," at the Wingspread Conference Center in Racine, Wisconsin. Our goal was to bring together stakeholders representing a variety of perspectives to explore how educators are using data and technology tools to make decisions that will lead to lasting improvements in student performance. Participants included researchers, policymakers, practitioners, vendors, and representatives from funding agencies. The National Science Foundation and the Spencer Foundation, in addition to the Johnson Foundation, which supports the Wingspread Conference Center, provided funding for the meeting.

Versions of all the chapters except one in this volume were prepared for the conference. The chapter by Abbott (chapter 14) is the only addition to this volume, a fitting keystone which provides a systemic state-management view, a perspective not represented at the meeting. Fundamental to the creation of a data culture is the recognition that school districts are complex, dynamic learning organizations that must be understood as a system (Abbott, chapter 14; Mandinach & Cline, 1994; Petrides, Nodine, Nguyen, Karaglani, & Gluck, 2005; Senge, Cambron-McCabe, Lucas, Smith, Dutton, & Kleiner, 2000), which means recognizing the interconnections among the system's components, its hierarchical structure, and the dynamic nature of change over time. The notion of systems in the creation of data cultures permeates several chapters (Hupert et al., chapter 8; Long et al., chapter 12; Mandinach, Honey, Light, & Brunner, chapter 2).

This volume is organized into five parts. The first part, "The Foundations for Data-Driven Decision Making," includes two chapters that provide foundational material on data-driven decision making and accountability. The chapter by Mandinach and colleagues presents a conceptual framework through which to view data-driven decision making. It describes how data are transformed into information and ultimately to usable knowledge, a framework based on a 3-year project sponsored by the National Science Foundation. The second chapter, by Confrey, provides a legal and historical foundation for the accountability movement and discusses how to achieve equity in educational assessment by ensuring fair testing.

The second part, "Data-Driven Decision Making and Change," focuses on how practitioners use data to promote changes designed to bring about improvements in students' learning. The first chapter in this part, by Carrigg and Kurabinski, describes how educators in New Jersey created literacy assessment teams to examine a variety of data to improve programs for students most in need. The second chapter describes how one small suburban district in New York uses data to create a data culture to address persistent achievement gap issues. This chapter, by King, the former superintendent, and Amon, an elementary school principal, presents a model of how informed and creative educators can effect change by using data to address misconceptions about pressing educational problems. The final chapter in this part, by Young, presents case studies of how two schools in California use data to inform practice, describing how grade-level teams and leadership impact data use and the creation of data cultures.

The third part, "Digital Resources: Technology to Facilitate Data-Driven Decision Making," examines how digital resources for data-driven decision making can be used to inform teaching in the classroom. The first chapter, by Crawford and colleagues, describes how technology can support teaching in data-rich environments by chronicling past, current, and future applications that can be implemented in classrooms and used by teachers to inform instruction. The second chapter, by Hupert and colleagues, examines the impact of using handheld computers to deliver, collect, and analyze early childhood literacy assessments. The chapter uses two different data sources to look systematically at questions of impact on teachers' teaching and student performance. The final chapter in this part, by Thorpe and Honey, describes an ongoing collaboration among New York's public television station Thirteen/WNET, the Grow Network, and CCT that links digital video clips to assessment information.

The fourth part, "Creating Data Cultures," describes how school districts have created data cultures through a variety of technology-based tools. The first chapter, by Wayman and colleagues, grounded in the work of Wayman and Stringfield on technology solutions for data-driven decision making (Stringfield, Wayman, & Yakimowski-Srebnick, 2005; Wayman et al., 2004), describes how the Corpus Christi, Texas, school district uses data for accountability purposes and the types of data systems that support data-driven inquiry. The next chapter, by Bertfield and Merrill, also examines data use in the Corpus Christi Independent School District and compares it with data use in the School District of Philadelphia, focusing on how information management systems were adopted in the two districts and helped to create data-using cultures. The third chapter, by Long and colleagues, chronicles the creation of a data culture in the Tucson Unified School District, stimulated by the development of their data warehouse and student information system. Using systems thinking as an analytical tool, it describes the components, variables, and issues of creating a data culture and outlines how data are used at various levels of the school district and how certain functionalities of the technology facilitate or impede data use. The final chapter in this part, by Moody and Dede, is based on research conducted in the Milwaukee Public Schools. It depicts some of the obstacles that inhibit the use of data and the creation of data cultures.

The final part, "Data-Driven Decision Making and Educational Reform," features a chapter on organizational change. The author, David Abbott, is the Deputy Commissioner and General Counsel for the Rhode Island Department of Education. This chapter, a thoughtful and thought-provoking treatise on educational reform, represents the state perspective on data-driven decision making and the necessary organizational infrastructure and systemic reform required to create effective data cultures.

This volume and the Wingspread Conference were made possible by the support of the National Science Foundation under REC 03356653, the Spencer Foundation, and the Johnson Foundation. We would like especially to thank Elmima Johnson, our program officer at the National Science Foundation; Paul Goren, vice president at the Spencer Foundation; and Carole Johnson, program officer for education at the Johnson Foundation. We would like to thank the advisory board (Jere Confrey, Susan Goldman, Jim Pellegrino, Bill Penuel, Sam Stringfield, and Jeff Wayman) for the National Science Foundation project, which strengthened our work, as well as some of the school-based professionals (Shazia Miller, Phyllis Chasser, Lisa Long, and Sherry King) without whom the work would not have progressed. We would like to thank Carol Shookhoff for her invaluable editorial work on the book, which helped to make this a stronger volume. We also would like to thank Louisa Anderson, who helped to organize the conference; Laura Bryant for all her assistance to keep the project functioning, as well as her never ending support; Chad Fasca for his editorial assistance; Laura Sanderson for all her support and help throughout the project; and project staff contributors (Cornelia Brunner, Cricket Heinze, Daniel Light, Hannah Nudell, and Luz Rivas). We would like to acknowledge Brian Ellerbeck at Teachers College Press for his interest in these papers, and his recognition of the timeliness of data-driven decision making as an increasingly important issue in education today. Ellen Mandinach would like to acknowledge and thank her new affiliation, the CNA Corporation, for its support during the final stages of the book's development, and Eli Gruber for all his love, support, understanding, and patience. Margaret Honey would like to acknowledge her new affiliation, Wireless Generation. Finally, we would like to acknowledge all the educators in our projects and beyond who work to make sense of the data they encounter daily in their professional practices. These individuals are faced with the daunting challenge of transforming data into usable knowledge to inform the work they do with their students day in and day out. They are the true pioneers.

REFERENCES

Bernhardt, V. L. (2003a). *Data analysis for continuous school improvement* (2nd ed.). Larchmont, NY: Eye On Education.

Bernhardt, V. L. (2003b). *Using data to improve student learning in elementary schools*. Larchmont, NY: Eye On Education.

Berry, B., Fuller, E., & Reeves, C. (2007, October). *Linking teacher and student data to improve teacher and teaching quality*. Austin, TX: Data Quality Campaign.

Boudett, K. P., City, E. A., & Murnane, R. J. (Eds.). (2005). *Data wise: A step-by-step guide to using assessment results to improve teaching and learning*. Cambridge, MA: Harvard Education Press.

Confrey, J., & Makar, K. M. (2005). Critiquing and improving the use of data from high-stakes tests with the aid of dynamic statistics software. In C. Dede, J. P. Honan, & L. C. Peters (Eds.), *Scaling up success: Lessons learned from technology-based educational improvement* (pp. 198–226). San Francisco: Jossey-Bass.

Creighton, T. B. (2006). *Schools and data: The educator's guide for using data to improve decision making* (2nd ed.). Thousand Oaks, CA: Corwin Press.

Data Quality Campaign. (2006a, October). *Creating longitudinal data systems: Lessons learned by leading states*. Austin, TX: Author.

Data Quality Campaign. (2006b). *Creating longitudinal data systems: Using data to improve student achievement*. Austin, TX: Author.

Depka, E. (2006). *The data guidebook for teachers and leaders: Tools for continuous improvement*. Thousand Oaks, CA: Corwin Press.

Earl, L. A., & Katz, S. (2006). *Leading schools in a data-rich world: Harnessing data for school improvement*. Thousand Oaks, CA: Corwin Press.

Education Commission of the States. (2000). *Informing practices & improving results with data-driven decisions*. Denver, CO: Author. Retrieved April 19, 2007, from http://www.ecs.org/clearinghouse/31/12/3112.htm

Firestone, W. A., & Gonzalez, R. A. (2007). Culture and processes affecting data use in school districts. In P. A. Moss (Ed.), *Evidence and decision making: The 106th yearbook of the National Society for the Study of Education, Part I* (pp. 132–154). Malden, MA: Blackwell.

Firestone, W. A., & Louis, K. S. (1999). Schools as cultures. In J. Murphy & K. S. Louis (Eds.), *Handbook of research on educational administration* (2nd ed., pp. 297–323). San Francisco: Jossey-Bass.

Fullan, M. (2000). The three stories of education reform. *Phi Delta Kappan, 81*(8), 581–584.

Grow Network. (2007). *More about Grow*. Retrieved February 27, 2007, from http://info.grow.net/grow.html

Holcomb, E. L. (2004). *Getting excited about data: Combining people, passion, and proof to maximize student achievement* (2nd ed.). Thousand Oaks, CA: Corwin Press.

Ikemoto, G. S., & Marsh, J. A. (2007). Cutting through the "data driven" mantra: Different conceptions of data-driven decision-making. In P. A. Moss (Ed.), *Evidence and decision making: The 106th yearbook of the National Society for the Study of Education, Part I* (pp. 105–131). Malden, MA: Blackwell.

Knapp, M. S., Copland, M. A., & Swinnerton, J. A. (2007). Understanding the promise and dynamics of data-informed leadership. In P. A. Moss (Ed.), *Evidence and decision making: The 106th yearbook of the National Society for the Study of Education, Part I*. Malden, MA: Blackwell.

Laird, E. (2006, September). *Data use drives school and district improvement*. Austin, TX: Data Quality Campaign.

L'Orange, H. P. (2007, January). *P–16 data systems: An alignment status report*. Austin, TX: Data Quality Campaign.

Love, N. (2002). *Using data/getting results: A practical guide for school improvement in mathematics and science*. Norwood, MA: Christopher-Gordon.

Love, N., Stiles, K. E., Mundry, S., & DiRanna, K. (in press). *A data coach's guide to closing achievement gaps: Unleashing the power of collaborative inquiry*. Thousand Oaks, CA: Corwin Press.

Mandinach, E. B., & Cline, H. F. (1994). *Classroom dynamics: Implementing a technology based learning environment*. Hillsdale, NJ: Erlbaum.

Mandinach, E. B., Honey, M., Light, D., Heinze, J., & Rivas, L. (2005, November–December). *Technology-based tools that facilitate data-driven instructional decision making*. Paper presented at the ICCE Conference, Singapore.

Means, B., & Padilla, C. (2006). *Study of education data systems and decision making*. Menlo Park, CA: SRI International.

Moss, P. A., Girard, B. J., & Haniford, L. C. (2006). Validity in educational assessment. *Review of Research in Education, 30*(1), 109–162.

Nichols, S. L., & Berliner, D. C. (2007). *Collateral damage: How high-stakes testing corrupts America's schools*. Cambridge, MA: Harvard Education Press.

No Child Left Behind Act of 2001. (2001). Retrieved January 30, 2002, from http://www.nclb.gov

Petrides, L. A. (2006, April). Using data to improve instruction. *THE Journal*. Retrieved April 9, 2007, from http://thejournal.com/articles/18239

Petrides, L. A., Nodine, T., Nguyen, L., Karaglani, A., & Gluck, R. (2005). *Anatomy of school system improvement: Performance-driven practices in urban school districts*. Half Moon Bay, CA: Institute for the Study of Knowledge Management in Education.

Picciano, A. G. (2005). *Data-driven decision making for effective school leaders*. Upper Saddle River, NJ: Prentice Hall.

Senge, P., Cambron-McCabe, N., Lucas, T., Smith, B., Dutton, J., & Kleiner, A. (2000). *Schools that learn*. New York: Doubleday.

Spellings, M. A. (2005, June 14). *Seeing the data, meeting the challenge*. Speech given at the Indiana High School Summit: Redesigning Indiana's High Schools, Indianapolis. Retrieved April 18, 2007, from http://www.ed.gov/news/speeches/2005/06/06142005.html

Stecher, B. M., & Hamilton, L. S. (2006). *Using test-score data in the classroom* (WR-375-EDU). Santa Monica, CA: RAND Education.

Stringfield, S., Wayman, J. C., & Yakimowski-Srebnick, M. E. (2005). Scaling up data use in classrooms, schools, and districts. In C. Dede, J. P. Honan, & L. C. Peters (Eds.), *Scaling up success: Lessons learned from technology-based educational improvement* (pp. 133–152). San Francisco: Jossey-Bass.

Wayman, J. C. (Ed.). (2005). [Special issue]. *Journal of Education for Students Placed at Risk, 10*(3).

Wayman, J. C. (Ed.) (2006). Data use for school improvement [Special issue]. *American Journal of Education, 112*(4).

Wayman, J. C., Stringfield, S., & Yakimowski, M. (2004). *Software enabling school improvement through analysis of student data* (CRESPAR Tech. Rep. No. 67). Baltimore: Johns Hopkins University. Retrieved on December 1, 2006, from http://www.csos.jhu.edu/crespar/techReports/Report67.pdf

Webb, N. (2002, April). *Assessment literacy in a standards-based urban education setting*. Paper presented at the annual meeting of the American Educational Research Association, New Orleans.

Whitehurst, G. J. (2006, March). *State and national activities: Current status and future directions*. Speech given at the meeting, Improving Educational Outcomes: Why Longitudinal Data Systems Are Necessary. Washington, DC.

Wireless Generation. (2007). *Solutions overview*. Retrieved February 27, 2007, from http://info.grow.net/grow.html

PART I

The Foundations for Data-Driven Decision Making

CHAPTER 2

A Conceptual Framework
for Data-Driven Decision Making

Ellen B. Mandinach, Margaret Honey,
Daniel Light & Cornelia Brunner

This chapter builds on a project sponsored by the National Science Foundation (NSF) to explore data-driven decision making to help understand the process of creating data cultures in educational institutions (Mandinach, Honey, Light, Heinze, & Nudell, 2005; Mandinach, Honey, Light, Heinze, & Rivas, 2005). An outgrowth of this work and the work of other projects from the EDC Center for Children and Technology (CCT) as well as that of others in this volume, including the project advisory board, has been the development of a conceptual framework for data-driven decision making. One of the goals in this project has been to use the data we have collected in six sites across the country to develop and refine our conceptual model. We present our model, couched in the context of data-driven decision making in classrooms, schools, and districts. There is no question that state and federal mandates also influence decision making, as do many other variables. To that end, the Institute of Education Sciences in the U.S. Department of Education is stimulating the use of data-driven decision making at the state level with its development program for longitudinal data systems (Whitehurst, 2006).

The objective of this chapter is to capture the dynamic, interactive nature and the complexities of how schools make decisions, across all levels of the districts, across various stakeholders, given the many influences and the contextual surrounds, using systems thinking as an analytical perspective (Mandinach, 2005; Mandinach & Cline, 1994). The conceptual model is grounded in the principles of systems thinking. For the purposes of this chapter, the conceptual model focuses solely on the classroom, school, and district levels of decision making, recognizing how the affordances of technology-based tools can facilitate, support, and enable decisions across stakeholders.

We first explore the literature that has helped to inform our thinking about the conceptual model of data-driven decision making. We then present our model, focusing on its various components—the necessary skills and decision feedback loop, the organizational levels within a school district, and the characteristics of the technology-based tools that impact decision making.

THE NEED FOR EFFECTIVE DATA-DRIVEN PRACTICES

Research on Systemic Reform and Data Systems

One consequence of the standards and accountability movement is that district and school administrators are being asked to think very differently about educational decision making and to use data to inform everything from resource allocation to instructional practice. O'Day (2002) notes the complexity of the mechanisms by which accountability is used in school improvement. Researchers (Mitchell, Lee, & Herman, 2000) at the UCLA Center for Research on Evaluation, Standards, and Student Testing (CRESST) note:

> Data-based decision making and use of data for continuous improvement are the operating concepts of the day. School leaders are expected to chart the effectiveness of their strategies and use complex and often conflicting state, district, and local assessments to monitor and assure progress. These new expectations, that schools monitor their efforts to enable all students to achieve, assume that school leaders and teachers are ready and able to use data to understand where students are academically and why, and to establish improvement plans that are targeted, responsive, and flexible. (p. 22)

As other CRESST researchers note, "Despite both the mandates and the rhetoric, schools are woefully underprepared to engage in such inquiry. The practice of applying large-scale data to classroom practice is virtually nonexistent" (Herman & Gribbons, 2001, p. 1).

The literature on systemic efforts to improve schools has been focused on the role of data in developing, guiding, and sustaining organizational change that leads to improvements in student learning (Massell, 1998). Initial interest was on data for accountability (Fullan & Stiegelbauer, 1991; Schmoker, 1996), but the debate around measurement-driven instruction in the 1980s was an early attempt to use assessment data to improve instructional decision making (Popham, Cruse, Rankin, Sandifer, & Williams, 1985; Shepard, 1991). As is often the case, however, human desires far outpaced actual capabilities. For assessment data to be useful for instructional planning, they need to be current, accurate, and in the hands of knowledgeable decision makers at the appropriate levels. Yet school systems rarely have had the capacity to process and disseminate data in an efficient and timely manner (Ackley, 2001; Thorn, 2002).

Recently, the education community has again become interested in data-driven instructional decision making, largely because growing numbers of school systems and states are improving their capacity to process and disseminate data (Ackley, 2001; Thorn, 2002). This trend has been further accelerated by the requirements of NCLB (2001) to use data to improve school performance (Hamilton, Stecher, & Klein, 2002) and by the initiative from the Institute of Education Sciences to fund and create statewide longitudinal data systems (Whitehurst, 2006). Further, advances in school networking infrastructures and online data warehousing have made it feasible to create systems that use assessment data to support decision making, by providing timely information and presentation and analysis tools to educators across multiple levels of the system.

The research on data systems and tools to support instructional decisions is a young, emerging field. There is a growing body of literature on data-driven decision making and on the use of such data systems, tools, and warehouses to support decision-making processes in schools. Two special issues of journals were published recently on and devoted to the topic (Wayman, 2005b, 2006).

Stringfield, Wayman, and Yakimowski (2004) and Wayman, Stringfield, and Yakimowski-Srebnick (2005) describe, classify, and evaluate these emerging tools, while Hamilton and colleagues (2002) offer a brief review of the literature on using test-based accountability data for decision making. As of yet, there is little evaluation across cases of these data tools in application. A number of initiatives are being implemented across the country for which research is in various stages of development and maturity. These projects include the Quality School Portfolio (QSP) developed at CRESST (Mitchell & Lee, 1998), IBM's Reinventing Education initiative in Broward County, Florida (Spielvogel, Brunner, Pasnik, Keane, Friedman, Jeffers, John, & Hermos, 2001), and the work of the Texas Education Agency and South Carolina Department of Education (Spielvogel & Pasnik, 1999). Work has been conducted on data-driven tools in New York (Brunner, Fasca, Heinze, Honey, Light, Mandinach, & Wexler, 2005; Honey, 2001; Honey, Brunner, Light, Kim, McDermott, Heinze, Breiter, & Mandinach, 2002), Minneapolis (Heistad & Spicuzza, 2003), Boston (Murnane, Sharkey, & Boudett, 2005; Sharkey & Murnane, 2003), Milwaukee (Mason, 2001, 2002; Moody & Dede, chapter 13; Thorn, 2002; Webb, 2002), and other locations (Chen, Heritage, & Lee, 2005; Lachat & Smith, 2005; Streifer & Schumann, 2005; Wayman, 2005a).

Wayman and colleagues (2004) provide one of the first comprehensive reviews of the tools available, identifying some of the technical and usability issues districts face when selecting a data application to support instructional planning. Technical challenges include data storage, data entry, analysis, and presentation. Other challenges include the quality and interpretation of data, and the relationship between data and instructional practices (Cromey, 2000). Work done on the QSP in Milwaukee indicates that educators are hesitant to base decisions that affect students on data they do not believe are entirely reliable and accurate (Choppin, 2002). Alignment of data for instructional purposes is another issue. The standardized test data provided in many of these data systems are often not originally intended for diagnostic or instructional purposes (Popham, 1999; Schmoker, 2000). Educators' knowledge and training in the use of data are also confounding factors. While teachers and administrators need not be experts in psychometrics, they must have some level of assessment literacy (Webb, 2002) and data literacy (Mandinach, Rivas, Light, & Heinze, 2006). Most educators, however, are trained in neither testing nor measurement, and therefore assessment literacy is a major concern (Popham, 1999). Data literacy is also a growing concern. Educators generally have not received formal training in fundamental statistical principles and the concepts that underlie the interrogation of data.

While the debate about the merits of using state-mandated testing data for diagnostic purposes continues, responding to accountability requirements remains a daily challenge that schools and districts must address (Pellegrino, Chudowsky, & Glaser, 2001; Stiggins, 2002). Although high-stakes accountability mandates are not new, the NCLB legislation places public schools under intensified external scrutiny that has real consequences (Fullan, 2000; Nichols & Berliner, 2007). Not only are failing schools identified, but parents are given the option of removing their children from such schools or using school resources to hire tutors and other forms of educational support. District and school administrators are struggling to respond to these heightened expectations, which by design call for different thinking about the potential of accountability data to inform improvements in teaching and learning. It is clear that NCLB is requiring schools to give new weight to accountability information and to develop intervention strategies that can target the children most in need. Yet it is important to distinguish between assessment *for* learning and assessment *of* learning (Nichols & Berliner, 2007; Petrides, 2006). The former is more aligned with accountability, noting what and how students learn, in contrast to the latter, which is more aligned with instruction and improvement of learning. These assessments and their resulting data ostensibly serve different purposes and yield different forms of data-driven decision making. Further, different technology-based applications tend to support and privilege particular perspectives. The growing interest in data-driven decision-making tools is no doubt a direct response to these mounting pressures (Stringfield et al., 2005).

Research on the Factors Influencing Data Use

The development and implementation of data-driven, decision-making tools are only two of the necessary steps toward effective use of data by educators. Several barriers have been identified (Lim, 2003), including access issues, technical expertise, and training (Choppin, 2002; Cromey, 2000; Mason, 2002; Wayman, 2005a). The lack of training for teachers in how to use data to improve student performance has posed a long-term problem (Schafer & Lissitz, 1987; Wise, Lukin, & Roos, 1991). It is rare to find schools in which teachers routinely engage in thinking critically about the relationship between instructional practices and student outcomes (Confrey & Makar, 2005; Hammerman & Rubin, 2002; Kearns & Harvey, 2000). Further, we know very little about the cognitive strategies teachers employ to transform data into usable knowledge and practice (Cizek, 2001; Herman & Gribbons, 2001). And, as noted earlier, the types of data-driven, decision-making tools proliferating in schools do not provide the kind of detailed data on individual students that could help teachers gather systematic evidence about the effectiveness of particular instructional strategies.

Recent research conducted at CCT has found that school administrators use high-stakes test data to understand general patterns of performance, identifying class-, grade-, and schoolwide strengths and weaknesses, as a basis for allocating resources and planning professional development and other kinds of targeted intervention activities (e.g., after-school remediation, summer school attendance, etc.). Teachers, in contrast, are wary of using any single data source, such as high-stakes test data, to make decisions about their students' strengths and weaknesses. Their preference is to engage multiple sources of data—homework assignments, in-class tests, classroom performances, as well as impressionistic, anecdotal, and experiential information—to inform their thinking about student learning (Brunner et al., 2005; Honey et al., 2002; Light, Wexler, & Heinze, 2004). While this approach to data yields a richer profile of individual student performance, it also has a downside. Our research and that of others (Confrey & Makar, 2002, 2005; Hammerman & Rubin, 2002, 2003) suggest that teachers are more inclined to examine factors that contribute to individual patterns of behavior and to think on a case-by-case basis than to look for patterns in data at different levels of aggregation, such as classroom-wide patterns. This kind of examination has a positive influence on teachers' ability to individualize instruction. It does, however, make it difficult to move beyond the micro level to the macro level to impact larger groups of students.

Helping all schools and students achieve, regardless of ethnic and socioeconomic background, requires that we identify and develop processes and practices that support teachers' deep and sustained examination of data in ways that are aligned to local instructional goals. Confrey and Makar (2005) and Hammerman and Rubin (2002, 2003) found that teachers need to develop fluency in the use of data. Confrey and Makar (2002) found that novice teachers tend to focus on data from individual students, mean scores, and passing rates, while ignoring distributions. The ability to examine a distribution as an aggregate, taking in the shape of the entire distribution rather than focusing on individual students, is seen as a critical skill. But while looking at an aggregate measure such as a mean gives a more representative view of the entire distribution, it risks ignoring how some poor student performances balance out good performances because the mean does not indicate variability. Confrey, Makar, and Kazak (2004) found that reporting only means, and the percentage passing high-stakes tests, can lead to stereotyping of disaggregated subgroups. Thus, there is a need for practitioners to understand the concepts of variation and distribution when examining data to be used to inform instructional practice. When people look at data that combine a number of different groups, they can miss differences among the groups. Understanding what constitutes a significant difference among groups and how to interpret interactions are also critical skills. It is important to define the groups carefully and then examine the distributions of the groups separately to discern potential differences. Understanding that there is normal variability in every process is yet another core skill. Small changes from one time to the next, such as those that occur when retaking the same test, can indicate nothing or something significant. The key is deciding when to pay attention to the differences. These are important skills, especially now, given the mandates of NCLB.

There is no question that data-driven decision making is a complex undertaking, even for the trained educator. As Secada (2001) notes, data should be used to inform educators' decisions, not to replace them, and this process requires time and effort. Educators must have specific uses in mind when examining data, and the decisions they make must be both strategic and timely. Fundamentally, this line of reasoning goes back to the basic definition of validity (Cronbach, 1976; Messick, 1989), which states that validity resides more in test score interpretation than in test construction. Extending beyond the more traditional psychometric definitions, consequential validity focuses on the potential impacts of decisions made from testing data. The hallmark of data fluency is understanding how data should be used, the interpretations that can be made from those data, and how such interpretations can be used to guide different types of decisions. For school personnel, a central component in this process is asking good questions about the data, analyzing the data accurately, and then applying the results appropriately (Mason, 2001).

The use of data in meaningful and actionable ways assumes at least some level of facility with and knowledge about assessment information. While teachers and administrators need not be experts in psychometrics, they must have some knowledge of general testing concepts, such as reliability and validity. Further, with the proliferation of accountability requirements from the local, state, and federal levels, there is a need for teachers and administrators to be conversant with and make use of the plethora of student assessment data. Fullan (2000) argues that teachers must become assessment literate, and that focusing on student work through assessment is a trait of a good school. According to Fullan and Stiegelbauer (1991), assessment literacy is a key step to improving student learning. Further, the appropriate individuals must be armed with the appropriate data. End users must recognize the power and limitations of data, ranging from summative to formative, standardized to informal, high-stakes to classroom-based, and annual to daily (Love, Stiles, Mundry, & DiRanna, in press). Even if districts have meaningful formative assessments, placing the data in coherent formats is still a major challenge (Ackley, 2001). Thus, the potential power in data-driven tools makes it all the more important to support users in collecting, analyzing, and interrogating data effectively.

CONCEPTUAL FRAMEWORK

In the course of the NSF project, we sought to understand the skills required of practitioners to transform data into actionable knowledge. Thus, we developed and refined a conceptual framework based on an iterative model of feedback among six skills hypothesized to be necessary for data-driven decision making. While describing the skills and strategies educators use, it became clear that we also needed to examine how different dimensions of data-driven technology tools support those strategies. It is our contention that the processes involved in transforming data into usable knowledge are closely aligned to, and informed, facilitated, or even impeded by, characteristics of the technology-based tools used for data-driven decision making.

The conceptual framework for data-driven decision making, founded on the notion of what it means for an educator to be data-driven, is depicted in Figure 2.1. We posit that individuals, regardless of where they are within a school system, have questions, issues, or problems for which data must be collected and examined to make informed decisions. This need crosses levels of the organization from the classroom to the school, and to the central administration. As mentioned above, the model presented here depicts decisions made within districts, focusing on the classroom, building, and district levels. No doubt many variables at the federal, state, and local levels can and will impact local decisions, but our intention here is to examine local decisions. The broader range of decisions is being explored through a systems-based evaluation methodology that examines how different external influences impact the implementation of data-driven decision making at the district level

Figure 2.1. Conceptual Framework for Data-Driven Decision Making

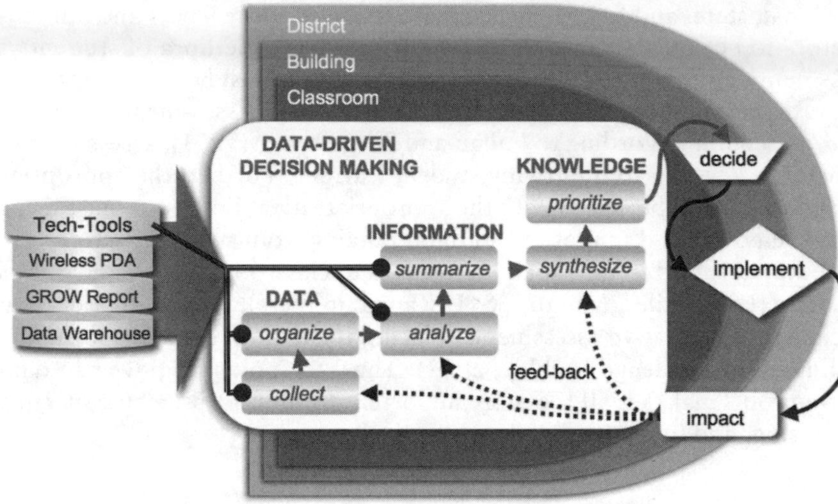

(see Long, Rivas, Light, & Mandinach, chapter 12, for an example of this framework).

The conceptual model presented here has evolved over time, informed by the work of colleagues, project advisory board members, and others. The model is informed also by data we have collected in the NSF project. Colleagues at CCT (Light et al., 2004) have examined organization and management theory in the use of data. In developing the conceptual framework for the use and transformation of data, we have drawn upon the work of Ackoff (1989), Drucker (1989), and a former CCT visiting scholar (Breiter, 2003). According to Ackoff (1989), data, information, and knowledge form a continuum in which data are transformed to information, and ultimately to knowledge that can be applied to make decisions. As Light and colleagues (2004) note:

- *Data* exist in a raw state. They do not have meaning in and of itself, and therefore, can exist in any form, usable or not. Whether or not data become information depends on the understanding of the person looking at the data.
- *Information* is data that is given meaning when connected to a context. It is data used to comprehend and organize our environment, unveiling an understanding of relations between data and context. Alone, however, it does not carry any implications for future action.

- *Knowledge* is the collection of information deemed useful, and eventually used to guide action. Knowledge is created through a sequential process. In relation to test information, the teacher's ability to see connections between students' scores on different item-skills analysis and classroom instruction, and then act on them, represents knowledge. (p. 3)

The continuum provides a logical progression from raw data to their transformation into usable knowledge.

Components of the Framework

The data-to-knowledge continuum is the foundation for the conceptual framework. It is grounded within the context of the classroom, the school, and the district, all of which use different data in different ways to make decisions. The role of the technology-based tools is to enable, support, and facilitate decision making by various stakeholders in different parts of the model.

DATA-DRIVEN DECISION-MAKING SKILLS. As seen in Figure 2.1, the data-to-knowledge continuum includes six skills or components that we have identified as crucial to the decision-making process. Two skills are aligned with each point along the continuum. At the data level, the two relevant skills are *collect* and *organize*; at the information level, *analyze* and *summarize*; and at the knowledge level, *synthesize* and *prioritize*.

A stakeholder, whether a classroom teacher, a principal, or a district administrator, is faced with an issue, a question, or a problem for which the *collection* of data could be helpful. The stakeholder must decide what data to collect; that is, decisions must be made about what will inform the issue. The individual then may decide to collect new data or interrogate existing data. For a classroom teacher, this might mean giving students an assignment or activity to highlight a particular learning problem. For a central administrator, it may mean drilling down into the district data warehouse or surveying parents to answer a particular question. Once the data have been collected, it is necessary to *organize* them in some systematic way to make sense of them. It is difficult, if not impossible, to extract meaning from raw data that have not been pulled together in some sensible manner. This organizational scheme enables the stakeholder then to convert the raw data into information from which meaning can be extracted.

The stakeholder takes the organizational scheme created from the raw data and *analyzes* those data for informational purposes. A teacher may analyze results from a classroom exercise. A principal may examine standardized test results across classes in a particular grade. A district administrator may analyze trends in performance for various cohorts of students to determine the likelihood of attaining adequate yearly progress (AYP). The scope of the analyses may be broad or constrained, depending on the type of inquiry and the role of the decision maker. Regardless of the depth and breadth, all accumulated information needs to be *summarized*. Educators are bombarded with information from all directions and many sources. It is therefore vital to have concise and targeted summaries of information that then can be transformed into usable knowledge, the final stage along the continuum. The summaries can be created by the end user or another stakeholder for the purpose of further transformation into knowledge.

To turn information into knowledge, the stakeholder must *synthesize* the available information. That is, the stakeholder attempts to concatenate or unify the amassed data or information into a usable entity. A teacher may pull together student portfolios to examine the work before deciding on a course of instruction. A principal or central administrator may examine a report that contains multiple sources of information on achievement before deciding how to allocate instructional resources. The final step is to *prioritize* the knowledge, which often requires judging the value of the accumulated information and knowledge; that is, determining the relative importance of the information and possible actionable solutions. Prioritizing allows decision makers to determine what is the most important, most pressing, most prudent, or most rational solution to a particular educational problem at a given time. A teacher may determine that it is more important first to remediate a student's literacy deficit before attempting to address other, less pressing learning issues. A principal may determine that it is more important to focus on one curriculum as opposed to another, based on teacher response and student performance. The superintendent may decide that the greatest potential for solving the minority achievement gap is to allocate resources disproportionately to the most needy schools.

The outcome of this six-step process, moving from data to information to knowledge, is a *decision*. The decision is then *implemented*, or in some instances may fail to be implemented for other external reasons, such as a lack of resources. The implementation results in some sort of outcome or *impact*. Depending on the impact, the decision maker may decide that he or she needs to return to one of the six steps, thereby creating a feedback loop. The stakeholder may need to collect more data, reanalyze the information, or resynthesize the knowledge. Because of the feedback loops, data-driven decision making is seen as an iterative process with data leading to a decision, implementation of that decision, determination of the impact, and perhaps the need to work through some or all of the six processes again.

LEVELS OF THE SCHOOL SYSTEM. The type of decisions and the form of data collected may differ depending on the particular stakeholder and the level at which the decision is being made. How the data are aligned across the levels of the district will influence the utility of the data. For example, the model of use for accountability will determine how the data factor into the decision-making process. That is, the data may be used for facilitation, for progress monitoring, or even for punitive purposes. There are likely to be different stakeholders at different levels. There also are likely to be different feedback loops (i.e., the iterations within the decision-making processes) for different stakeholders and at different levels of the school hierarchy. The feedback loops will depend on the implementation model and context of the data-driven decision making. Data that teachers need may differ from what a building or central administrator may need. The questions asked will differ. Although many questions and the utility of the data may be embedded within a particular level of the school district, interactions across the levels are likely. Building-level decisions will impact the classroom level, just as classroom-level decisions will impact the building level. District-level decisions will impact the building level and indirectly or directly affect what happens in the classroom. The model is one of dynamic interconnections among and between components of the system.

For example, the district administration may decide to introduce a new quarterly assessment for all grades to determine how students are doing in math or in reading. In this example of a top-down decision, issues impacting the decision might include the resources necessary to carry out such an assessment program, the potential information to be gained, personnel issues around who will develop the assessments and who will score them, and the like. The building personnel then have to carry out the decision. A principal or school curriculum person has to allocate time in the schedule for the administration and scoring of the assessments and determine how the resulting data will be used at the school level to inform instruction and perhaps other decisions. The classroom teachers have to implement the assessments, collect the data, and score the tests. It is then up to them to use those data to help remediate particular learning deficits for particular students. In this example, the closer to the data a stakeholder is, the more instructional validity the decisions will have due to proximity to the data and the ability to transform the data into information and then to actionable knowledge.

With cross-level decision making, top-down decisions will be more prevalent than bottom-up decisions. That is, classroom teachers probably will make fewer decisions that directly influence a decision made at the district level. There will, however, be many within-level decisions. No doubt the cultural surround and context that translate into rationales, needs, and purposes will determine who uses the data, how they are used, and the sorts of interactions across levels of the stakeholders. A shared and explicit vision for the use of data is vital to the creation of an effective data culture.

SALIENT CHARACTERISTICS OF TECHNOLOGY-BASED TOOLS. The potentials and added value of using technology to support, enable, and facilitate data-driven decision making are becoming increasingly clear (Wayman et al., 2004). Such tools that have the potential to support data mining that otherwise would be impossible are seen as enabling devices for good practice (Wayman, Conoly, Gasko, & Stringfield, chapter 10). But as with many innovations, when it comes to answering the questions, "Does technology work?" or "What is the impact of the technology?" the answer is always, "It depends."

One issue that we have debated is whether the data and the tools are separable. Some argue that the data are embedded within the tools and thus the two are inextricably linked and must be treated together. Others have argued that although the tools influence the data available or the data being sought influence the tools selected for use, they should be treated as independent. We posit that complex interactions are at play here, functioning in a multivariate world. Just as there are data by information by needs by value interactions, there also are person by data by tool by context interactions. These interactions relate to the context and values of a school district where decisions are made about the importance of particular kinds of data and the types of technology-based tools that will enable the interrogation of those data.

The affordances of the technology should facilitate the use of the tool and align with the type of data, the contextual surrounds, and the goals for data and tool use. Different characteristics, functions, and capacities of a tool will facilitate or impede its use. For example, if a tool is too labor-intensive, individuals are unlikely to use the application. This project and prior work at CCT (Light et al., 2004) have highlighted six functionalities that impact the usefulness of a tool and are key to the decision-making process: (1) accessibility, (2) length of the feedback loop, (3) comprehensibility, (4) flexibility, (5) alignment; and (6) links to instruction.

Accessibility means how easy the tool is to access and use. For example, one data warehouse we have examined has a difficult user interface. No matter how simple the inquiry, practitioners must ask a designated data person in the school to interrogate the data. For highly complex inquiries, they must ask a statistician in the research department for assistance.

Length of the feedback loop means the amount of time between when the data are collected and when the end user receives them in a meaningful form. Progress monitoring via handheld devices enables teachers to collect and analyze early childhood literacy or mathematics assessment data and immediately transform those data into actionable knowledge (see Hupert, Heinze, Gunn, & Stewart, chapter 8). These handhelds bridge the all-too-familiar abyss between assessment and instruction (Mandinach & Snow, 1999). Instruction and assessment become intertwined and instantaneous.

In contrast, when a standardized test is administered in the spring and the data are delivered in a reporting system to teachers in the autumn, the substantial delay in the feedback loop minimizes the utility of the data to inform instructional strategies for particular students (Brunner et al., 2005; Light et al., 2004; Mandinach, Honey, Light, Heinze, & Nudell, 2005). Such data often are referred to as being dead on arrival. The tighter the feedback loop provided by the application and the more recent the data, the more informative and instructionally valid the data are likely to be.

Comprehensibility refers to how easily the presentation of the data is understood or interpreted. Often many different presentation modes improve comprehensibility, such as the inclusion of graphics, tables, and the ability to aggregate the data in different ways. The handhelds provide multiple modes of presentation. Once data are downloaded to a website, teachers or administrators can view the data in a variety of ways, some graphic, some tabular, and with different levels of aggregation (i.e., by the individual student or by classroom level).

Similarly, *flexibility* refers to how easily a tool allows the user to manipulate the data. In terms of both comprehensibility and flexibility, take, for example, the two data warehouses the project has examined (Mandinach, Honey, Light, Heinze, & Nudell, 2005). In one instance, the data entered into the warehouse are presented at an individual-student level, with no provision for the end user to aggregate the data at the classroom, grade, or school levels. To aggregate at any level, the end user must ask the district's research and assessment department to make a special data run.[1] In contrast, the other warehouse has the flexibility to aggregate data at multiple levels, enabling end users to explore the data themselves. The greater the flexibility, the more comprehensible the data become for even the most novice user.

Alignment refers to how well the tool enables the alignment of the data to the objectives of the stakeholders, making the data useful, meaningful, and of high quality. Scope and accuracy are important factors here. The data must have the depth and breadth to be useful, all the while being vetted as accurate. Both data warehouses we examined contain the data deemed essential to the districts' goals: standardized achievement test scores that determine the districts' AYP status, as well as many more data sources that reflect local objectives.

The final tool characteristic is *links to instruction*. The data need to be connected to practice, the way the data from the handhelds can directly inform instruction. Some data from the warehouses, such as the quarterly writing and mathematics assessments, may be linked to instruction; other data, including some standardized achievement tests that are not fully aligned to standards and instruction, may be much farther removed from instruction.

Given these capacities and functions of tools, a key issue is whether the application enables effective interrogation of data that match the specified objectives of end users. New applications are being developed and used. What becomes clear is that the selection of a tool is a complex decision based on many factors. The characteristics of the tools will impact how the data are being examined, the types of questions that can be asked, and by whom. The tool also determines the type of data that can be examined and how the data are organized and transformed into information and knowledge. Conversely, the type of data sought determines the choice of tool that will support those data. The needs, values, and objectives of the users and the district play a major role in the selection process. Some tools provide access only to student data that are aligned with standards and instruction, while others are broader in scope and move well beyond student information management systems (see Wayman et al., 2004, for a comprehensive review of the possibilities).

Districts need a vision and plan for how data-driven decision making will be implemented and sustained, for what purposes and goals, and by whom. The selection of appropriate tools must align with those objectives. No single tool may meet all the goals. Take, for example, one of our project sites. Its district was using a particular application of interest, a test-reporting system. We soon learned that it also was using handhelds and developing its own data warehouse, that is, implementing a triangulation strategy of using different tools to meet different information needs.[2] One data warehouse site also adopted handhelds to provide immediate diagnostic information. For some districts a single tool will suffice. These decisions must be based on the objectives, needs, and resources of each site and its targeted users.

NEXT STEPS

The framework presented here elaborates on the data-driven skills and acknowledges the impact of the tool and its affordances on data-driven decision making, the outcomes of the decision-making process, the importance of feedback loops, and the differences among the levels of end users within a district.

Our goal has been to use this conceptual model as the foundation for understanding the systemic nature of data-driven decision making and the creation of data cultures within school and district settings (Mandinach, 2005; Mandinach & Cline, 1994; Senge, Cambron-McCabe, Lucas, Smith, Dutton, & Kleiner, 2000). The framework depicts the dynamic nature of data-driven decision making and the complex patterns of interactions among contextual variables, including the impact of the technology-based tools. Fundamental to the systems perspective is the idea of interrelationship, feedback, and context.

Taking the conceptual framework to the next step, we have constructed systems maps for each site to determine the relative importance of various components and influences as the districts have implemented the technology-based tools and data-driven decision making (Long et al., chapter 12; Mandinach et al., 2006). The systems-based framework recognizes and attempts to capture the dynamic and multivariate nature of phenomena and the hierarchical contextual surround that influences school districts as complex and evolving systems, just as the conceptual model presented here recognizes the interrelations among the components of data-driven decision making.

The systems-based framework extends the conceptual model beyond the school district to include the state and federal levels, acknowledging the importance of these influences and the need to examine the interconnections within and across levels. More important, the framework attempts to capture and model the many contextual variables and inputs that influence the way stakeholders at various levels make decisions, how these decisions occur within a data culture, and how the external factors influence internal implementation of data-driven decision making.

Data-driven decision making surely will be an important tool for educators in the years to come. The development of new technology-based applications for end users at all levels of educational institutions can only serve to promote and support effective data-driven decision making and the creation of data cultures. Understanding the processes by which data-driven decision making occurs and the factors that contribute to, facilitate, or impede the development of effective data cultures can only assist decision makers at all levels of the educational system.

NOTES

The research on which this chapter is based was funded by the National Science Foundation under Grant No. REC 03356653. Any opinions, findings, conclusions, and recommendations expressed in this material are those of the authors and do not necessarily reflect the views of the NSF. The authors would like to acknowledge the contributions of the staff and sites of the NSF evaluation framework project and other colleagues—Juliette Heinze, Hannah Nudell, and Luz Ruvas. The authors also would like to thank the anonymous reviewers, Hugh Cline, and Susanne Lajoie for their helpful comments.

1. Based on feedback from our research, the district has begun development to remediate this problem by allowing for easier aggregation of data across units of analysis.

2. This district ultimately discontinued the use of the test-reporting system because it failed to meet the district's data needs.

REFERENCES

Ackley, D. (2001). Data analysis demystified. *Leadership, 31*(2), 28–29, 37–38.

Ackoff, R. L. (1989). From data to wisdom. *Journal of Applied Systems Analysis, 16*, 3–9.

Breiter, A. (2003). *Information–knowledge–sense-making: A theoretical analysis from management/business literature.* Unpublished manuscript, University of Bremen, Institute for Information Management, Bremen, Germany.

Brunner, C., Fasca, C., Heinze, J., Honey, M., Light, D., Mandinach, E., & Wexler, D. (2005). Linking data and learning: The Grow Network study. *Journal of Education for Students Placed at Risk, 10*(3), 241–267.

Chen, E., Hermitage, M., & Lee, J. (2005). Identifying and monitoring students' learning needs with technology. *Journal of Education for Students Placed at Risk, 10*(3), 309–332.

Choppin, J. (2002, April). *Data use in practice: Examples from the school level.* Paper presented at the annual meeting of the American Educational Research Association, New Orleans.

Cizek, G. J. (2001). Conjectures on the rise and fall of standards setting: An introduction to context and practice. In G. J. Cizek (Ed.), *Setting performance standards: Concepts, methods, and perspectives* (pp. 3–18). Mahwah, NJ: Erlbaum.

Confrey, J., & Makar, K. (2002). Developing secondary teachers' statistical inquiry through immersion in high-stakes accountability data. In D. Mewborn, P. Sztajn, & D. White (Eds.), *Proceedings of the twenty-fourth annual meeting of the North American Chapter of the International Group for the Psychology of Mathematics Education PME-NA24* (pp. 1267–1279), 3.

Confrey, J., & Makar, K. (2005). Critiquing and improving the use of data from high-stakes tests with the aid of dynamic statistics software. In C. Dede, J. P. Honan, & L. C. Peters (Eds.), *Scaling up success: Lessons learned from technology-based educational improvement* (pp. 198–226). San Francisco: Jossey-Bass.

Confrey, J., Makar, K., & Kazak, S. (2004). Undertaking data analysis of student outcomes as professional development for teachers. *ZDM, 36*(1), 1–9.

Cromey, A. (2000). *Using student assessment data: What can we learn from schools?* Oak Brook, IL: North Central Regional Educational Laboratory.

Cronbach, L. J. (1976). Test validation. In R. L. Thorndike (Ed.), *Educational measurement* (2nd ed., pp. 443–507). Washington, DC: American Council of Education.

Drucker, P. F. (1989). *The new realities: In government and politics/in economics and business/in society and world view.* New York: Harper & Row.

Fullan, M. (2000). The three stories of education reform. *Phi Delta Kappan, 81*(8), 581–584.

Fullan, M., & Stiegelbauer, S. M. (1991). *The new meaning of educational change* (2nd ed.). Toronto/New York: Ontario Institute for Studies in Education/Teachers College Press.

Hamilton, L. S., Stecher, B. M., & Klein, S. P. (2002). *Making sense of test-based accountability in education.* Santa Monica, CA: Rand Education.

Hammerman, J. K., & Rubin, A. (2002). Visualizing a statistical world. *Hands On!, 25*(2).

Hammerman, J. K., & Rubin, A. (2003). *Reasoning in the presence of variability.* Paper presented at the Third International Research Forum on Statistical Reasoning, Thinking, and Literacy (SRTL-3), Lincoln, NE.

Heistad, D., & Spicuzza, R. (2003, April). *Beyond zip code analyses: What good measurement has to offer and how it can enhance the instructional delivery to all students.* Paper presented at the annual meeting of the American Educational Research Association, Chicago.

Herman, J., & Gribbons, B. (2001). *Lessons learned in using data to support school inquiry and continuous improvement: Final report to the Stuart Foundation* (CSE Tech. Rep. 535). Los Angeles: Center for the Study of Evaluation, UCLA.

Honey, M. (2001). *The consortium for technology in the preparation of teachers: Exploring the potential of handheld technology for preservice education.* New York: EDC/Center for Children and Technology.

Honey, M., Brunner, C., Light, D., Kim, C., McDermott, M., Heinze, C., Breiter, A., & Mandinach, E. (2002). *Linking data and learning: The Grow Network study.* New York: EDC/Center for Children and Technology.

Kearns, D. T., & Harvey, J. (2000). *A legacy of learning.* Washington, DC: Brookings Institution Press.

Lachat, M. A., & Smith, S. (2005). Practices that support data use in urban high schools. *Journal of Education for Students Placed at Risk, 10*(3), 333 349.

Light, D., Wexler, D., & Heinze, J. (2004, April). *How practitioners interpret and link data to instruction: Research findings on New York City Schools' implementation of the Grow Network.* Paper presented at the annual meeting of the American Educational Research Association, San Diego, CA.

Lim, C. (2003). Data for decisions are just a click away. *ENC Focus, 10*(1). Retrieved October 2, 2007, from www.goenc.com/focus/

Love, N., Stiles, K. E., Mundry, S., & DiRanna, K. (in press). *A data coach's guide to closing achievement gaps: Unleashing the power of collaborative inquiry.* Thousand Oaks, CA: Corwin Press.

Mandinach, E. B. (2005). The development of effective evaluation methods for e-learning: A concept paper and action plan. *Teachers College Record, 107*(8), 1814–1835.

Mandinach, E. B., & Cline, H. F. (1994). *Classroom dynamics: Implementing a technology based learning environment.* Hillsdale, NJ: Erlbaum.

Mandinach, E. B., Honey, M., Light, D., Heinze, J. C., & Nudell, H. (2005, April). *Data-driven instructional decision making using technology-based tools.* Paper presented at the annual meeting of the American Educational Research Association, Montreal.

Mandinach, E. B., Honey, M., Light, D., Heinze, J. C., & Rivas, R. (2005, June). *Creating an evaluation framework for data-driven instructional decision making.* Paper presented at the meeting of the National Educational Computing Conference, Philadelphia.

Mandinach, E. B., Rivas, L., Light, D., & Heinze, J. C. (2006, April). *The impact of data-driven decision making tools on educational practice: A systems analysis of six school districts.* Paper presented at the annual meeting of the American Educational Research Association, San Francisco.

Mandinach, E. B., & Snow, R. E. (1999). *Integrating instruction and assessment for classrooms and courses: Programs and prospects for research* (Special Monograph). Princeton, NJ: Educational Testing Service.

Mason, S. A. (2001, Spring). Turning data into knowledge: Lessons from six Milwaukee public schools. *Using data for educational decision making: Newsletter of the Comprehensive Center–Region VI, 6,* 3–6.

Mason, S. A. (2002). *Turning data into knowledge: Lessons from six Milwaukee public schools* (WP 2002–3). Madison: University of Wisconsin, Wisconsin Center for Education Research.

Massell, D. (1998). *State strategies for building capacity in education: Progress and continuing challenges* (CPRE Research Report RR-41). Philadelphia: University of Pennsylvania, Consortium for Policy Research in Education.

Messick, S. (1989). Validity. In R. L. Linn (Ed.), *Educational measurement* (3rd ed., pp. 13–103). New York: Macmillan.

Mitchell, D., & Lee, J. (1998, September). *Quality school portfolio: Reporting on school goals and student achievement.* Paper presented at the CRESST Conference, Los Angeles. Retrieved May 12, 2003, from http://cse.ucla.ed/andmore_set.htm

Mitchell, D., Lee, J., & Herman, J. (2000, October). *Computer software systems and using data to support school reform.* Paper prepared for Wingspread meeting, Technology's Role in Urban School Reform: Achieving Equity and Quality. New York: EDC Center for Children and Technology.

Murnane, R. J., Sharkey, N. S., & Boudett, K. P. (2005). Using student-assessment results to improve instruction: Lessons from a workshop. *Journal of Education for Students Placed at Risk, 10*(3), 269–280.

Nichols, S. L., & Berliner, D. C. (2007). *Collateral damage: How high-stakes testing corrupts America's schools.* Cambridge, MA: Harvard Education Press.

No Child Left Behind Act of 2001. (2001). Retrieved January 30, 2002, from http://www.nclb.gov

O'Day, J. A. (2002). Complexity, accountability, and school improvement. *Harvard Educational Review, 72*(3), 293–329.

Pellegrino, J. W., Chudowsky, N., & Glaser, R. (2001). *Knowing what students know: The science and design of educational assessment.* Washington, DC: National Academy Press.

Petrides, L. A. (2006, April). Using data to improve instruction. *THE Journal.* Retrieved April 9, 2007, from http://thejournal.com/articles/18239

Popham, W. J. (1999). Why standardized tests don't measure educational quality. *Educational Leadership, 56*(6), 8–15.

Popham, W. J., Cruse, K. L., Rankin, S. C., Sandifer, P. D., & Williams, R. L. (1985). Measurement-driven instruction. *Phi Delta Kappan, 66,* 628–634.

Schafer, W. D., & Lissitz, R. W. (1987). Measurement training for school personnel: Recommendations and reality. *Journal of Teacher Education, 38*(3), 57–63.

Schmoker, M. J. (1996). *Results: The key to continuous school improvement.* Alexandria, VA: Association for Supervision and Curriculum Development.

Schmoker, M. (2000). The results we want. *Educational Leadership, 57*(5), 62–65.

Secada, W. (2001, Spring). From the director. *Using data for educational decision making: Newsletter of the Comprehensive Center–Region VI, 6,* 1–2.

Senge, P., Cambron-McCabe, N., Lucas, T., Smith, B., Dutton, J., & Kleiner, A. (2000). *Schools that learn*. New York: Doubleday.

Sharkey, N., & Murnane, R. (2003, April). *Helping K–12 educators learn from assessment data*. Paper presented at the annual meeting of the American Educational Research Association, Chicago.

Shepard, L. (1991). *Will national tests improve student learning?* (CSE Tech. Rep. 342). Los Angeles: Center for the Study of Evaluation, UCLA.

Spielvogel, R., Brunner, C., Pasnik, S., Keane, J. T., Friedman, W., Jeffers, L., John, K., & Hermos, J. (2001). *IBM's reinventing education grant partnership initiative: Individual site reports*. New York: EDC/Center for Children and Technology.

Spielvogel, R., & Pasnik, S. (1999). *From the school room to the state house: Data warehouse solutions for informed decision making in education*. New York: EDC/Center for Children and Technology.

Stiggins, R. (2002). Assessment crisis: The absence of assessment for learning. *Phi Delta Kappan, 83*(10), 758–765.

Streifer, P. A., & Schumann, J. A. (2005). Using data mining to identify actionable information: Breaking new ground in data-driven decision making. *Journal of Education for Students Placed at Risk, 10*(3), 281–293.

Stringfield, S., Wayman, J. C., & Yakimowski-Srebnick, M. E. (2005). Scaling up data use in classrooms, schools, and districts. In C. Dede, J. P. Honan, & L. C. Peters (Eds.), *Scaling up success: Lessons learned from technology-based educational improvement* (pp. 133–152). San Francisco: Jossey-Bass.

Thorn, C. (2002). *Data use in the classroom: The challenges of implementing data-based decision making at the school level*. Madison: University of Wisconsin, Wisconsin Center for Education Research.

Wayman, J. C. (2005a). Involving teachers in data-driven decision making: Using computer data systems to support teacher inquiry and reflection. *Journal of Education for Students Placed at Risk, 10*(3), 295–308.

Wayman, J. C. (Ed.). (2005b). [Special issue]. *Journal of Education for Students Placed at Risk, 10*(3).

Wayman, J. C. (Ed.). (2006). Data use for school improvement [Special issue]. *American Journal of Education, 112*(4).

Wayman, J. C., Stringfield, S., & Yakimowski, M. (2004). *Software enabling school improvement through analysis of student data* (CRESPAR Tech. Rep. No. 67). Baltimore: Johns Hopkins University, Center for Research on the Education of Students Placed at Risk. Retrieved January 30, 2004, from www.csos.jhu.edu/crespar/techReports/Report67.pdf

Webb, N. (2002, April). *Assessment literacy in a standards-based urban education setting*. Paper presented at the annual meeting of the American Educational Research Association, New Orleans.

Whitehurst, G. J. (2006, March). *State and national activities: Current status and future directions*. Speech given at the meeting, Improving Educational Outcomes: Why Longitudinal Data Systems Are Necessary. Washington, DC.

Wise, S. L., Lukin, L. E., & Roos, L. L. (1991). Teacher beliefs about training in testing and measurement. *Journal of Teacher Education, 42*(1), 37–42.

CHAPTER 3

Framing Effective and Fair Data Use from High-Stakes Testing in Its Historical, Legal, and Technical Context

Jere Confrey

In theory, data-driven decision making based on sufficient and available data from test results is a powerful route to fairer and more effective practice. The challenges to realizing this goal, however, are too often underestimated. Challenges include specifying the theories, empirical skills, and interpretive experiences necessary for practitioners to make valid, fair, and reliable use of data in the interests of their students. These are not straightforward tasks, however; even researchers and assessment specialists have not adequately addressed the relationships among using tests for various purposes, fostering equity, and clarifying fundamental measurement constructs such as validity and fairness.

The enactment of No Child Left Behind (NCLB), our current federal legislative mandate for testing and accountability, complicated the issues further: In most states, a single test is now used for multiple purposes, such as accountability of teachers and schools, decisions on student progress, feedback to teachers on curricular and instructional programs, and so on. Researchers know that the practice of using tests for multiple purposes results in trade-offs and compromises in interpreting the results fairly and validly. However, to my knowledge, we have not analyzed carefully and fully the implications of these trade-offs for their potential detrimental effects on students, especially those from underrepresented groups. In light of this situation, providing guidance to practitioners around data use is both sorely needed and supremely difficult.

Too often practitioners and lay people believe all tests are the same, especially in mathematics, where a student's performance on a set of items is cast simply as an objective representation of what the student knows.

Assessment specialists know this is not the case. However, assessment specialists are seldom content experts, and in many states, curriculum specialists have few interactions with testing divisions, leaving a gap between standards and assessments. These splits among diverse groups of professionals contribute to a fragmented testing system. Practitioners at the school level then are charged with correctly interpreting and implementing test results. The situation is further complicated because too often the historical/cultural roots of testing are ignored by test proponents, permitting them to cast data as purely informational rather than as political/interpretive. Data, however, are always interpretive and must be situated in a context that permits adequate explanation; testing systems, and the resultant data use and interpretation, should acknowledge this.

Two examples illustrate this point. The first example is a high-performing high school in a wealthy section of a Texas city that was classified as low-performing on the basis of the performance of a relatively small group of African-American students. The solution, touted in the newspapers as effective and innovative, was to require all African-American students, even those who had passed, to participate in lunch-hour tutoring. The school claimed benefits for all, some through conducting the tutoring and others through receiving it. At another high school in that district, in a poorer section of town with a majority of Hispanic students, the performance of a small group of African-Americans on the state test narrowly caused the school to become low-performing. Although far more Hispanic students failed the test than African-Americans, the state demanded that the school write a plan that would address the need for improvement of the African-American students, but that ignored the needs of the far more numerous Hispanic students who likewise failed. Both remedies were flawed in that the remedy for low performance was inequitable. In the first case, the plan obligated every member of the low-performing group to participate in remediation regardless of their performance; in the second, the plan ignored a substantial portion of the students in need of assistance. These examples illustrate the need for a theory of equity as a means to interpret data and to guide the actions taken in response to test results.

Thus, we are challenged to share expertise across diverse communities of practice by creating some common understandings about equity, testing, and data use. To contribute to this effort, I begin by distinguishing three common uses of testing and linking each to its implicit treatment of the key measurement constructs of validity and fairness. Each is set in its historical/cultural context to more fully illustrate the differences in use, and each is tied to its proponents' underlying views of how to use testing to promote equity. Then I seek to show that those views of equity are not consistent with one another and that the linking of these different uses into a single test, as a consequence of NCLB, resulted in deleterious tensions in data use and interpretation. To resolve some of those tensions, the last section of the chapter proposes two partial solutions.

The approach in this chapter—to span communities of practice and to bridge technical and statistical with historical/cultural analysis—requires us to link issues of knowledge, politics, and discourse, fundamental pieces of competent data-driven decision making. Latour (1999) proposed the notions of "hybrids," networks, and the activities of translation and mediation among varied groups of specialists as necessary elements in addressing persistent and complex social issues. Considering how to promote effective data use by practitioners, and how to strengthen their voices in relation to data collection and interpretation, could be characterized as an example of the type of hybridization he advocated. It is in sharp contrast to the reductionist view in which we treat education as a form of business-like accounting of the "bottom line."

The approach can be viewed as part of a larger plan to help remedy the contradictions inherent in the hybrid NCLB by promoting three measures. The first is to articulate clearly the *practical interpretive skills* that educators need to make valid, fair, and reliable use of data in the interests of students. The second is to develop and apply the *construct of instructional validity* to measure opportunity to learn and instructional guidance, for both students and teachers. The third, to exert pressure for systemic improvement, is to propose a *students' bill of assessment rights*, to ensure that students and their parents have some recourse to the consequences of high-stakes testing if improvements in the assessment system are not forthcoming.

VALIDITY, FAIRNESS, EQUITY, AND THREE HISTORICAL USES OF TESTING

There are three different traditions of testing in the United States relevant to the current discussion. They are (1) *selection testing*, to identify individuals qualified for specialized programs and opportunities, including postsecondary education; (2) *monitoring*, to watch over national trends in student achievement (NAEP and TIMSS); and (3) *certification*, to ascertain minimum competency of students. In this section, each tradition of testing is placed in its historical/cultural context, and its ties to the promotion of equity, as understood by its proponents, are articulated. First, I briefly review two fundamental testing constructs, validity and fairness, which underlie all tests, as a means to disentangle each type of test and describe how these constructs are construed and achieved. The third construct of testing, reliability, is not addressed in this chapter.[1] Finally, I define equity so that it can serve as a lens by which to conduct data interpretation and action.

Validity, Fairness, and Equity Defined

Validity is defined as "an integrated judgment based on the degree to which empirical evidence and theoretical rationales support the adequacy and appropriateness of interpretations and actions based on test scores or other modes of assessment" (Messick, 1990, p. 1). By implying that the *inferences* drawn from a test—not the test itself—are validated by combining empirical evidence, observation, and argument, Messick's definition ties validity fundamentally to the purpose, use, and interpretation of a test. A simple example of an invalid test use would be to use a driver's licensing test (and hence the possession of a driver's license) as a requirement for voting.

Fairness in testing requires that all students have an equal chance to demonstrate their knowledge and skills on a test, and thus that the test results not underestimate or overestimate students' knowledge in systematic ways attributable to their membership in a subgroup (National Research Council, 1999). For example, testing a hearing-impaired student by reading directions out loud would be unfair. Or, situating applications of mathematics concepts in contexts unfamiliar to particular subgroups would be unfair. Validity and fairness are therefore key elements in examining the different uses of tests.

The concept of equity, as used in this chapter, is associated with a broader concept of justice for all members of society: how to ensure that the quality of students' educational opportunities is not restricted by their membership in a group based on factors such as race, gender, or class. Equity, by this definition, concerns a comparison among groups, and, as a *quality* of opportunity, can be only imprecisely and incompletely gauged by measurements of *quantities* such as test scores. Test scores are limited in that they are estimates of what students know, based on how students respond to particular items in the test setting, and further because they are measures of the *outcomes* of a system rather than measures of the educational system itself, within which opportunity accrues. Seeking equity obligates one to distinguish and address two distinct sources of inequities: the inertia of historical conditions and traditions that need to be redressed, and the impetus of some members of advantaged groups to protect their own privileges by perpetuating, tolerating, endorsing, and/or contributing to inequities. Data use in the service of equity must always keep these distinctions in mind: It is imperative to avoid mistaking narrowing the gap in scores *by any means* as a goal of equity instead of the broader provision of equity of opportunity. Further, since validity is concerned with the inferences drawn from tests, and fairness is concerned with opportunities to demonstrate proficiency, both are intertwined with equity and need to be unpacked in relation to data use and interpretation.

Purposes of Testing

Many people do not distinguish among different purposes of tests. By selecting three historical episodes of testing, I seek to demonstrate how different
test purposes interact with the concepts of validity and fairness, and, further, document that in all three traditions, proponents sought to increase
equity, albeit different conceptions of equity and configurations of validity
and fairness. I will argue that by combining all three functions of testing into
a single testing and accountability system as mandated by NCLB, lawmakers
have contributed to increased tensions and contradictions that hamper the
effectiveness of the law and make data use contradictory and ambiguous. In
the final two sections, I offer a few suggestions to address these limitations.

SELECTION TESTING. The Educational Testing Service (ETS) and the College Board are probably the best-known examples of selection testing
(Lemann, 2000). Until the 1940s, entrance to Ivy League colleges, which led
to the most prominent positions in finance, law, and other professions, was
limited essentially to those with inherited wealth and power. In the late 1930s,
James Bryant Conant, the first president of Harvard from a modest financial and class background, sought a means to open higher education to those
with talent but who lacked the social and economic privilege that were pre-
requisites for higher education. He was entranced by Thomas Jefferson's
distinction between "a natural aristocracy among men [grounded in] virtue
and talents" and "an artificial aristocracy founded on wealth and birth,
without either virtue or talents." Jefferson had written, "May we not even
say that that form of government is the best which provides the most ef-
fectually for a pure selection of these natural aristoi into the offices of government?" (Malone, 1981, p. 239). Conant thus wanted to economically
diversify the elite student population (although his vision still excluded
women, Jews, and African-Americans).

To create a natural aristoi or meritocracy (Young, 1994), Conant sought
a test that would identify individuals of talent and competence regardless of
their background. For this purpose he recruited Henry Chauncey, an assistant
dean at Harvard who subsequently became the first president of ETS, whose
convictions about testing were expressed as follows: "We seem . . . to have
arrived at the period in Man's history when human affairs can be studied as
impartially and scientifically as physical phenomena" (Lemann, 2000, p. 68).

This belief in a scientific and impartial test led researchers at ETS to
develop the concept of "aptitude" (as distinct from intelligence) to measure
proclivity to learn, and to claim aptitude's independence from different curricula in various geographic locations and its resistance to bias from socioeconomic background. However, the impartiality of the SAT was belied by
the fact that a forerunner of the test was altered (by adding a practical sci-

ence section) to select more young men from farms for the military (Lemann, 2000, p. 6), while the SAT itself was not changed to respond to differences in performance by African-Americans (p. 52) or by young women on the mathematics portions (Dwyer, 1976, as cited by FairTest.org, 2003).

The selection testing did evolve with a view toward equity in terms of achieving increased representation of diverse groups across the award pool. Equity in this context is based on the premise that by background, preparation, or proclivity, people can be tested for their fitness to gain access to restricted opportunities. However, it does not necessarily address the question of whether individual applicants have been provided equal consideration or equivalent opportunities to learn. In selection testing, this view of equity incorporates a paradoxical perspective, as recounted by Lemann (2000): "This was the fundamental clash: between the promise of opportunity and the reality that, from a point early in the lives of most people, opportunity would be limited" (p. 65). Validity in the context of selection testing is restricted to determining whether those who are selected do well in subsequent opportunities; whether others, not selected, could have done equally well is not addressed.

Within this restricted view of validity, tests of selectivity must be scrutinized carefully for fairness. These tests involve direct competition among test takers; those whose knowledge can be demonstrated most easily in testing conditions will fare best. Those who cannot perform well within the dominant testing format will not be provided equal opportunities. Thus, debates over tests of selectivity often focus on item selection and format as one of the most direct means to improve fairness.

SATs, since they are designed and utilized by only a portion of the population, are not used to monitor the educational system. Further, they cannot be used for certification, as no systematic attempt is made to "cover" the material. In fact, items are selected primarily for their ability to "discriminate" among students. Discriminate in this sense is a technical term indicating that the items result in wide distributions of results (high discrimination) rather than in all students getting the item correct or all students getting it incorrect (low discrimination).

TESTING FOR MONITORING. The use of testing for monitoring can be illustrated by the periodic National Assessment for Educational Progress (NAEP), known as "the Nation's Report Card." It is administered by the Commissioner of Educational Statistics of the National Center for Educational Statistics (NCES). According to the Web site of the National Assessment Governing Board, the NAEP since 1973 has gathered information about student achievement in order to "inform citizens about the nature of students' comprehension of the subject, inform curriculum specialists about the level and nature of student understanding, and inform policymakers about factors related to schooling and its effect on student proficiency" (National Assessment Governing Board, 2004). NAEP data are collected by sampling the overall student population, and they have no impact on a student's record; hence the assessment is not used for certification or selectivity.

To illustrate the relationships between equity and monitoring in NAEP-based discussions, I selected two contributions to the proceedings of a national conference held in 1998 examining the "significant differences in black and white student achievement" (Grissmer & Ross, 2000, p. xi). In one chapter, Raudenbush (2000) reported that the results of the NAEP's trial state assessments (TSA) were interpreted too often as measures of program effectiveness across the states without adequate consideration of demographic differences. Raudenbush sought to connect the gaps in performance with resource inequities. To do so, he confirmed that NAEP data show that socially disadvantaged and ethnic-minority students are "at high risk of poor performance" (p. 6), and then linked these results to "substantial evidence of inequality in access to these resources [favorable disciplinary climates, eighth-grade algebra, teacher preparation, and emphasis on reasoning] as a function of social background [parent's educational levels] and ethnicity" (p. 36). This suggests that if a policy does not take variations in school resources into consideration, as should be the case in the application of a national law such as NCLB, the attributions from comparisons of test scores across states could be misleading.

At the same conference, Smith (2000), then U.S. Undersecretary for Education, noted that while the achievement gap had narrowed significantly between 1971 and 1988, it remained unchanged in the 1990s. He hypothesized that increases in poverty, the end of northward migration to stronger schools, and the number of states using minimum competency tests were some possible explanations for the stall in progress. Further, he reviewed the fundamental elements of the standards-based movement—establishing challenging state content and performance standards, aligning assessments to these, and then addressing the necessary elements of curriculum and teacher training—and then outlined the challenges such changes implied for NAEP and other national assessments. He called for more sophisticated assessments that: (a) align with content standards, (b) stipulate adequate performance levels for those standards, (c) "become more real" in relation to validation, with authentic uses of the knowledge and skills, and (d) draw on "the intersection of reasonable theories of the content area, human development, human learning, and pedagogy" (Smith, 2000, p. 275).

These two studies of the NAEP, an assessment designed to monitor progress, illustrate further the complex relationship between test purpose on one hand and data interpretation and decision making on the other. Raudenbush (2000) illustrated that school factors concerning quality instruction can be masked when data on test performance, accumulated at the state level, are compared, even allowing for adjustments of scores for economic or racial differences. In the absence of measurements on variations in resources, it is easy to imagine how practitioners could make unwarranted attributions about students and/ or groups. Similarly, Smith's argument suggests that if the bar for performance is set too low (using minimum competency tests), progress in reducing the gaps can slow down; but if the bar is to be raised to reflect a change to standards-based instruction and hence to be more responsive to the needs of today's society, then other changes also will be needed to ensure equity, including changes in how items are assessed and how much professional development will be needed for teachers to instruct properly.

In terms of equity, the NAEP looks at national trends in order to focus on inputs by: (a) drawing valid data-based conclusions that recognize the interconnectedness of demographic factors and school quality; (b) explaining data trends in terms of other large-scale events and patterns; and (c) anticipating needs for changes in monitoring protocols to ensure that the indicators remain appropriate. Because the NAEP has no high-stakes consequences for individual students, equity dimensions consist of how to report current status to the public and how to anticipate necessary changes to alleviate patterns of inequity at the broad policy level. Without high-stakes consequences for individual students or districts, the validity of the NAEP tests is difficult to assess. It rests on the quality of the experts who guide the development of the tests. In their current form, they cannot be used for certification or for selectivity. However, within NCLB, all states are mandated to participate in the NAEP as a means to independently validate their own tests; the question of cross-validation of these two types of tests is currently under examination (Hoff, 2007; Nettles, Domenech, Haertel, Kopp, Paulson, Ravitch, Ward, Whirry, & Wolf, 2002).

CERTIFICATION TESTING. A third tradition of testing, certification of proficiency (or competency), arose historically from the "back-to-basics" movement and its ties to "minimum competency" goals in the 1980s. Testing was mandated by state agencies for all students, in order to certify competencies considered essential for citizenry and work, and that had been taught multiple times during each student's school years. If a student failed to demonstrate competency at the appropriate level, he or she either was not promoted to the next grade or ultimately was denied graduation from high school. The rationale for the tests, and for the consequences to individual students, included strong equity rhetoric that asserted that permitting youth to graduate without adequate skills was a neglect of our responsibilities to them and a betrayal of their trust.

The accountability movement, which aimed to create a means to hold schools responsible for the level of performance of their students, is closely associated with certification testing. Within this perspective, schools and/or teachers are provided incentives or sanctions depending on how their students fare on certification tests.

Competency testing has been contested in the courts on the grounds of discriminatory effects on individuals, and the courts thereby have provided guidelines concerning proper use. As stated in the NRC report *High Stakes Testing*, "There is often no single legal view on what constitutes non-discriminatory or appropriate test use . . . legal rules, like psychometric norms and notions of sound educational policy and practice, are constantly evolving" (National Research Council, 1999, p. 51). Typically, however, the courts generally use the following three indicators of discrimination in their decision making: (1) a present intent to discriminate; (2) a policy that preserves and projects the effects of prior illegal discrimination; and (3) evidence of a disproportionate adverse impact with evidence of inadequate justification for the differences and the availability of a reasonable alternative. A major challenge for a plaintiff is to demonstrate convincingly that "the decision-maker selected or reaffirmed a particular course of action *at least in part 'because of,'* not merely 'in spite of' its adverse effects on the group disproportionately affected" (National Research Council, 1999, emphasis in the original).

One landmark case (*Debra P. v. Turlington*, 1979) challenged Florida's high school graduation test, which during the mid-1970s Blacks were 10 times as likely as Whites to fail. The courts ruled that the test had preserved the effects of illegally segregated schools attended by the students in grades 1 through 5. This case established two requirements about input for competency tests: adequate notice and evidence of curricular validity. Adequate notice means students must be informed several years in advance how a test that determines promotion or graduation will be changed. Curricular validity means that the content of the test must match what the schools are teaching. *Debra P.* required the state to demonstrate curricular validity.

G.I. Forum v. Texas Education Agency (2000) also challenged certification testing (Phillips, 2000; Valencia & Bernal, 2000). U.S. District Judge Edward C. Prado ruled that there was evidence of disparate impact on different subgroups. Further, he ruled that a high school diploma is a form of property right, which established individual rights regarding issues of equity. However, in seeking to determine whether discrimination had been intentional, he ruled that: (a) the Texas Education Agency (TEA) had provided sufficient notice of test content; (b) evidence of predictive validity was not required; (c) the test's construction was consistent with professional standards, including the setting of the pass rate; (d) in providing students with multiple repetitions of the test, TEA avoided reliance on a single score; (e) test-driven instruction and remediation were valid practices; (f) the empirical evidence supported progress; (g) accountability provided uniformity across the state; and finally (h) no viable alternative was available. Overall, the judge determined that the practice of certification testing is acceptable to the degree that the state "demonstrated an educational necessity for the test," and to the degree that the test has a "manifest relationship to classroom education."

Prado's ruling reveals the inherent dilemma in applying tests of certification in schools. Education is meant to be a source of educational opportunity. However, educational rewards, passage to a new grade or award of a diploma, are meant to signal accomplishments. Hence the ruling documented that membership in particular less economically advantaged subgroups leads to failure at disparate rates, and there is a basis to look for injustice. Further, he acknowledged that because the award of a high school diploma clearly is associated with better-paying work, more stable family situations, and personal identity benefits (National Research Council, 1999), denial of that benefit is the denial of a property right by schools. However, his finding in favor of the Texas Education Agency finally determined that for a state to successfully counter such a judicial challenge, the state need only establish the validity of the test relative to state standards, provide adequate advance notice of changes in the test, and meet professional standards of test construction, a relatively closed system with only internal validity. While this ruling, in effect, released the state to attempt to ameliorate the problem as well as it knew how, the judge declared that a test must bear a "manifest relationship to classroom education" (*G.I. Forum v. Texas Education Agency*, 2000). In so stating, the judge left open the question of how the test's relationship to classroom education should be defined. Further, in stating that his ruling was predicated on the absence of the plaintiff's proof that a better alternative existed, he perhaps signaled that a better solution would be desirable.

These three histories show how all three uses of testing—selection, monitoring, certification—had roots, to one degree or another, in issues of equity. However, in each case, the meaning of equity shifts. Only the monitoring function of testing seems to fully meet the definition of equity as "a broader concept of justice for all members of society: how to ensure that the quality of students' educational opportunities is not restricted by their membership in a group based on factors such as race, gender, class." Monitoring testing as embedded in the NAEP explicitly provides for the examination of gaps in performance of subgroups, with a broad consideration of the factors affecting educational performance, as seen in the Raudenbush and Smith contributions.

On the other hand, selection testing was developed specifically to address a vision of equity, albeit a much narrower one, namely, the aim of diversity in the selected population to which the opportunities and rewards of advanced education are provided. Selection testing does not specify that the diversity of the selected group must reflect the representative proportions of that group in the national population. In fact, recent legal cases dealing with affirmative action would specifically prevent this consideration (Lewin, 2006).

This view is reminiscent of the concept of the "talented tenth" promulgated by Du Bois (1903/1996) many years ago.

Finally, in certification testing, success provides individuals with assurance that their performances have met required standards, at which point benefits are assigned (passage to a new grade, graduation, etc.). Conversely, failure on a certification test is supposed to indicate that a student has not successfully learned the material and should be held responsible; consequently, benefits, including certain rights, may be withheld. So far, equity consideration within certification testing (in the legal environment) requires only that schools and the states do the best that they can, and it allows for the fact that disparate impacts, while unfortunate, may be tolerated. The failure of a student on a certification test legitimates retention in a grade or refusal of a diploma. However, without assurances that instructional opportunity to learn, adequate resources, and quality instruction have been provided to members of any particular subgroup of the population, the equity dimension of certification testing remains underdeveloped and flawed. In the next section, these flaws will be shown to become more problematic as the content on these tests becomes more challenging. These flaws will be addressed only by taking up the challenge implicit in the judge's ruling: to demand that testing and accountability bear a stronger "manifest relationship to classroom education." By doing so, we should be able to develop proven alternative approaches that draw a more complete and satisfactory view of equity.

Considerations of Equity in Relation to No Child Left Behind

The No Child Left Behind legislation, modeled on the Texas accountability system, was passed with broad bipartisan support in Congress. As currently enacted, the Act requires annual testing of children in grades 3 through 8. High stakes are associated with student performance in terms of school-level accountability. Failure to make adequate annual progress can result in support for students to move to other schools. In many instances, financial incentives and sanctions for districts are used to stimulate improvements in scores. For instance, failing districts can be required to pay for students to attend better schools. Whether individual students also are held accountable is determined by each state; high-stakes consequences can include retention at grade or withholding of the high school diploma.

By formally appending the accountability movement to the standards-based movement, NCLB created a *standards-based* accountability system. States are free to select their own standards, so long as the assessment system is aligned with those standards. How to achieve the required improvement in performance is the responsibility of individual locales. NCLB explicitly states that equity in educational excellence is its primary goal, with testing for proficiency as the secondary and instrumental goal: The purpose of the law is "to ensure that all children have a fair, equal, and significant opportunity to obtain a high-quality education and reach, at a minimum, proficiency on challenging state achievement standards and state academic assessments" (NCLB, 2001).

NCLB strengthens Title I accountability by requiring states to implement statewide accountability systems covering all public schools and students. The law requires:

- challenging state standards in reading and mathematics;
- annual testing for all students in grades 3–8;
- annual statewide progress objectives ensuring that all groups of students reach proficiency within 12 years;
- assessment results and state progress objectives must be broken out by poverty, race, ethnicity, disability, and limited English proficiency, to ensure that no group is left behind;
- school districts and schools that fail to make adequate yearly progress (AYP) toward state proficiency goals will, over time, be subject to improvement, corrective action, and restructuring measures aimed at getting them back on course to meet state standards; and
- schools that meet or exceed AYP objectives or close achievement gaps will be eligible for state academic achievement awards.

NCLB has compressed elements of all three testing traditions into one law. The heart of the law builds upon the tradition of certification, wherein a student must demonstrate annual progress toward specified proficiency levels. While some states have implemented NCLB without individual consequences for students (high stakes), most have not. Then, by situating certification of performance within a strong accountability system (i.e., by holding schools accountable for the performance of their entire student population as well as for the performance of subgroups), a more indirect proficiency standard is applied. The requirement for reporting AYP toward full proficiency in 2012 incorporates a monitoring function. Finally, as states define "challenging standards," we are witnessing a shift in the kinds of items tested, from the predominantly multiple-choice, low-level items of minimum competency to more constructed response items and increased emphasis on higher-level thinking skills and more difficult concepts. While these changes are not being used explicitly for selection purposes, the use of these types of items for all children injects an element of selective testing into the mix.

When multiple uses of testing are combined, conflicts, trade-offs, and tensions are likely to arise. This is especially true when these different uses evolve from different perspectives on equity, validity, and fairness. These tensions are felt most intensely by schools in threat of being labeled as nonperforming and slated for improvement, corrective action, or restructuring, or by schools labeled as persistently failing. For instance, when tests are used for monitoring within an accountability system and the requirement is for a certain percentage to reach designated cutoff points, schools may choose strategically to sacrifice some of the weakest students and concentrate on those most likely to pass, known as the "bubble kids." Clearly, the certification aspect of testing for those sacrificed individuals is coming into conflict with the monitoring provisions.

Similarly, if items previously used for selectivity are incorporated into the testing under NCLB for purposes of certification, then one must question whether those items have been adequately validated for use with a broader segment of the population. For instance, psychometricians select items based on their ability to differentiate among test takers, based on the typical sample tested. Will the same items differentiate properly among the broader segment of the population? A second tension, interjected with the change to more challenging standards, and hence toward testing that mirrors testing for selectivity, that might emerge at upper grades concerns whether all students have had adequate opportunities to learn the material. In *G. I. Forum v. Texas Education Agency*, Judge Prado found 3 years to be sufficient notice of curricular changes if these changes are broadly disseminated to practitioners, and he did not require evidence that all students had opportunities to learn. However, that case was based on minimum competency testing. While minimum competency items typically are taught repeatedly over a number of years, standards-based challenging items often are taught only once (such as in a beginning algebra class). Under such a scenario, it becomes likely that some students will miss items because the associated topics were not taught to them proficiently, or perhaps not taught at all, because many schools in high-poverty rural or urban settings lack qualified or even sufficient numbers of teachers.

Finally, when monitoring is undertaken with more challenging content, the issues cited by Marshall Smith (2000) come into play. That is, assessments will have to change to adequately and fairly assess these more complex skills.

In summary, compressing the three traditions of testing into one testing system has created inherent trade-offs, even conflicts, among the interests of administrators, teachers, and students, including those in different subgroups, within the educational system. To craft a solution to these tensions, contradictions, and unwise practices—with the goal of both coherence and equity within the educational system in the context of No Child Left Behind—much closer attention must be paid to what actually happens in the classroom. The legal precedent in *G.I. Forum v. Texas Education Agency* made the consideration of the links between testing and practice an issue of equity by requiring a manifest relation to classroom practice. To ensure that students are treated fairly, then, the link between testing and classroom instruction must be conceptualized and investigated.

The questions addressed in the rest of this chapter are: How can issues of fairness and equity in our current accountability system be more directly linked to classroom practices? What are the roles of data collection, data use, and interpretation in this process? and, as we move to resolve the inequities and tensions to create a more coherent system, What is necessary to protect the interests and rights of individual students?

INSTRUCTIONAL VALIDITY:
OPPORTUNITY TO LEARN AND INSTRUCTIONAL GUIDANCE

Fairness in educational accountability testing can exist only if the system takes instructional validity into consideration. That is, do the contents of a test address what is being taught, or do inputs correspond to outputs? (In the language of testing professionals, while statistical inequities can be documented using current monitoring methods, equity can be achieved only in circumstances in which the degree of validity can be examined and aligned with the test's purposes.) Instructional validity assesses whether the enacted curriculum has prepared students adequately for the test; thus it requires establishing the relationship between what occurs in classrooms during instruction and students' performance on the test. Under the rubric of instructional validity falls the determination of whether students have been given an opportunity to learn the material: whether (a) the instruction has been accurate, engaging, and challenging; (b) students have been provided adequate opportunities to demonstrate and refine their knowledge; (c) key examples and known misconceptions have been addressed and opportunity to gain automaticity has been provided; and finally (d) ways of organizing and structuring the material for effective and efficient understanding and recall have been put in place.

The relationship between instruction and assessment is bidirectional, in that how one teaches affects performance on the test, but past performance on the test, as well as anticipation of new testing, affects instruction. Therefore, it is helpful to break instructional validity into two components: (1) opportunity to learn and (2) instructional guidance. Opportunity to learn addresses whether students have been taught the material adequately prior to testing, while instructional guidance addresses whether students' performance on prior tests leads to improvements in instruction over time (equity for a group) and remediation (equity for an individual).

Instructional validity must be a central construct in ensuring that accountability systems are driving school improvement toward both improved coherence and improved equity. If, as discussed previously, certification testing with individual and school consequences is to be cast as an educational necessity, then, as Judge Prado ruled, it must bear a manifest relationship to classroom practices. While curricular validity may be sufficient for minimum competency testing, instructional validity must be established for standards-based assessment.

State agencies are understandably reluctant to see instructional validity cast as a necessary element of accountability systems: Documenting classroom instruction is costly and unreliable. However, separating instructional validity into two categories—opportunity to learn and instructional guidance—makes solutions more economically feasible. Teachers should be expected to certify that they have taught mandated topics over the course of the year. This can be accomplished inexpensively by simply asking teachers at least twice a year (at semester and year end) to complete a checklist to certify that they have taught what is on the state content standards. By using a moderate grain size (10 to 20 topics per year), teachers should be able to complete this task with reasonably high reliability and validity. This checklist would be a measure of opportunity to learn.

Certainly, teaching a topic does not ensure that students will learn it: Learning in schools depends heavily on instructional quality. At this time, we have no cost-effective and efficient means to assess the quality of instruction, but we do have an alternative method. Adequate instructional guidance for teachers is available in the previous year's test and should be provided in a timely, valid, and reliable way, so that teachers are able to provide better instruction to the next class (Elmore & Rothman, 1999). If test data demonstrate failure of a teacher's students year after year, we can begin to presume that the instructional quality is falling short—another threat to the validity of conclusions drawn from a test and their consequences for the individual student. Further, with instructional guidance, teachers can tailor instruction to the tested material to an appropriate degree. Note that this is not "teaching to the test," but teaching in ways consistent with what is tested and how it is scored. Teaching to the test results in narrowing instruction to items tested on previous tests; teaching in ways that are *consistent* would, for example, use a similar item format in classroom assessments as a regular part of instruction, would address commonly documented misconceptions from previous years, and would focus instruction on difficult topics.

Moreover, since in most cases students are provided with multiple opportunities to pass graduation tests, the issue of instructional guidance also applies to teachers' providing feedback to individual students. While this information may not reach the level of diagnostic information, it at least should provide screening and progress monitoring, which are prerequisite to diagnostic assessment (Learning Point Associates, n.d.). Locating instructional guidance within the concept of instructional validity fine-tunes opportunity-to-learn measures. If a district, school, or teacher consistently certifies a teacher's content coverage, but test data indicate consistent failure by that teacher's students, the discrepancy provides a basis for re-evaluating the instructional quality. In the end, it is widely believed by most researchers that instructional quality is the most salient factor in ensuring instructional validity (Elmore, 2002).

I have argued that high-stakes tests, with consequences for students, for teachers or schools, and for districts, should be linked to instructional practice in order to ensure that the issue of validity is addressed adequately. I have suggested that this be done through a combination of means to measure opportunity to learn and to use test results to produce and provide adequate instructional guidance. These two improvements would give teachers the information necessary to improve their own instructional quality and to monitor the progress of individual students. Together these improvements would link the test contents to "a manifest demonstrable relation to classroom education" in a much more coherent way than they are at the present time, would improve our ability to detect and address educational inequities to which some groups of students are subject, and, overall, would improve the educational validity of NCLB's use of testing as an "educational necessity." They also would open the door to a next step in improving the equity dimension of testing, which would be to engage in remediation that works. At the current time, remediation funds are dramatically underutilized in NCLB, and part of that may be because teachers have little way to target their interventions effectively. If they knew whether a student had received an opportunity to learn the material and if they knew better how the student fared on tests in particular content areas and in relation to particular problems, they could be more successful in applying this knowledge to help students effectively.

DO WE NEED A STUDENT'S BILL OF TESTING RIGHTS?

The NCLB system as currently enacted is far from perfect, from a number of perspectives, some of which have been described above. A fundamental weakness in NCLB is the absence of accountability of the tests themselves, in particular with regard to ensuring that the high-stakes assessments required under NCLB are instructionally valid and that the testing system is structured to provide adequate instructional guidance. In failing to address issues of instructional validity, NCLB predisposes our educational systems to persistent and additional inequities for subgroups and individuals, system-wide and in specific locales, because it fails to make data available for decision making that is coherent with the types of improvement demanded by the testing system.

Legal action to redress perceived wrongs or inequities in the testing system is expensive and time-consuming, and cannot exert sufficient pressure on the various educational systems and governing bodies to make them change. Even when disparities among subgroups are demonstrated, educational necessity and compliance with (inadequate) professional practices have permitted the system to move only slowly. Perhaps the best solution would be to empower students, and their parents on their behalf, to hold test makers, and the state educational officers who negotiate the massively expensive test contracts, accountable for the structure of and the data available from these high-stakes tests. In a number of places in the country, we have seen how students' refusal to participate in testing has been an effective form of civil disobedience. Perhaps what researchers could do to assist test makers, state educational agencies, and legislators to improve the testing system would be to provide students and parents a professional basis for choosing to act to remedy weak or deleterious testing practices. In the next section, when I refer to tests of certification, I intend that they are all tests in which consequences accrue to (a) individual students for passing a grade or graduating, or (b) schools and districts for purposes of examining AYP based on the aggregation of students' individual scores.

In this spirit, I propose a students' bill of testing rights.

Testing with high-stakes consequences for individual students should be permitted only if the data from the tests can be used properly to provide instructional guidance, increase instructional validity, improve equity for individuals' membership groups, and ensure fairness for individuals.

- No single test of certification should be used to make decisions that could harm a child's potential to achieve. Repeated administration of the same test does not constitute multiple measures, although it can be an useful component of the overall system. Instead, other indicators (teacher recommendations, other test scores, performance measures, grades) should be factored into the retention/promotion decision, while new and better forms of testing are developed.
- For all tests that determine certification, all items must be released to teachers and schools soon after the completion of testing each year. Too many mistakes have been found in released tests to trust their accuracy and correctness (FairTest.org, 2003; Hoff, 2003). Item release must be accompanied by item analyses, including the correct answers and the percentage of students selecting each distractor.
- All tests of certification must provide valid information to students, parents, and teachers at the level of content strands. Whole-test scores are too broad to provide instructional guidance.

- All tests of certification must provide evidence that they are fully sampling the state or district curricular standards in two ways: from the variety of topics mandated, and from the types of process skills needed, so as to ensure that valid certification and not teaching to the test occurs.
- All tests of certification that disaggregate by subgroup must provide a means to examine the same information for all combinations of the relevant demographic characteristics by mean and standard deviation (grade, school, race, socioeconomic status [SES], special education status) over time. These tests also should be disaggregated by performance level to ensure that all performance levels (high, medium, and low) are served adequately.
- All tests of certification must make transparent their methods of setting cut points, including the data used to make the cut point, and any adjustments made on the basis of grade-level consistency.
- Following weak test results, all students should be provided the opportunity to receive remediation based on their individual performances, using proven strategies. Students should not be required to receive remediation based only on the aggregate performance of a subgroup to which they belong. The requirement for remediation should be based on their individual scores.
- All public release of monitoring tests also must report the demographic information for a district and the level of resources made available relative to the relevant demographic characteristics.

CONCLUSIONS

In its current form, NCLB is riddled with contradictions around issues of equity, due to its compression of multiple test uses into a single high-stakes test for each state. The resolution of the contradictions depends on the development of a clear, concise idea of instructional validity, which should encompass documentation of opportunity to learn and clear specifications for the development of instructional guidance from test results. However, clarity in instructional guidance requires improved clarity in our understanding of equity and how it relates to data interpretation and use.

Researchers and practitioners have key roles to play in driving the system to develop approaches that in fact do produce sound instructional guidance in relation to the multiple levels of the system (a class, a school, a district, and the nation). Further, certain current practices in many states—nonrelease of test items, lack of validity at the level of content strands, failure to examine data trends for cross-tabulated subgroups, the failure to demonstrate adequate levels of representative sampling of the state curricular standards—

should be vigorously challenged. To ensure this, I propose a students' bill of testing rights, so that students and parents can pressure politicians and state administrators to make progress on the issues raised herein.

We must enlist teachers as critical actors for improving this system. They can do this, however, only if they are provided the best data possible, in formats that both inform their efforts to instruct students and assist in building their own capacity to do so.

It will take networks of experts to grapple with the legal, historical, technical, practice-based, cognitive-science-based, and ethical challenges that face us in ensuring that our system of education is serving our children adequately. Data use has a key role to play in this process, but only if we look carefully and knowledgeably at what the data mean and the inputs that produce them.

NOTES

I would like to acknowledge the assistance of Dr. Alan Maloney in revising and editing this chapter.

1. Reliability, the third fundamental construct, has a more technical definition as a calculation to gauge the likelihood that a student will achieve the same outcome on two different administrations of the same test. While debates surround which technical formula to use, the issue of reliability and equity tends to be less controversial and will not be treated in this analysis.

REFERENCES

Debra P. v. Turlington, 474 F. Supp. 244 (M.D. Fla. 1979); aff'd in part and rev'd in part, 644 F.2d 397 (5th Cir. 1981); rem'd, 564 F. Supp. 177 (M.D. Fla. 1983); aff'd, 730 F.2d 1405 (11th Cir. 1984).

Du Bois, W. E. B. (1996). The talented tenth. In Henry Louis Gates Jr. and Cornel West, The future of the race (133–158). New York: Vintage. (Original work 1903)

Dwyer, C. A. (1976, March). Test content in mathematics and science: The consideration of sex. Paper presented at the annual meeting of the American Educational Research Association, San Francisco.

Elmore, R. F. (2002). Bridging the gap between standards and achievement. Washington, DC: Albert Shanker Institute.

Elmore, R. F., & Rothman, R. (Eds.). (1999). Testing, teaching, and learning: A guide for states and school districts. Washington, DC: National Academy Press.

FairTest.org. (2003). NY test fiasco prompts calls to reassess high stakes. Retrieved February 20, 2007, from http://www.fairtest.org/examarts/Summer%2003/regents.html

G.I. Forum v. Texas Education Agency, 87 F. Supp. 2D 667 (W.D. Texas 2000).

Grissmer, D. W., & Ross, J. M. (Eds.). (2000). *Analytic issues in the assessment of student achievement.* Washington, DC: National Center for Educational Statistics.

Hoff, D. J. (2003, November 5). Flaws could spell trouble for N.Y. Regents exams. *Education Week, 23*(10), 22, 27.

Hoff, D. J. (2007, April 18). Not all agree on meaning of NCLB proficiency. *Education Week, 26*(33), 1, 23.

Latour, B. (1999). *Pandora's hope: Essays on the reality of social science studies.* Cambridge, MA: Harvard University Press.

Learning Point Associates. (n.d.). Starting points for meeting the requirements of NCLB. Retrieved February 24, 2007, from http://www.learningpt.org/page.php ?pageID=220

Lemann, N. (2000). *The big test: The secret history of the American meritocracy.* New York: Farrar, Strauss, & Giroux.

Lewin, T. (2006, October 31). Campaign to end race preferences splits Michigan. *The New York Times,* p. 1.

Malone, D. (1981). *The sage of Monticello.* Boston: Little, Brown, and Company.

Messick, S. (1990). *Validity of test interpretation and use.* Princeton, NJ: Educational Testing Service.

National Assessment Governing Board. (2004). Mathematics framework for the 2005 national assessment of educational progress. Retrieved February 12, 2007, from http://www.nagb.org/frameworks/m_framework_05/chap1.html#intro

National Research Council. (1999). *High stakes: Testing for tracking, promotion, and graduation.* Washington, DC: National Academy Press.

Nettles, M., Domenech, D., Haertel, E., Kopp, N., Paulson, D., Ravitch, D., Ward, M., Whirry, M., & Wolf, D. P. (2002). Using the national assessment of educational progress to confirm state test results: A report of the ad hoc committee on confirming test results. Retrieved April 19, 2007, from http://www.nagb .org/pubs/color_document.pdf

No Child Left Behind Act of 2001. (2001). Retrieved April 2007 from http:// www.ed.gov/nclb/overview/intro/execsumm.html

Phillips, S. E. (Ed.). (2000). *Defending a high school graduation test: G.I. Forum v. Texas Education Agency* (Vol. 13). Mahwah, NJ: Erlbaum.

Raudenbush, S. (2000). Synthesizing results from the NAEP trial state data. In D. W. Grissmer & J. M. Ross (Eds.), *Analytic issues in the assessment of student achievement* (pp. 3–42). Washington, D.C.: National Center for Educational Statistics.

Smith, M. (2000). Assessment trends in a contemporary policy context. In D. W. Grissmer & J. M. Ross (Eds.), *Analytic issues in the assessment of student achievement* (pp. 249–278). Washington, D.C.: National Center for Educational Statistics.

Valencia, R. R., & Bernal, E. M. (Eds.). (2000). *The Texas assessment of academic skills (TAAS) case: Perspectives of plaintiffs' experts* (Vol. 22). Thousand Oaks, CA: Sage.

Young, M. (1994). *The rise of the meritocracy.* Edison, NJ: Transaction.

PART II

Data-Driven Decision Making and Change

CHAPTER 4

The Role of Comparative Data in Changing the Educational Reform Conversation

Fred Carrigg & Mary Jane Kurabinski

In 1990, the New Jersey Supreme Court handed down a landmark decision (*Abbott v. Burke II*) declaring the state's educational system unconstitutional because it denied students in 28 urban districts their guaranteed right to a "thorough and efficient" education. It was the second in a series of decisions, known collectively as the Abbott rulings,[1] that would drive efforts to address the needs of New Jersey's most underserved schools.

New Jersey responded by providing additional funding guaranteeing that poor urban school districts—which became known as the Abbott districts—received funding at least equal to per-pupil spending in the state's wealthiest districts. However, more than a decade after *Abbott v. Burke II* and billions of additional dollars beyond allocated state equalization aid, many urban students were still not achieving the same levels of academic success as their suburban counterparts. In 2003, the Court ordered the New Jersey Department of Education (NJ DOE) to address the lowest-performing elementary Abbott schools.

The NJ DOE shifted its attention from merely formulaic funding to focus instead on instructional practices. It examined both quantitative and qualitative assessment data on literacy in collaboration with district and school administrative staff to help effect change at all levels of the educational structure for the most educationally deficient Abbott schools.[2]

Roughly 4 years later, state scores on the fourth-grade literacy test have improved slightly, but the Abbott district gains have been significantly larger (New Jersey Department of Education, 2005; see Table 4.1).

Table 4.1. Grade 4—New Jersey ASK (Assessment of Skills and
Knowledge) Language Arts Literacy

NJ State

	2003	2004	2005	2003–2005
All	77.6	82.1	81.6	+4.0
GE	86.3	90.3	88.9	+2.6
LEP	31.4	48.6	46.2	+14.8
SE	41.5	48.9	48.7	+7.2

Abbott

	2003	2004	2005	2003–2005
All	55.8	64.0	65.9	+10.1
GE	67.1	75.3	76.3	+9.2
LEP	26.5	45.1	43.9	+17.4
SE	18.0	25.2	27.9	+9.9

Low-Performing Districts (LPD) / Low-Performing Schools (LPS)

	2003	2004	2005	2003–2005
All	39.2	51.5	55.0	+15.8
GE	47.5	61.2	62.6	+15.1
LEP	11.0	31.9	33.3	+22.3
SE	7.8	14.0	19.9	+12.1

Note: Prepared by Fred Carrigg, August 2005.

FORGING PARTNERSHIPS

When the 2003 decision came down, the NJ DOE's newly formed Office of
Urban Literacy was charged with improving the literacy programs in the
Abbott elementary schools. The Office of Urban Literacy targeted 42 elementary schools in 12 Abbott districts where more than half of the general education students scored "partially proficient" in language arts literacy on the
fourth-grade state test.[3]
    The Office of Urban Literacy recognized that it first must address the
misgivings that haunt local responsiveness to school reform. State interven-

tions historically have been ineffectual because schools and districts view these efforts as shallow and short-term. Senior-level district and school administrators are generally resentful, defensive, and unwilling to collaborate with state intervention teams. Discussions often bog down with digressions into the intractable socioeconomic differences between have and have-not districts and schools.

To overcome local skepticism and resentment, the Office of Urban Literacy developed partnerships with districts and schools by creating what became known as Literacy Assessment Teams (LATs). Each of the 42 targeted schools was examined by staff from the Office of Urban Literacy and staff from the central office of the local district, who worked collaboratively with staff from the individual school. The school personnel always included the principal and usually the reading specialist, literacy coach, and/or ESL/ bilingual teacher. The district personnel always included the superintendent, central office supervisors and administrators, and in most cases the assistant superintendent in charge of curriculum and instruction. Together, the Literacy Assessment Teams investigated the root causes for the lack of academic achievement in literacy and developed recommendations for program changes at the district, school, and classroom levels designed to result in immediate as well as long-term improvement. So that the findings would carry weight, the Office of Urban Literacy made sure that the recommendations on how to improve student achievement were concrete, and gave the district equal say in the final report.[4]

THE ROLE OF DATA

The comprehensive review of the literacy programs compared data at as many levels as possible, including similar districts and schools with similar populations and programs. The data reviewed needed to reach the teacher and student levels and needed to be gathered not just to evaluate but also to inform instruction. School and classroom visits were conducted to validate findings or identify mitigating circumstances.

The Literacy Assessment Teams collected and analyzed a variety of data sets, including state and summative off-year assessments from New Jersey school districts, comparing results with previous years as well as between identical populations or subgroups. Disaggregating the data across subgroups had a profound effect. Confronting schools with multiple discrete comparisons—data from districts of similar size, economic status, and racial/ethnic composition—redirected discussion from home and background circumstances (factors beyond school control) to curricula, structures, teaching practices, and other educational components that needed improvement.

Over time, a five-step review procedure emerged:

- Collection and disaggregation of data. The LATs collected and analyzed state, standardized, and local assessments to identify potential
areas of concern. The collected data were disaggregated across populations, including racial/ethnic groups, gender, English-language
learner (ELL) students, and special education students. The LATs
made school and classroom visits to verify findings or identify mitigating circumstances; they also looked to see whether the schools were
using structures and teaching practices aligned with the state's Intensive Early Literacy.[5] It is worth noting that in most cases visits to
schools and classrooms bore out the potential problems identified
through analysis of the data.
- Review of comprehensive reading programs. The LATs gathered information on the district and/or school's comprehensive reading program. They examined how the program intended to address all
students, including limited-English-proficiency students and students
with disabilities, as well as the program's level of implementation. The
recommendations in the final report to the district were predicated
on the strengths and weaknesses specific to populations and programs
as revealed by the data; they also included suggestions about the effective use of the district's chosen comprehensive reading program.[6]
- Examination of delivery of instruction. To address the delivery of
instruction, the LATs examined organizational patterns and structures
(e.g., a 90-minute literacy block, district-level or school-level guidance on "read-alouds" during the block) so that their recommendations would take these elements into consideration and, ultimately,
be effective at improving current practice in the schools.
- Review of assessment's role in informing instruction. The state required four levels of assessment—screening, ongoing, diagnostic, and
standardized—to inform statements and recommendations that would
build on the strengths of students while addressing weaknesses. The
LATs looked closely at assessment practices at the student level to
determine whether and how they informed instruction; for example,
Are students screened for potential reading difficulties? Are portfolios used and, if so, are they aligned with the curriculum?
- Review of professional development. The LATs reviewed the district's
current professional development practices, across all teacher populations (novice, veteran, and master teachers; general education, special education, ESL, bilingual, etc.). Their observations, combined with
other district data, led to the development of appropriate and comprehensive district-level and/or school-level professional development
plans. For example, if schools didn't routinely screen their K–3 stu-

dents for reading, the district planned a professional development workshop on how to administer and evaluate screenings. If district policy was to screen but a particular school did not, the district would provide professional development for that school.

In addition, the district Literacy Assessment Teams reviewed the organization and instructional guidance offered to determine whether those systems supported or deterred academic achievement. Team members analyzed the results of the data, including the observations from the visit protocol, and the current level of student performance in order to develop recommendations to assist the schools and districts. Based on these reviews, the focused visits, and the comparative data, district and Office of Urban Literacy staff formulated recommendations to improve instruction at the classroom level. These recommendations created the framework for the development of targeted, district-wide plans for improvement.

COMPARATIVE ANALYSIS: A TALE OF TWO DISTRICTS

The analysis described here is based on sample composites of actual fourth-grade state assessment data[7] for two Abbott districts. For purposes of confidentiality we refer to them as Districts A and B (New Jersey Department of Education, 2005). District A's general education students consistently have underperformed compared with the state average. Administrators frequently argue, with substantial justification, that students in urban districts face a host of challenges not encountered by the general population of New Jersey. In 2003, the year of the first LAT interventions, the state of New Jersey was approximately 62% White with equal percentages of African-American (17%) and Latino students (17%) as well as 4% Asian, but many of the Abbott districts were, and are still, more than 80% minority.[8] Furthermore, as in the rest of the nation, economically disadvantaged students are clustered in urban settings. Thus, Abbott districts differ substantially in their average demographics and economics from other districts throughout the state. For these reasons, simply comparing the average state results with the average results of Abbott districts as a whole would not be enlightening. A more nuanced comparison was critical.

As in many states, the NJ DOE differentiates districts based on socioeconomic status with a "district factor grouping" (DFG) ranging from A to J: DFG A indicates the lowest income, and DFG J, the most affluent. Most Abbott districts are DFG A, so comparisons to other DFG A districts and other Abbott districts would provide a critical lens on the results in Districts A and B.

The LAT reports used data from tables that give multiple comparisons, for language arts literacy, of the different program placement categories:

general education (GE), special education (SE), and limited English proficiency (LEP).[9] The District A report was completed in March 2004, when data for Spring 2004 were not yet available (see Table 4.2).

Based on the data from District A, the Office of Urban Literacy and central district staff recorded the following observations in the LAT final report.

GENERAL EDUCATION. From 2001 to 2002 District A's percent of general education students demonstrating proficiency increased by 6.6%, thus outpacing the rate of growth at the state level, but not keeping pace with other DFG A and Abbott districts. In 2003, the district decreased by 6.4% in the number of general education students achieving proficiency. The district outperformed the DFG A but not the Abbott comparison groups, while continuing to fall well below the state average, by 19.6%.

SPECIAL EDUCATION. In 2002, District A's number of special education students demonstrating proficiency increased by 11.5%, thus exceeding the rate of growth achieved by the state, DFG A districts, and Abbott districts. However, in 2003, the district decreased by 12.4% in the number of special education students achieving proficiency. The district also performed below the DFG A, Abbott, and state averages.

LIMITED ENGLISH PROFICIENCY. District A's number of limited-English-proficient students demonstrating proficiency increased by 4.6% in 2002, thus keeping pace with all comparative groups. In 2003, though, the district decreased by 24.2% in the number of LEP students demonstrating proficiency. The district also performed well below all comparative groups, all of which lost ground in 2003. A possible explanation is that, contrary to past policy, the pool of LEP students was increased to include first-year new entrants (see discussion below about Table 4.1).

Table 4.2. Percentage Proficient and Advanced Proficient—District A

	GE				SE				LEP			
	2001	2002	2003	2004	2001	2002	2003	2004	2001	2002	2003	2004
District	66.3	72.9	66.5	73.6	14.5	26.0	13.6	14.1	39.4	44.0	19.8	35.2
State	85.3	86.3	86.1	90.3	45.7	42.6	40.6	49.1	40.2	44.7	31.3	48.7
DFG A	61.3	68.9	65.8	74.3	18.8	20.1	17.6	23.0	34.0	41.3	26.9	44.6
Abbott	62.6	69.8	67.1	75.3	20.0	20.3	18.0	25.2	34.9	41.1	26.5	45.9

Note: Years represent the end of school terms; 2001 means the 2000–01 school year.
Source: NJ DOE.

District B's LAT report was issued in December 2004 and included Spring 2004 data (see Table 4.3). The Office of Urban Literacy and central district offices made the following observations.

GENERAL EDUCATION. District B's passing rate for general education students was consistently better than other DFG A districts, although the gap is narrowing. This is also true of a comparison between the district and the Abbott average pass rate. It appears that in 2004, District B made real gains in closing the gap between its scores and the state average pass rate.

SPECIAL EDUCATION. The district's passing rate for special education students fluctuated from year to year, mirroring the Abbott rates, but remained well below state averages. This is an area of concern; the special education population has not experienced the stability/growth of the general education group.

LIMITED ENGLISH PROFICIENCY. The district's passing rate for LEP students fluctuated, but essentially mirrored the passing rates of all comparable groups. Note, however, the changes in the reporting of LEP scores from year to year, as explained later about Table 4.1.

District A's performance mirrored that of comparable districts serving a similar population of low socioeconomic students. Performance jumped in 2001–02 and then again in 2003–04 for the general education students, but performance for subgroups did not follow the same pattern. In contrast, District B consistently outperformed the comparison groups; however, it remains below the state average. The issue no longer can be haves versus have-nots. Confronted with multiple discrete comparisons like these, based on districts of similar size, economic status, and racial/ethnic composition, educators shift their conversations from home and background to curriculum, structures, teaching practices, and so on, which can be examined for

Table 4.3. Percentage Proficient and Advanced Proficient—District B

	GE				SE				LEP			
	2001	2002	2003	2004	2001	2002	2003	2004	2001	2002	2003	2004
District	72.0	72.3	71.2	79.4	18.6	16.6	21.5	23.3	40.3	35.2	29.5	47.8
State	85.3	86.3	86.1	90.3	45.7	42.6	40.6	49.1	40.2	44.7	31.3	48.7
DFG A	61.3	68.9	65.8	74.3	18.8	20.1	17.6	23.0	34.0	41.3	26.9	44.6
Abbott	62.6	69.8	67.1	75.3	20.0	20.3	18.0	25.2	34.9	41.1	26.5	45.9

Source: NJ DOE.

enhancement. The comparative data show that District A has clear issues to address and offer a persuasive argument to all stakeholders that further probing within the district is needed to determine strengths and weaknesses that relate directly to program design and instruction.

Schools Within Districts

When a school within a district with a typical student population in the general education program has reversed the district trend and is improving, the question is: What is the school doing differently so that while the district pass rate has fallen, the school's pass rate has improved? On the other hand, if the school's pass rate for special education students is extremely low when compared with all comparison groups (see Table 4.4), the follow-up visit to the school will look to see what is going well in general education classes and how services are provided to children with disabilities.

In addition to looking at performance based on program participation, similar analyses are conducted based on gender and racial/ethnic subgroups (see Tables 4.5 and 4.6).

We regularly find a tremendous gap between the genders in low-performing urban schools (see Table 4.5). In this example, the performance difference between males and females mirrors state averages for 2002 and 2003. The gap between male and female performance grew in 2004, with improved scores by female students.

Table 4.6 shows African-Americans in this school underperforming compared with African-Americans in the district and the state. Latino students at the school significantly underperformed in similar comparisons, although the gap began to close at this school in 2004. Racial/ethnic sub-

Table 4.4. Percentage Proficient and Advanced Proficient—
School X in District A

	2000-2001			2001-2002			2002-2003			2003-2004		
	GE $n=47$	SE $n=15$	LEP $n=2$	GE $n=40$	SE $n=5$	LEP $n=1$	GE $n=30$	SE $n=17$	LEP $n=8$	GE $n=41$	SE $n=4$	LEP $n=10$
School X	29.8	20.0	n/a	45.0	n/a	n/a	70.0	5.9	n/a	78.0	n/a	n/a
District	66.3	14.5	39.4	72.9	26.0	44.0	66.5	13.6	19.8	73.6	14.1	35.2
State	85.3	45.7	40.2	86.3	42.6	44.7	86.1	40.6	31.3	90.3	49.1	48.7
DFG A	61.3	18.8	34.0	68.9	20.1	41.3	65.8	17.6	26.9	74.3	23.0	44.6
Abbott	62.6	20.0	34.9	69.8	20.3	41.1	67.1	18.0	26.5	75.3	25.2	45.9

Source: NJ DOE Cycle II Report.

Table 4.5. Percentage Proficient and Advanced Proficient in 2002–2004 Disaggregated by Gender Subgroup—School X in District A

	2002		2003		2004	
	Males $n = 23$	Females $n = 23$	Males $n = 30$	Females $n = 25$	Males $n = 32$	Females $n = 22$
School X	35.3	47.6	37.7	45.8	39.1	62.5
District	56.4	71.7	44.9	61.3	53.7	64.6
State	73.9	84.6	71.9	83.0	77.9	86.5

groups are often overrepresented in program placement categories such as special education and LEP. When ethnicity converges with programs, the Literacy Assessment Teams often find that schools need to review carefully their programs to ensure that structures, curricula, and teaching practices are appropriate.

With these multiyear data, we now can pose the critical question: What are other schools in District A doing so that these subgroups are achieving at significantly higher levels than at School X?

When subgroups do not perform as well as the general education students, the LATs would suggest that schools investigate possibilities for improving subgroup performance by, for example, reviewing the classroom libraries. Is there a gender gap in the selection of books? Are books available that are self-motivating and engaging for boys, or are the offerings inadvertently tilted toward girls? Similarly, in a school with a predominance of Latinos or African-Americans, are there books that nonstereotypically engage and include these subgroups?

Table 4.6. Percentage Proficient and Advanced Proficient in 2002–2004 Disaggregated by Racial/Ethnic Subgroup—School X in District A

	2002		2003		2004	
	African-American $n = 16$	Hispanic $n = 29$	African-American $n = 17$	Hispanic $n = 38$	African-American $n = 17$	Hispanic $n = 37$
School X	35.7	46.9	45.0	36.6	45.1	57.1
District	61.6	74.7	50.6	52.1	54.7	59.6
State	60.7	67.4	57.6	62.3	66.6	68.9

DIGGING DEEPER: ANALYSIS OF CLUSTERS

Another analysis of the data is at the cluster level (see Table 4.7). The NJ DOE clusters certain types of questions and tasks on its literacy test into two subgroups: those pertaining to writing and those pertaining to reading. The reading cluster is subdivided further into two groups: working with text and analyzing text. While the working-with-text questions usually address literal and lower-level comprehension, the analyzing-text group asks questions associated with multiple-step or higher-order thinking skills, such as making inferences and synthesizing information. The NJ DOE provides "mean" score cluster-comparative data. Although the number and items in a cluster change each year, preventing horizontal multiyear comparisons, for any given year the comparison is valid. Analyzing several individual years of subclusters presents an opportunity to discover patterns in the data, and patterns support the formulation of recommendations at the district and/or school level.

In the writing cluster, District A has swung back and forth from outperforming to underperforming the DFG A and the just proficient mean,[10] a trend at the school level as well. The Literacy Assessment Teams identified performance on the writing portion of the state test as a problem at both the school and the district level. When results from schools throughout the district were compared with the just proficient mean, a pattern emerged indicating that writing was a problem across the district and not localized at individual schools. Based on this closer look at the data, and the subtest data in particular, the LATs decided that District A should implement a districtwide writing initiative, focusing on the process and product of writing. In

Table 4.7. Literacy Mean Scores for General Education Students

	Writing			Reading			Working with Text			Analyzing Text		
	2002	2003	2004	2002	2003	2004	2002	2003	2004	2002	2003	2004
School X	10.4	9.4	9.3	9.2	8.8	9.9	4.7	4.2	3.3	4.5	4.6	6.6
JPM*	10.9	10.0	9.0	9.1	8.0	10.0	4.5	3.9	3.3	4.6	4.1	6.6
District	12.2	9.8	10.5	10.7	8.2	11.2	5.3	3.8	3.6	5.5	4.4	7.6
DFG A	11.8	9.9	10.3	10.4	8.5	11.7	5.1	4.0	3.9	5.3	4.5	7.9
State	12.8	11.7	11.5	12.7	11.4	14.1	6.1	5.2	4.6	6.6	6.3	9.5

* just proficient mean
Source: Cycle II Reports.

2003–04, District A implemented a program focused on writing and the district writing mean improved.

The two subclusters—working with text and analyzing text—are more opaque. Test items are not released, so we cannot conduct an item analysis to uncover what students are finding particularly difficult. Since so many indicators, such as literal comprehension, are buried within these larger clusters, basing specific recommendations on comparative mean performance is murky and unlikely to produce anything directly useful at either the school or the district level.

Digging Deeper: Using Analysis of Items to Pinpoint Problems and Inform Instruction

The investigations discussed above focused on passing rates using criterion-referenced state tests. In brief, they tell us how well students are doing compared with other students in the state. However, the inability to tease out information about discrete reading skills led the team to investigate a second set of summative assessment data to help answer remaining questions. The state assessments were administered only at grades 4, 8, and 11. Abbott districts were required to administer a state-approved, norm-referenced or criterion-referenced summative assessment annually in the grades not taking the state test. Most districts—Abbott and non-Abbott—opted for the same nationally available test in the elementary-level grades—K, 1, and 2.

The test publisher reports out data in various ways, including:

- National percentile at the district, school, and student level;
- Objective summary report at the national, school, and classroom level; and
- Item analysis summary with comparisons to the national, district, school, and classroom level, including broad categories such as basic understanding, analyze text, and identify reading strategies, with each broad category containing selected items that measure student attainment of specific skills such as stated information.

Tables 4.8 and 4.9 represent second-grade assessment results in one composite, fictitious school and district, from the norm-referenced, off-year summative assessment used by most districts in New Jersey.

The Literacy Assessment Teams found the item analysis comparisons to be the most informative data about literacy because they segregate discrete reading skill acquisition from general observations. The district team compared student responses on test questions, noting discrepancies and instances when most students chose the same incorrect answer. Patterns of

Table 4.8. Percentage Correct and Difference on Specific
Assessment Items

	Nation	District	School	Difference: District-Nation	Difference: School-Nation
Reading Objective					
02 Basic Understanding					
05 stated information	94	98	84	+4	−10
16 stated information	72	79	76	+7	+4
17 stated information	63	67	52	+4	−11
18 stated information	69	78	76	+9	+7
31 sequence	48	50	47	+2	−1
47 stated information	69	72	70	+3	+1
48 stated information	65	72	78	+7	+13
50 vocabulary	75	84	87	+9	+12

answers often revealed instructional issues that went deeper than the intent
of the test questions.

Throughout the districts, the most common, widespread issue was that
many students stumbled when items contained Tier 2 vocabulary words.[11]
For example, in an item assessing stated information, students were asked
to read a sentence and then identify the opposite of the underlined word *shrill*.

Table 4.9. Percentage Correct and Difference on Specific
Assessment Items

	Nation	District	School	Difference: District-Nation	Difference: School-Nation
03 Analyze Text					
06 conclusions	90	94	94	+4	+4
07 conclusions	86	82	78	−4	−8
29 story elements/character	75	77	79	+2	+4
30 cause/effect	74	86	82	+12	+8
45 main idea/theme	57	59	48	+2	−11
46 conclusions	69	78	88	+9	+19

In the district where the item analysis was conducted, 80% of the stated information questions were answered correctly by most students. However, a majority got the same stated information question wrong. A further look showed that other questions about opposite meaning were answered correctly most of the time. The underlying reason for the incorrect response was vocabulary. Students did not know the meaning of *shrill* and so could not determine accurately its opposite, even though they understood the concept of opposite. The test developers had distributed Tier 2 vocabulary into various skill groups, which both inadvertently masked the problem and negatively affected student scores in a number of skill areas. The LATs recognized that a fundamental building block of vocabulary—knowledge of key words—was essential to performing the comprehension tasks being measured.

In another pattern, the LAT noticed that students overwhelmingly chose an incorrect response to an analyze-text question. After discussion, team members concluded that students were having difficulty finding an answer embedded in the middle of the text. This suggested that teachers were emphasizing finding answers at the beginning or end of passages, overshadowing other possibilities.

In yet another instance, items in the middle or end of very long passages were answered incorrectly by a majority of children. The team looked at the district's instructional materials and concluded that students were exposed almost exclusively to short reading passages and had not developed the stamina needed to stay with longer passages. The LAT recommended that students be asked to read and respond to longer passages as part of their regular instructional program.

In some cases, site visits to verify issues uncovered alternative contributors to a problem, such as late-decodable words containing unusual grapheme representations, for example, /ough/. In this particular case, the teaching of phonics and word meaning was discontinued too soon, before many of the more difficult grapheme arrangements had been studied.

Discrete assessments at a micro level can indicate exactly where the process of becoming a proficient reader breaks down. Item analysis tells a school district what it is doing well and pinpoints areas that need instructional focus. When patterns are discerned across a district, the LAT recommends a district-level change in curriculum. If the issue is isolated at a school, the recommendation is to assess school-level fidelity to the district curriculum model and specific teacher practices in implementation. Item analysis further allows a district, a school, or a teacher to detect issues relevant to subgroups of the student body, for example, special education students or English-language learners, so that instruction can be targeted to specific issues that challenge students who are part of these subgroups. By making targeted instruction possible, item analysis brings the focus of instruction back to the specific needs of the learners in each classroom.

In the 2003 court ruling, the state mandated that each of the 12 under-performing districts develop an Intensive Early Literacy (IEL) plan in accordance with the state paradigm and submit that plan for state approval. The Literacy Assessment Teams' powerful combination of data analysis with the qualitative assessment resulted in all 12 districts earning state approval for their IEL plans. The plans were collaborations among the schools, districts, and the NJ DOE, a significant transformation from the all-too-often combative, confrontational relations between local districts and the state education department that marked prior efforts at improvement.

State scores have improved slightly since 2003, but Abbott gains are greater. The subset of the combined scores of the 42 low-performing schools shows the greatest improvement for the comparable groups. Spurred by these encouraging results, Abbott districts not mandated by court order have undertaken LAT reviews.

Table 4.1 shows the progress that has been made and sustained over the 2 years since the implementation of IEL recommendations, using the comparative analysis approach and qualitative review. The numbers in the table represent the pass rates on the state test of districts/schools that underwent LAT review and collaboratively developed and implemented IEL plans. Low-performing district/low-performing school (LPD/LPS) and LEP data are defined as follows:

- *LPD/LPS.* Any school with 50% or more general education students "below proficient" are designated "low-performing." Any district with 25% of its schools designated "low-performing" is designated a low-performing district.
- *LEP Data.* In 2003, all students (4,111) categorized as LEP were included in reported data.

In 2004, all students (5,306) categorized as LEP were included; however, districts were allowed to include exited ELLs up to 3 years. This ruling on the definition of LEP skewed the results because some districts included exited ELLs as LEP and some did not (including exited ELLs improved reported results).

In 2005, the State of New Jersey said the districts no longer should include students who had been in the country for 1 year or less. Some schools included these students; some didn't. No exited ELLs were included in the LEP category (3,447 students).

For 3 years, the LEP data were actually about different students, depending on which district they were coming from and the state and federal guidance. (Note the difference in the number of students tested from year to year.)

LESSONS LEARNED

Many districts and schools regard data collection as a compulsory compliance activity. When used properly, however, data can be invaluable in pointing the way to improvement. For example:

- State and federal regulations on collecting data have created an opportunity to focus districts and schools on evidence.
- Comparative data analysis has the power to change the conversation among stakeholders, redirecting the focus away from societal ills toward how to improve student performance based on the use of scientifically based best practice.
- Qualitative assessments based on school and classroom visits have made administrators and teachers reflective about current practice and enabled them to re-evaluate curriculum and benchmarks, often raising expectations.
- Item analysis of nationally norm-referenced assessments can pinpoint areas of specific instructional weakness at district, school, and classroom levels.

In conclusion, we believe that a balanced approach to data—using multiple sources, matching quantitative data analysis with in-depth qualitative reviews at the school level—has been successful because it makes sense to school- and district-level administrators. The comparative achievement data analysis establishes a clear need for change and challenges stakeholders to look beyond environmental, societal, and subgroup laments and instead create solutions based on data that improve student performance. Once the conversations focus on student achievement, district- and school-level guidance and support, teacher practices, and instructional strategies, genuine educational reform shifts from possible to probable.

NOTES

1. For more on the Abbott rulings, see http://www.edlawcenter.org/ELCPublic/AbbottvBurke/AbbottHistory.htm
2. To suggest that efforts in New Jersey do not emanate from the realities of No Child Left Behind would be disingenuous. However, it is also true that New Jersey state-level testing preceded NCLB, and the breadth and depth of data analysis reported exceed NCLB mandates.
3. The scores of special education students and English-language learners were not included in the results of the literacy portion of the NJ ESPA (Elementary School Proficiency Assessment) fourth-grade test, Spring 2002 administration; if they had been included, the percentage deemed inadequate would have been even higher.

4. No substantive findings were changed, but the districts could add nuance and explanation. If, for example, the LAT found that district schools were not implementing a 90-minute literacy block, the district might change the wording to note that district policy stipulated 90-minute blocks but that individual schools had not implemented these.

5. The LATs deliberately chose not to observe individual teachers because the Office was looking at student-level information to identify district-wide issues. During a classroom visit, the team would randomly ask students to read aloud. Thus the LAT would directly observe whether students could word-read and whether they could comprehend at literal and analytical levels. The school personnel present could corroborate the reports at the central district office.

6. For example, a district might have purchased a comprehensive reading program with a good Spanish component but might not have been using this component with its majority Hispanic population. The report would indicate that using the Spanish component would be effective and appropriate.

7. The state assessment—the Elementary School Proficiency Assessment/Assessment of Skills and Knowledge (ESPA/ASK)—measures both language arts and math, but for our purposes, we consider only the language arts literacy results.

8. Since 2003, New Jersey has become slightly less White and slightly more Latino.

9. The categories are defined as follows: GE–all students except those categorized as special education or limited English proficient; SE–classified students with disabilities; LEP–English-language learners below the state's cut points on a state-approved English-language proficiency test.

10. The just proficient mean is the average (mean) number of points received in each cluster by all students in the state who fell at the cutoff between partially proficient and proficient.

11. Tier 2 vocabulary words are words that appear frequently in books but less frequently in conversation; for example, *fortune* for *luck*, or *splendid* for *nice*, or *excursion* for *trip*. They often are accessed (or used) by more-mature language users, providing more precision and specificity in speaking and writing.

REFERENCES

Abbott v. Burke II. (1990). 119 N.J. 287, 575 A.2d 359.

New Jersey Department of Education. (2005). *New Jersey school report cards.* Retrieved September 2005 from http://education.state.nj.us/rc/

CHAPTER 5

Assessment Data: A Tool for Student and Teacher Growth

Sherry P. King with Carrie Amon

Mamaroneck, New York, is a suburban community about 25 miles north of New York City. Beautiful homes and country clubs line the Long Island Sound; the schools, which share fields and playgrounds with the community, enjoy an excellent reputation; Starbucks and upscale restaurants nestle next to Italian delicatessens and butchers that have been in the community for two generations. However, the popular perception of affluence and stability is only part of the picture of the school district. There are middle-class homes throughout the three municipalities (the town of Mamaroneck, the village of Mamaroneck, and the town of Larchmont), and subsidized/mixed housing adjacent to the district's middle school. In one portion of the village of Mamaroneck, there are homes converted into many small rooms housing Latino families or groups of laborers living together in tight, substandard quarters. This area of the village historically has been home to different immigrant groups, and the three municipalities and the school district have been proud of the diversity. Since several affluent neighboring communities are much more homogeneous, many residents believe this to be a community of choice for those seeking high-quality schools with a diverse student body.

Each month the Local Social Summit, a volunteer group that addresses social concerns of the community, meets in a diner. One meeting, which included all of the municipal leaders, school officials, and interested community members, focused on the growing tension over how to deal with Latino day laborers who gather in a local park hoping for work. The village of Mamaroneck officials wanted to curtail the presence of the laborers in order to preserve the quality of life in the community; others believed that developing a more welcoming treatment of the Latino population would enhance the quality of life. Some of the village officials cited complaints they received from residents about excessive garbage in the area where the laborers gathered to seek employment. They told of mothers saying they were afraid to walk their children past large groups of men, and of laborers urinating in the park. The Hispanic Resource Center, a local advocacy group, had already begun to bring more order rather than try to disperse them. They also complained that a strong police presence was intimidating to workers and potential employers. The village wanted the schools to keep children living in illegal residences out of school, even though monitoring how many people live at a particular address is beyond the school's purview; other members of the Summit wanted the schools to add programs to support second-language learners and children in economic need. The division in the community mirrors some of the struggles of a school system committed to educating to the highest standards all its students in a diverse community. This commitment entails working to maintain the highest levels of challenge while at the same time opening the doors to the most rigorous programs to a wider variety of students.

Over the past decade, long before No Child Left Behind called for disaggregating data for subgroups, the leadership of the Mamaroneck Public Schools understood that finding ways to raise the achievement of its minority students was necessary to maintain the district's "high-achieving" profile. While the achievement levels of its 18% of children of color easily could be hidden in the data, the community, in its commitment to diversity—as evident in its funding of breakfast programs, after-school programs, summer programs, and more staffing for the elementary school with the largest number of poor and second-language learners—was determined to use its resources, its professional capacity, and its will to increase achievement for minority students, who were also the district's most economically disadvantaged students. That kind of commitment raises many complex issues.

The four elementary schools are zoned by neighborhood. Of these, Mamaroneck Avenue School has the most diverse population, with students from subsidized housing as well as from homes abutting a world-class golf course. Of its 503 students, 225 are of Caucasian, 225 of Latino, 29 of African-American, and 24 of Asian descent. Close to 40% (195) of the students in the school are eligible for free lunch. Virtually all of the eligible students are children of color.

On my first night as superintendent of schools, I attended a meeting at Mamaroneck Avenue School. The principal, a reading teacher, and a testing expert were explaining to a large group of angry, mostly White parents their strategy for dealing with students who scored below the state standard on reading tests. A parent stood up, turned to the back of the room where I was sitting with a board member, and asked when the board was going to change the school's attendance patterns so his children would not have to attend school with children who did not speak English and could not read. Diplomacy was called for; I told the parents that I recognized they were worried that, with all of the attention to bringing some students up to standard, time and resources would be diverted from helping their children achieve at even higher levels. I promised that as a district we would do both, and that we would share our work and progress toward that end with the public.

The route to fulfilling that promise of having all children improve in achievement has been complicated, but the progress of Mamaroneck Avenue School, and its link to the use of assessment data, tells a story of what is possible. One major element, an examination of the achievements in English language arts with a specific focus on how data analysis contributed to the growth of teachers and students, illustrates the power of using formative assessment data, providing targeted professional development, and, with those supports, holding teachers accountable for student growth.

At its simplest level, the reading scores showed that this elementary school's literacy instruction was inadequate. Many students of color were reading below the already low state standards. In addition, few of the White, middle-class students were achieving at as high a level as their peers in the district's other elementary schools. A first step in the transformation of the school was the appointment of an administrator whose sole focus was instruction. That leader, Carrie Amon, who since has become principal of Mamaroneck Avenue School, saw that teachers needed to understand and implement a consistent and coherent literacy program. She helped teachers build classroom libraries; altered the school schedule to provide 90-minute literacy blocks, even though that caused some tension with art and physical education teachers at first; and made explicit her expectations about what should happen during those blocks.

She organized monthly, 2-hour, grade-level team meetings, which continue to this day. Each meeting follows the same format: During the first 30 to 45 minutes, student achievement is discussed, beginning with charts of individual students' academic success. This part of the meeting includes the full grade-level team of special needs teachers, social worker, psychologist, ESL teacher, classroom teachers, and administrators. Special service providers (speech, occupational, and physical therapists) are invited as the need arises. The entire team looks closely at students who are not meeting academic expectations and at trends of growth or lack of growth. The team also looks at high achievers to see whether instruction is meeting their needs as reflected in their continued growth, and shares teaching strategies for pushing and challenging those students. For the following hour and 15 minutes, the classroom teachers and administrators stay to discuss instructional practice. These discussions might relate directly to the prior conversation, or might follow up on classroom visits by administrators. The district also hires literacy consultants to help teachers expand their teaching practices. Some of the discussion may be related to the observations of those consultants.

All discussions begin with data from monthly reading assessments administered by the teachers. Prior to meeting regularly as a team and using data as the basis for analysis, meetings were sporadic, there was rarely an agenda, and much of the conversation was about the logistics of class trips, discipline, or other administrative concerns. When the focus was on student achievement, teachers shared impressions about how well students were reading, but had no systematic assessment data to support these ideas. One of Amon's early goals for the grade-level meetings was to replace impressions with more objective information. The school and district chose the Developmental Reading Assessment (DRA; Pearson Learning, 2007) as the quantitative measure it would use. Assessing reading ability is complex. The DRA measures two different reading levels: independent and instructional. The independent level measures a student's ability to read without instruction; the instructional level measures a student's ability to read with explicit help from a teacher. That explicit help includes strategies that allow the student to engage with more complex texts on his or her own. The instructional level thus is always higher than the independent level, and instruction is designed to move the child to a higher independent level because of the new reading strategies he or she has gained.

Initially, the teachers brought only the independent reading-level results as measured on the DRA to the monthly grade-level meetings. To collect reliable data, the first task was to help teachers learn to administer the DRA, which requires knowledge of the instrument and what it measures. Administering the DRA also requires a classroom structure that allows the teacher to assess a few students while others are engaged in independent work. This structure forces teachers to create tasks that allow children to work independently and practice skills while the teacher works with other students either in small groups or individually. At Mamaroneck Avenue School, simply gathering reliable data—without analysis—thus required changing classroom practice significantly, which was accomplished through an enormous amount of staff development, modeling, and in-class support for the new organizational structures.

Once reliable data were available, Amon decided that sharing the process of analysis was important for teachers. She believed that teachers sharing successful strategies and areas of frustration would build a powerful learning community. She also believed that some teachers did not have high enough expectations for their students and that seeing how much students in other classes were growing would be an incentive for them to change their practices. She boldly created a large board in the faculty room where students' names were placed according to their independent reading level and their teacher, as seen in Figure 5.1.

Making student achievement public, even to teachers of a single grade level (the boards were covered between meetings so the information was not

Figure 5.1. Faculty Room Chart of Students and Their Reading Levels

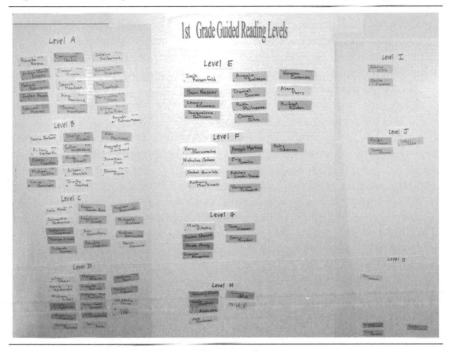

available to non-team members), runs counter to the culture of many schools because it threatens some teachers whose students are not making as much progress as others. Making data public also highlights disagreements, when, for example, the reading teacher has a different interpretation of a student's reading level than the classroom teacher has. Rather than allowing the differences to create tensions, Amon used them to open up discussions about assessment and instructional practice, seeing moments of open disagreement as opportunities for professional growth that would help children. For example, it was fairly typical at grade-level meetings for a teacher to bring evidence of a child's instructional level but insist that the child's lack of background and experience necessitated instruction at a lower level than the data suggested. In a meeting where such a discrepancy is presented, there is an opportunity for discussion about preteaching, the difference between instruction and independent reading, and the planning that is necessary to present a new, more demanding text to a student—the kind of reflection that rarely happens when a teacher works in isolation. The conversation gives other teachers a chance to share strategies they have used to achieve success. Without such open discussion, many teachers will continue to instruct at a lower level than the student's ability because the teachers want their students to experience success rather than struggle with the demands of more complicated texts. Also, because the data are focused on students, there is not a tone of judgment about the teacher, even though there is direct discussion of classroom practice. Demonstrating that data could be used productively on behalf of students, rather than punitively against teachers, was an important first lesson in using data to enhance student achievement.

Only about halfway through the second year did teachers become confident that test results were not being used against them and begin to come to meetings ready to share. During that second year, the teachers received professional development on guided reading, a component of balanced literacy. Balanced literacy is an instructional model that includes teaching the students, practice with the students, and opportunities for the students to model reading practices by themselves; sometimes this is described in shorthand as "to, with, and by." Within this model the teacher reads to the students in a read-aloud, modeling fluent reading. In a second component, shared reading, the child practices those skills with the teacher. Guided reading is a time when a teacher teaches direct skills to a small group of students according to their needs. That is the aspect of the model when the teacher helps students gain the skills within an instructional level to attain independence as readers. Finally, in independent reading, the children take all of those skills and practice on their own.

In the course of the monthly team meetings, the full grade-level team discovered that the data showed groups of students not making expected progress. A sizable number of students had been stuck at a particular independent reading level for several months. Because the data showed patterns of which the teachers were unaware, the teachers gained a new recognition that looking at data on a consistent basis could be useful to their classroom practice. In this case, they decided that to determine what was happening to those students who were "stuck," they needed to look more closely at additional kinds of data about what was happening in the classroom.

The first effort of those teachers to look more deeply at what was happening in their classrooms to students who weren't improving at the expected rate, involved videotaping students reading as a way to jointly examine both teacher practice and student behaviors during instruction. When the tapes were shown at the team meetings, teachers, principal, reading specialist, and outside consultant created separate "running records," a process of coding student errors and corrections while students read, to help determine reading levels. The principal observed that teachers tended to insist that a student's reading level was lower than the data suggested, even when the whole group compared "running records" and discussed the difference between independent and instructional reading levels. These moments of discrepancy led the principal to hypothesize that teachers were focusing their instruction at too low a level and were not doing enough teaching. Her hunch was that teachers were inadvertently keeping students at their independent reading level.

One fundamental concept of balanced literacy is that students work in reading groups at an instructional level, but in guided reading groups teachers teach to the next higher level. Analyzing the data on reading achievement against tapes of students actually reading indicated that (1) not all teachers understood the workings of balanced literacy; (2) some were having difficulty balancing individual and guided reading strategies; and (3) while teachers had done much reading with students, many students required more explicit teaching. For example, teachers may be teaching young readers the strategy of using pictures as clues to understanding words. In explicit teaching, the teacher would begin the lesson by telling students that the day's lesson was to learn to use pictures as clues to understanding words. She would be clear about why readers use the strategy, would practice using the strategy with the students, then would ask the students to practice the strategy on their own. In explicit teaching, teachers continually remind students what skill they are learning and why the skill is necessary for good readers.

While data can help uncover assumptions and practices that affect student learning, changing those practices requires focused attention, persistence, and continued accountability. In the year following the school's recognition that reading instruction had to be improved, the long-term outside reading consultant changed his strategy from primarily providing teacher workshops to going into first-grade classes to model guided reading groups for teachers. He chose texts at the next higher level than students' independent reading level and showed teachers that if the book they chose for instruction was too difficult, they could flip into a shared reading lesson, which would give students more teacher support, instead of moving to a lower-level book. During this first year of focusing on changing classroom practice based on achievement data, teachers were willing to try this strategy with students they considered strong readers—who subsequently made large leaps in their reading levels as measured on the DRA—but were not willing to stay with more difficult texts for struggling readers. By year two, teachers were bringing both independent and instructional reading levels to the monthly team meetings, a change that reflected their increased understanding that they needed to work on their teaching strategies together with evidence of student growth.

Using data to improve student growth is complicated because the needs of teachers in the process of change must be balanced against the rights of citizens. On the one hand, if schools intend to examine in-depth connections between teacher practice and student results, staff need a safe space out of the public eye in which to learn, develop, and implement new strategies. On the other hand, public schools require public accountability, which means letting taxpayers know how we are faring in bringing all our students to higher levels of achievement. In a district like Mamaroneck, which willingly allocated additional resources and attention to the issue of minority achievement, teachers should be able to see whether their hard work was reaping benefits in terms of student achievement, the Board of Education and parents should see whether their financial commitment was paying off, and parents should be able to see whether the students in the school were now doing as well as their counterparts in other schools in the district. Moreover, the district wanted to avoid any possibility of "throwing money" at a social problem without determining whether its intended recipients benefited. In short, the Board of Education wanted to make sure the reading efforts at Mamaroneck Avenue School remained focused on improving reading scores, not making an affluent community feel good about itself for spending money rather than creating real change.

The district decided to report publicly on student progress four times a year. The goal was to increase parental trust in the school by presenting the real story of achievement without concealing areas where the school was facing difficulties. The administration also wanted to use the opportunity of public reporting to maintain a sense of urgency among the staff.

Explaining student progress clearly to the community was the next challenge. Over the years, the school developed a number of different presentations. For example, Figure 5.2 displays children's growth over time as measured by the DRA.

In this figure, each little dot represents a child. With each subsequent presentation, the graph shows the movement of change from left to right, from lower to higher reading levels for each child. It shows in changing quarterly reports that some children jump several reading levels in one interval, while others move a single level, and still others remain static.

Initially, this report was a breath of fresh air because it made public the real state of reading achievement in the school and demonstrated that the teachers now knew the actual reading levels of every child in the school. Over time, however, this form of reporting to the community proved insufficient in the eyes of the school administration, who thought it was important for parents to understand the reading levels better and to know what kind of books they should expect to see at different grade levels. As a result, in the second year, the school added samples of student work to show the community what different levels of work look like so that the abstract notion of "levels" made more concrete sense. In the third year, the presentation further included video clips of students reading at different grade levels, again making the abstract independent reading levels come to life.

The students at Mamaroneck Avenue School and their teachers made great strides during the years of initial implementation of the data-based approach to literacy work. The fourth-grade test scores increased from 52% to 68% at or above state standards in the first 2 years (see Figure 5.3). The school could now demonstrate that students generally grew at least one

Figure 5.2. Children's Growth over Time on the DRA

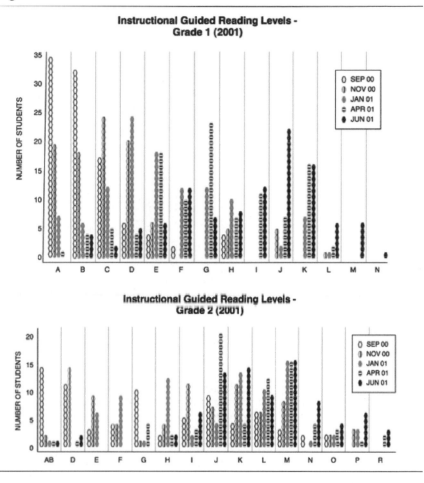

grade level each year they were in school. The gap was no longer widening, as it had been in previous years. On the other hand, the test scores also showed that the school was still unable to make up for the unmet language-learning needs that many of the students had upon entering school, resulting in lagging test scores despite the steady improvement in reading levels. So, while students grew a year or more in reading during the academic year, they did not necessarily come up to grade level if they entered the year reading more than a year below grade level. Even with summer school, bridging that gap was difficult, which led the school to focus more attention on pre-K and kindergarten reading. The school recognized that students'

Figure 5.3. Comparison over Time of Performance

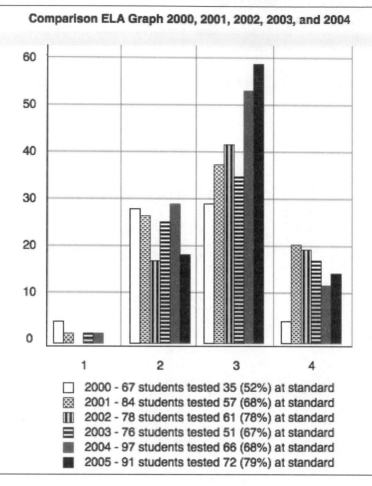

Comparison ELA Graph 2000, 2001, 2002, 2003, and 2004

☐ 2000 - 67 students tested 35 (52%) at standard
▨ 2001 - 84 students tested 57 (68%) at standard
▥ 2002 - 78 students tested 61 (78%) at standard
☰ 2003 - 76 students tested 51 (67%) at standard
▨ 2004 - 97 students tested 66 (68%) at standard
■ 2005 - 91 students tested 72 (79%) at standard

best hope for reading at standard was to leave kindergarten ready for first grade.

During the course of this journey into reading data, a long-time research partner, the EDC Center for Children and Technology, introduced us to visualization software, specifically TinkerPlots™ (Key Curriculum Press, 2006), which allowed the school to examine information in different ways. TinkerPlots™ is a case-based visualization tool. It consists of cases with attributes. Each case can represent a child, whose attributes can be defined flexibly to range from subscores on standardized tests to attendance data, to participation in special programs, and so on. The tool is designed to encourage very flexible questioning of the data. The cases are represented by data points that rearrange themselves according to three possible dimensions, one on each axis of the plot and a third expressed through the colors of the data points. Simply dragging any attribute to either axis causes the data points to rearrange themselves to reflect the relationships selected, and clicking on a third attribute colors the data points according to that attribute.

This process invites investigation of different possible relationships. Clicking on a data point calls up the full attribute record of the case next to the plot, allowing users to always see both the individual and the pattern of the group. This enables users to see immediately how individual students stand on any dimension and to consider the relationship between an individual and the rest of the group.

The most important affordance of this tool is its flexibility. Rather than forcing teachers to make sense of a data representation created by someone else, it enables them to formulate a hypothesis (e.g., maybe there is a relationship between these attributes) and check it immediately. This supports active data investigation rather than passive acceptance of data interpretations made by others. In addition, the availability of information about individual cases, as well as patterns among students, reassures teachers, who are not always comfortable thinking "across" students, that the patterns they are seeing in the data are real rather than artificial, because they can examine each individual case in a pattern to see whether they believe it to be true about that individual student.

Showing TinkerPlots™ to the community affords a similar flexibility. Instead of creating static slides representing data interpretations, teachers and administrators can conduct live data-analysis sessions and thus answer any questions community members may have about the meaning of the data. If a parent wants to know, for instance, whether a result is caused by a particular attribute (such as participation in a special program), administrators can show them the relationship simply by dragging that attribute into the plot. This increases the credibility of the data representation and permits rich discussions of what the data mean.

Figure 5.4 maps all the children's reading levels for one grade; levels A to C are considered below grade level, and levels G and H are considered above grade level.

Teachers, administrators, and parents could see at a glance what additional resources students at a particular grade level were receiving and how those services were distributed among the grade-level classes. The column with the "*" shows the students who entered the school and still needed to be assessed for additional services. The grey dots represent students receiving no additional services. Only eight students who tested below grade level on reading were not receiving extra services. This chart allowed the

Figure 5.4. Reading Levels

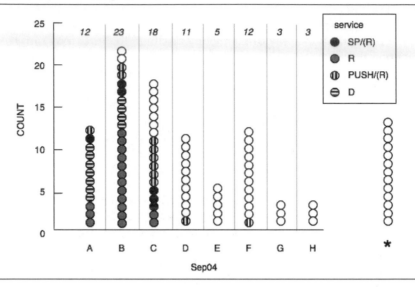

administration to supply a genuine answer to the question, What are you doing about the literacy achievement gap?

In 2004–05, the grade-level teams began using TinkerPlots™instead of charts for their discussions because data visualizations could be created "on the fly" as needed to question the data in new ways. Having built a culture that looks seriously at data on student achievement and having found a tool that allows easy investigation of multiple variables, the school has increased the likelihood that teachers, rather than just administrators, will use data to examine their own practice and their students' achievement. Since the essence of teaching and learning occurs in the classroom between teachers and students, having teachers see the link between the data and what they do with their students is essential to continual growth. At Mamaroneck Avenue School, where comparing the improvement in reading scores over the years by looking at data and practice had become a norm, the first-grade team understood that current students had not grown as much as first graders in prior years. This led to a discussion among teachers about what data they could look at to learn more about the children.

The data suggested a number of transition points that needed attention. For example, generally, 80% of the students left kindergarten ready to enter first grade reading on grade level, but only 60% actually entered at the same level the following September. This drop in skill level led the teachers to generate a number of questions about their students. Since many of the students were in a school-run summer program, teachers wondered what happened to them over the summer.

- Does the summer program keep students on their reading level?
- Is there a difference between students from homes where parents read and those where they don't read?
- Is there a difference between students who stay in this country and use English versus those who travel to home countries where they are immersed in Spanish?
- How far apart are the independent and instructional levels? More than one level of separation between the two suggests the need for greater instructional push. Teachers created a summer reading program to provide "just right" books for kindergarten students whose parents might not have access to them.
- If children are not in the school's summer program, they may not have access to books on their reading level. Teachers gave students exiting kindergarten three packs of books, and 3 days in the summer were scheduled for students to exchange their packs of books. In a recent year, 35 out of 90 students came to exchange them. Will more students come to the book exchange if they are offered additional opportunities to do so?

Generating such questions is an important outgrowth of the data-based work the teachers accomplished during the school year. Next, they need to figure out how to answer these questions by determining what data are relevant to the issues and then collecting those data. Because the data suggest that more accomplished readers come from homes where parents regularly read with their children, the school has taken steps to send home books in English and the children's native language, as well as books on tape, to encourage nightly reading at home. Teachers collect weekly reading logs, another form of data, in support of at-home reading. The teachers and administration recognize that educating parents, especially those who did not go to school in this country, is key to success in getting families to read at home. Knowing that they can look at and analyze collected information in a variety of ways using visualization tools like TinkerPlots™ has opened new possibilities for teachers to use data to guide classroom practice.

A second transitional area of concern has been third grade, where the reading levels of many students at Mamaroneck Avenue School remain the same for long periods of time. Using TinkerPlots™ to chart students moving from grade 2 to grade 3, teachers concentrated on the lower-level readers. While the research indicates that ten instructional sessions at any particular guided reading level should result in movement from that level, the school's experience was that student progress required more than ten instructional sessions. Focusing on students who did not progress led to an examination of the numbers of students at each reading level in each classroom as well as schedules for each class. Looking at the data, teachers saw that in some classes there were as many as seven clusters of students learning at different levels. The data highlighted the need to increase teacher contact time with the students for reading instruction. Could every student functioning below grade level receive reading instruction twice a day? If this was doable, would teachers be able to help students advance their reading levels in less time? Just as the earliest changes in the school required reorganizing the structures to allow 90-minute literacy blocks, this new recognition that the third-grade classes had so many levels within them was calling for new structures that have yet to be determined. In a 90-minute literacy block, a teacher can work with approximately two groups per day. Prior to examining the data, reading teachers simply pulled students from classes; there was no joint responsibility with the classroom teacher for ensuring that all students received explicit reading instruction on agreed-upon skills. The data changed practice by providing a common goal for all teachers working with a particular student, whether the regular classroom teacher, a special education teacher, or a reading specialist. Instead of acting separately, they could organize to provide focused reading instruction more than once a day, thus improving the chances that the student would grow more quickly as a reader.

After studying the clusters of students in third grade, some teachers found other pockets of time for reading instruction and shared with colleagues different ways to schedule the day to achieve more reading time. Another way that the study of data changed teacher practice was its use in breaking down the skills students needed in order to change levels. Teachers looked more closely at the skills students needed to advance in reading and what was standing in their way. For some number of students, especially second-language learners, teachers discovered that students were "stuck" because they lacked background knowledge, so that ten lessons were insufficient to move up to higher-level texts, which were longer and used more complex sentence structures. In addition, if students were reading a text that was set on a prairie and had no prior knowledge of what prairie life might look like, the teacher had to provide background information so students could have full access to the text. The data led to deeper analysis of the need for more explicit instruction in reading skills and context, which then led to change in classroom practice.

Seeing that students were stuck at a particular level was insufficient to change methodology. Disaggregating those scores into skills (more of an item analysis), and understanding that students could decode but had neither the contextual background nor the stamina to read and comprehend more complex reading passages, changed the teachers' strategies. Tracking the new strategies against future achievement data will tell the school whether the new strategies are working.

While the focus of this chapter is on the achievement at Mamaroneck Avenue School, it was not the only school in the district that used data to better support underachieving students. In another school, secondary math teachers assumed that their problem with a number of Latino students related to the students having come to this country with little experience in school or with English. The data showed that, in fact, one third of those Latino students had been in the Mamaroneck school system since kindergarten, spurring a rethinking of practice based on new understandings (King, 2001; King, Weitzman, & Keane, 2004). In this case, the new insight was that language was not the barrier to learning. In another example, the district decided that all eighth-grade students would be enrolled in the advanced earth science curriculum as part of the board's belief that all students can achieve at the same high standards given the proper supports. The results were eye-opening: Using TinkerPlots™ to examine all test data for eighth graders showed that a high number of second-language learners passed the rigorous state test in earth science, which is rich with complex vocabulary, yet did not meet state standards on the English exam at the same grade level. This anomaly raised new questions about instruction in English classes and taught the district about the positive value of high expectations.

Several lessons can be drawn from the experience of the Mamaroneck School District about the use of data. First, a culture of accountability, like the one developed at Mamaroneck Avenue School around student growth in reading, is neither an enemy of good classroom practice nor a panacea for student improvement. Rather, using data as a springboard for analysis is a vehicle for moving beyond impressions or even test results to rethink teacher practices in light of student achievement. Sharing data, making sense of them, and even disagreeing about their implications are important elements in the process of educational change on behalf of children. Second, if used constructively rather than punitively, data can become a catalyst for teachers to become more active researchers into their own practice. In this case, the Mamaroneck teachers were able to focus on the real problems of reading skills and move toward genuine differentiation of instruction based on actual student needs. Third, the process of using data to drive instructional practice is recursive and slower than any of us would like. It helps us move away from embedded assumptions into thoughtful diagnosis. From diagnosis, the process of changing practice and ascertaining that the new practices are achieving the desired results is slow and requires respectful persistence. Finally, each new accomplishment leads to a new cycle of inquiry based on new data.

REFERENCES

Key Curriculum Press. (2006). TinkerPlots [Computer software]. Emeryville, CA: Author. Retrieved March 3, 2007, from http://www.keypress.com/x5715.xml

King, S. P. (2001). Tracking data on student achievement: Questions and lessons. In B. Kallick & J. M. Wilson (Eds.), *Information technology for schools* (pp. 17–32). San Francisco: Jossey-Bass.

King, S. P., Weitzman, S., & Keane, L. (2004, November). Untracking earth science. *Educational Leadership*, 62, 66–69.

Pearson Learning. (2007). *Developmental reading assessment*. Retrieved March 3, 2007, from http://www.pearsonlearning.com/dra

CHAPTER 6

Supporting Teachers' Use of Data:
The Role of Organization and Policy

Viki M. Young

State and federal accountability policies place tremendous faith in the power of data—in particular, standardized test data—to effect school improvement. Practitioners, however, commonly object that standardized data lack instructional usefulness: Teachers note that familiarity with their students' in-class performance means that standardized test results are generally unenlightening; further, those data are obsolete on delivery because the students tested have already moved on to another teacher. Moreover, test results correlate to affluence and English proficiency, so that some teachers are skeptical about the fairness of the tests and the accuracy of their representation of student knowledge.[1]

How do practitioners define and act on data in everyday instruction-related work? Some examples suggest that quantitative test results constitute only a narrow conception of "data."

- Teachers examining student writing to understand what proficiency, as denoted in writing standards, tangibly means;
- Principals viewing videos of other principals leading staff development activities to improve their own capacity to help teachers learn;
- District leaders conducting classroom "walkthroughs" to gauge how well teachers understand and enact components of a literacy program.

Using a broad definition of data, then, I explore how organizational conditions, role definitions, and district and school policy facilitate or frustrate teachers' data use in instruction-related work. The data for this study come from embedded case studies of grade-level teacher teams in two schools in one California school district, Oak Park.[2]

This chapter elaborates the relationship between collaboration and trust among a team of teachers and their understandings of how to use various data for instruction. The cases also illustrate the strategic role of "agenda setting": the way school leaders articulate rationale, set expectations, and structure time and teachers' learning about data. For most teachers, using formal data is not a traditional instruction-related activity. Thus, providing teachers a rationale for using data and building understanding around which data to use and how may be a necessary and intentional early step.

Simply establishing an expectation for teachers to examine data, however, is insufficient to integrate data use into teachers' practices. The cases further suggest that district curriculum and assessment policies simultaneously both enrich the data environment and constrain teachers' abilities to respond to data analyses.

THE CASES:
FULTON AND HILLTOP SCHOOLS IN THE OAK PARK DISTRICT

Oak Park Unified School District is a midsized, urban K–12 district in the San Francisco Bay Area. Its demographics mirror those of the state. No one racial/ethnic group exceeds one-third of the student population, whereas students eligible for free or reduced-price lunch do. English learners hover at one-fifth of district enrollment. Real estate prices are climbing, exacerbating the district's wealth gap drawn along geographic lines. The two case study schools in Oak Park, Fulton and Hilltop, are located in the West End, the poorer section of town.

Fulton, an alternative K–8 program, draws its approximately 400 students citywide. Its demographics reflect those of the overall district, but the school's student population is changing, with increasing numbers of English learners (to 25% in 2003–04), Asians (to 27%), and students in poverty (to 35%).

By comparison, Hilltop Elementary has been one of the poorest schools in Oak Park for a quarter century, serving the predominantly African-American community in the West End. African-American students represent the school's largest single racial/ethnic group (44%), and 87% of Hilltop students are eligible for free or reduced-price lunch. English learners have increased to over one-third.

Oak Park Literacy and Assessment Programs

In 2003–04, Oak Park adopted Houghton-Mifflin (HM), one of two state-approved English language arts (ELA) programs. The district directed its K–2 teachers to implement the word work (phonics, vocabulary, spelling, and writing conventions) and comprehension portions with "fidelity," meaning that teachers must complete virtually all of the activities in sequence and according to a district-wide pacing guide. The HM program also recommends extended literacy blocks—2.5 hours at grade 2, for example—representing, in most Oak Park elementary schools, an increase in time for literacy and a decrease for all other subjects.

This new program contrasts markedly with the teacher-developed, individualistic literacy approach dominant in the district for at least the prior decade. Although the district adopted various programs during that time, district administrators recall, "There was no accountability for whether anyone ever used them or not," and "after 12 years, we've got a bunch of seniors who can't read!" The charge to use HM with fidelity is an attempt to create consistency district-wide, and to instill more direct instruction in comprehension strategies and phonics into the curriculum, which, the district argues, was lacking previously under teachers' primarily whole-language approach.[3]

In support of the new HM literacy program, the district created a K–2 assessment plan that features frequent and varied testing. Grade 2 students, for example, take

- Diagnostic tests on phonemic awareness and phonics decoding in the fall;
- End-of-story tests, approximately every other week, on story-specific vocabulary and comprehension;
- Theme skills tests, six per year, on phonics, conventions, vocabulary, and comprehension strategies covered in each of six thematic units included in the HM program;
- California Summative Tests, three per year, tied to state content standards and not specific to the Houghton-Mifflin program; and
- Fluency tests, three times per year, measuring accurate words per minute in individual oral reading, referenced to national norms.

The range in assessments provides the district with "multiple measures" and "a pretty balanced set," argues the district coordinator for assessment. The district aims to fulfill an *instructional* as well as a monitoring purpose with the new assessment program, by incorporating "curriculum-embedded assessments" in response to teachers' requests for formative assessment. Teachers, however, protest that the assessment schedule is too packed, leaving at times only 2 weeks of instruction between week-long tests.

The literacy adoption and new assessment program form the dominant context in understanding which data Oak Park teachers have available and which they choose to use.

Fulton School

Fulton's identity as an alternative school is palpable among the teacher and parent community. Building a program predicated on developing the "whole child" through cross-curricular instructional themes forged school traditions of teacher leadership and collaboration.

Further, as an initial member of a regional inquiry-based reform network in 1996, Fulton saw itself as a test-bed for the network's main tool, the Cycle of Inquiry (BASRC, n.d.).[4] The language of inquiry still permeates grade-level meetings and staff discussions, and teachers express comfort with critiquing and using multiple forms of data. Although overwhelmed by the Houghton-Mifflin program, the primary-grade teachers had a foundation on which to rest the new district assessment program.

The second-/third-grade team of six teachers—the focal team of this research project at Fulton—had been together for 4 years by 2003–04. All the members have long-term teaching experience, ranging from 12 years to more than 30 years. Each team member takes on a leadership role in some way, whether serving on committees or supporting fellow teachers. The school has three founding teachers still on staff, and two are on the second- /third-grade team. In short, this team feels ownership over the school and has strong roots across the district.

Each teacher has a "homeroom" of both second- and third-grade students.[5] Organized into two pods of three teachers, the teachers switch students within each pod for reading and math to create one smaller class of struggling second-grade students, one class of on-grade-level, second-grade and struggling third-grade students, and one class of on-grade-level, third-grade students.

Literacy Instruction in Second and Third Grade at Fulton

The school's "whole-student" mission clashes in significant ways with the district directive to implement HM with fidelity. The whole-class, teacher-centered instruction embedded in the HM materials collides with the Fulton teachers' orientation toward individual students and individual needs. The second- /third-grade team maintains flexible groupings, moving particular students between classes during the year if they progress rapidly or do not thrive. Rigidly following grade-specific curricula in sequence creates new barriers to moving students on the cusp of second- and third-grade skills—movement, the teachers argue, that allows them to better address students' needs.

Data Practices Among Fulton Second- /Third-Grade Team

Fulton's reform history helped root teachers' data practices squarely within their joint activity. Although they scan assessment results for their own students as the curriculum progresses, their most extensive uses of data occur during full-day, grade-level team meetings every 6 weeks. In part, sharing students as they do motivates them to use one another as resources in making sense of assessment data, student work, and their observations of students.

The team weaves various forms of data into the fabric of its joint activity, in grouping and regrouping students across classes, in writing individual intervention plans for students, and in "knowing students." Because the team assigns students to literacy classes based on skills level and instructional need, the teachers use the HM assessments to group and move students for instruction throughout the school year. They initially sorted the second- and third-grade students into "intensive," "strategic," and "benchmark" categories,[6] using the district-generated, student-level multiple measures report, as well as reading fluency tests from Spring 2003 and diagnostic results in phonemic awareness and phonics decoding skills from Fall 2004.

Delving deeper into the groupings, the team split the intensive category further, arguing that a student approaching the 50th percentile has substantively different needs from a student scoring at the 10th or even 25th percentile. They noted which students had existing individual intervention plans (IIPs) and individual educational plans (IEPs, for special education students), and created new IIPs for those who had neither. The teachers were "surprised at how many of our kids are in that lowest level and have not been identified yet, have not gotten purple folders [individualized intervention plans]." Their analysis by the benchmark, strategic, and intensive categories helped them identify students with the greatest academic needs but without an intervention plan. This gap in attention to student needs jarred the team enough to question, "Where does this happen, how are we breaking down?" They saw their response—filling out IIPs for all previously unidentified children—as an important "save."

Jointly, the second- /third-grade Fulton teachers reviewed all IIPs at the end of the year to evaluate whether students should continue an IIP moving into the next grade. They integrated the assessment results with their observations of particular students based on literacy class or homeroom to determine the specific need or needs that the IIP strategies should address. Although homeroom teachers take the lead in writing the IIPs, they work with a student's reading teacher (if it is someone else) to define the student's instructional needs and the actions to address those needs. The teachers who know a particular student discuss each individual child as they complete the IIP forms. They all compare their observations of the student and make a decision that reflects their collective level of concern.

Similarly, the Fulton team jointly decides whether to move a particular student to another class during the school year. They observe students for independence and for qualitatively deeper reading comprehension. One teacher explained that the teachers evaluate the [student's] comprehension of questions; the understanding and the ability to follow directions independently, to ask questions when you're not sure what's happening; a sample of the writing, to make sure that the student is capable of writing a complete sentence and understanding all those things. . . . And it's are you [the student] ready—are you ready for a bigger group? Or, do you need more of me checking everything?

The decision to move students between classes—which fundamentally shapes the student's opportunity to learn—involves a wide range of data, from student work samples to classroom behavior to classroom test results. The process illustrates Fulton teachers' diverse considerations as they strive to meet each individual student's needs, a goal that annual standardized test scores are ill suited to illuminate.

One pod's homework system further illustrates how authentic student work complements or mediates the Fulton teachers' understanding of formal assessment data. Switching students for literacy and math, as the grade-level team does, leaves approximately 5 hours during the week when students meet in their homeroom classes. The team believes that "it's really up to a teacher to take charge and make sure that they get to know that kid." In one pod, homeroom teachers are anxious that they "don't know the students" to whom they do not teach reading or math. The other pod overcomes that problem through a collaborative homework system that uses weekly student work as data on students' learning and needs.

The homework system requires close collaboration on both content and logistics. Every week, each teacher assigns reading and math homework to the students—drawn from across the three homerooms—to whom they teach those subjects. The homeroom teacher collates the assignments and, importantly, corrects the homework given by the other teachers to her homeroom students. The teachers thus see the work others are assigning and their expectations for student performance. On occasion, they give feedback to one another about the workload or difficulty of the homework. Correcting the assignments provides a concrete way for the homeroom teachers to experience—in a way quantitative assessments do not permit—the strengths and weaknesses of the homeroom students they do not teach in reading or math.

In addition, the Fulton team members exchange critiques of the district's formative assessments, revealing differences that reflect their beliefs about how students learn to read. For example, the team evaluates the assessments for data quality. Team members enumerate items that do not test the purported skills, such as a "writing skills" section on one test composed entirely of six questions on how to write the date, and a section on another test ostensibly asking students to use the dictionary but testing students on parts of speech. They question the age-appropriateness of the writing prompts, one of which asked students to write about an "unusual event": The third graders "bombed; they just sat there and couldn't think of what's unusual." The teachers also uniformly agree that the comprehension questions on the main theme skills tests are unhelpful because each test structures the section differently, precluding comparisons over time.

The teachers' discussions reveal that they judge the usefulness of the fluency data by whether their individual experiences corroborate or contradict the research. Maddie argues, "The greater the fluency, the greater the comprehension. At the beginning of the school year, if I had a child reading 25 words a minute and I asked him a comprehension question, the chances are 99% of the time they're not going to be able to answer it." In contrast, Samantha considers prosody (expression in oral reading) a better indicator of comprehension than fluency, which "doesn't correspond with who understands what they are reading." Lynne weighs fluency in conjunction with other comprehension work. Hillary values the fluency tests because they are standardized and thus give her a sense of how well students are doing relative to an external standard. She questions, however, the validity of the assessment for English learners, citing a student "who's trying to enunciate because that's what he's working on" as a second-language goal, which consequently depresses his fluency rate. John relies on the fluency results to identify readers who appear somewhat fluent on casual observation but actually are not meeting grade-level standards. The teachers thus use their own clinical experience to legitimize or question the validity of the fluency assessment.

This joint "meta" reflection allows the teachers to hear one another's perspectives. Although they reached no agreement about the worth of particular types of data—especially the fluency test—the discussions reflect, and likely reinforce, the importance the school places on using data. For these teachers, the question is not whether to use data, but which data. The sentiment that "if we had our druthers, I don't think we'd be using some of this [assessment] stuff that we're told to use," corresponds with a sense that other types of data would be more valuable to them.

Hilltop Elementary

A historically low-performing Title I school, Hilltop Elementary is transforming into a collaborative teacher learning community that brooks no excuses for student failure. In 2001 a new principal entered Hilltop with a clear agenda to "create an adult learning community" and a strong mandate for change under the school's improvement plan. Under her stewardship, the staff's work together—in their words—"became data- and standards-driven examination"; "it was not so isolated by grade level and content"; and the school became "a more academic place instead of a place of 'when's the next recess?'" This cultural shift is fundamental to Hilltop teachers' motivation to work with data—the premise of using data to improve is lodged in newfound optimism that they *can* improve.

The second-grade team, the focal team for the case study, comprises three teachers, one novice and two veterans with more than 25 years' experience each.

Second-Grade Literacy Instruction at Hilltop

School-specific conditions exacerbate the challenges of implementing the Houghton-Mifflin program at Hilltop. First, the school has split classes in the primary grades, which makes implementing Houghton-Mifflin with fidelity nearly impossible for either grade. Teachers stretch to fit in extended literacy blocks, address each grade somewhat separately, and teach at least some math as well. Second, many Hilltop students come from homes with few resources to support academic achievement. Thus teachers work to scaffold the HM materials, which are written at grade level, to make them accessible to their students. Third, high student mobility undermines teachers' efforts to follow the program in sequence because they need to fill in holes in reading development for newcomers arriving throughout the school year.

Data Practices Among the Hilltop Second-Grade Team

The second-grade team's data practices are explicit professional learning opportunities for the teachers. Frequent team meetings—3 full-day meetings during the year and 90-minute "collaboration times" approximately twice a month—begin to cultivate a data-oriented mind-set among the teachers. Building on the principal's learning-community goals and beliefs about data-driven instruction, the school's leadership council[7] structures the team meetings with guided activities that ask teachers to review collaboratively various types of data, such as student writing samples and journal responses, as well as district-required formative assessments. These activities are designed to give teachers experiences that build collaborative norms as well as trust and knowledge of how to integrate data analysis into instructional concerns.

At one meeting, for example, the second-grade teachers combined student work samples in literacy, sorted by the district's performance levels (beginning, approaching, proficient, and advanced). Then they individually reviewed the work in each performance level, observed any commonalities and inconsistencies in the representative work, and compared their observations. The teachers could see that advanced student work samples "have imagery, [the students] have a comfort with words," whereas "for low kids, there's a paucity of vocabulary compared to advanced," and "approaching is all over the place." This exercise also revealed to the teachers that "we all have very different work."

To continue the discussion of what proficient student performance looks like, while also addressing certain standards on the district report card, teachers decided to select specific Houghton-Mifflin worksheets as common assessments. They looked for multiple activities addressing a particular standard and examined the tasks relative to the scope and difficulty inherent in the content standard. For example, the worksheet on prefixes and suffixes includes only the suffixes "-er" and "-est," and the teachers complained that none of the worksheets covered a broad range of suffixes and prefixes. Further, the worksheet exercises demand only that students manipulate the word (e.g., adding "un" in front of each word) rather that using it so that "they know 'un' is 'not.'" These considerations suggest that using student work as data requires a set of criteria against which to judge the adequacy of the work. The teachers endeavored to develop common expectations, calibrated against the district's performance and content standards.

The teachers' individual orientations toward data reveal differences between expert and novice literacy teachers. Marjory's peers and the principal recognize her as a "master teacher." With her expertise, Marjory values assessment data that give her a measure of information she otherwise would not have. For example, "the fluency [test] . . . [for] some of my EL [English Language Learner] kids who can read but just have a lot of trouble with the comprehension, it gave me a measure for them, although I could listen to them read also." Marjory firmly believes in listening to students read as data. She circulates through the class with "a basket of books" and a notebook, writing down "mistakes, patterns, questions I asked them, level [of book] that's good for them." These data tell her that her students are "able to choose books on their independent reading level; that they're able to understand what they're reading and not just read the words, but actually read the sentences and with correct inflection." She "ask[s] them a few questions and see[s] what kinds of things they can decode." None of the district assessments furnish this kind of information.

In contrast, Joan, the novice teacher, struggles with how to make sense of all of the district assessment data. For example, she does not know how to determine a particular student's performance level on the midyear report card, in part because her experiences reading with the student give her a different picture than the formative assessments do. When the principal asks whether the student would be "beginning" in phonics, Joan is unsure because "on the themes test [the student] was OK." She asserts that "part of the problem is I don't know what I expect at this time of year." The data tell her that the student is struggling with reading and has some weaknesses in phonics skills, but the teacher is unsure whether that is a problem *at this time of year*.

Marjory, the expert teacher, approaches the problem differently, relying on oral reading as definitive data. The novice's summary that the student "knows how to attack a word, she knows how to decode, but she just isn't fluent," raises a red flag for Marjory, who argues that "when [second-grade] student[s] can decode, they are reading [with some level of fluency]; if they are below, they aren't reading at all." She suggests that Joan find the student's reading level by using leveled books and "if [students] are more than a half year behind, they are 'below' [for this time of year], but if they are less than a half year behind, then [they're] 'approaching' [for this time of year]." On the advice of the more experienced teacher, oral reading thus became the final arbiter in determining the student's performance level, mediating the district quantitative formative assessment results.

The frequent team meetings afforded the teachers the opportunity to share war stories—data of a different kind. Teachers often claim that the most valuable part of any professional development is the time spent talking with other teachers; they are eager to hear from their peers about what works in "real" classrooms. As Little (1990) points out, such stories are also appealing because recipients pick and choose which aspects to try out in the privacy of their own rooms. Stories do not carry implementation mandates. Teachers can break down the stories into constituent tips and tricks and adapt them for their own situations.

So in what ways could war stories constitute data rather than a mere collection of anecdotes?[8] If war stories could be catalogued into a metaphorical database by fields such as activity, purpose, student grouping, common student misconceptions, instructional time required, preparation time, materials, outcomes, and so forth, then perhaps we could begin to approximate how teachers use stories as data. The stories can evolve into data when teachers *situated within a community* swap them and treat the stories (or components thereof) as hypotheses; for example, would reading parties lead to improved fluency in our classrooms, Hilltop teachers asked, as they did for another teacher? A teacher trying out the idea then contributes her observations of student learning or successful implementation to the collective, figurative database so that other teachers have an increasing number of observations from which to infer the effectiveness of a particular tactic. In essence, as other teachers try out a given story in their own classrooms, it gains more validity in what Simons, Kushner, Jones, and James (2003) call "situated generalization," or is discarded by the community as an isolated success.

The Hilltop second-grade teachers held such conversations about improving students' reading fluency, for example. The teachers agreed to use "echo reading," where students repeat after the teacher reads, and reading "tea parties," where students practice a 2-minute passage at their independent reading level and then read it aloud to the class for feedback. After trying these strategies for 2 months, the teachers reported they were working "swimmingly," and that students' "expression is better, they're reading dialogue as dialogue." Teachers also highlighted student feedback to one another, such as "you read with a lot of expression," "you're doing better," and "you're stopping for punctuation." The team compared how they decide which students should read and how they manage student behavior during the activity. The three teachers varied slightly in how they organize the class for the reading party, such as having students practice with a partner, read in front of the whole class, or read in small groups. Their stories build the group's collective knowledge of the different ways reading parties can be implemented, the problems a specific implementation solves or creates, and the apparent effects on student learning. Their advice to one another derives usefulness from the teachers' shared student, curricular, assessment, and reform contexts.

FACILITATING TEACHERS' DATA USE:
ORGANIZATIONAL AND POLICY CONDITIONS

Key conditions that shape the grade-level teams' data practices arise from multiple levels of the school district hierarchy. As the teachers' most proximate context, team norms underpin whether and how teachers engage collaboratively in data analysis with the goal of improving instruction. By setting agendas and creating organizational capacity to support teachers' learning to use data, school leadership can further enable teachers to use various forms of data. And finally, district curriculum and assessment policies can enhance or inhibit teachers' data use.

Grade-Level Norms of Interaction

The teams' commitment to and level of joint work help shape the extent to which data use falls into legitimate group activity. In a profession traditionally characterized by isolated, private, and autonomous practice (Little, 1990; Lortie, 1975), simply the notion of grade-level teams represents reform. Compelling teachers in non-self-selected groups to work together on instructional matters normally reserved for individual prerogative requires conscious effort to negotiate which aspects of instruction-related activities fall under team jurisdiction. And as Little (1990) points out, the depth of such collaboration ranges dramatically from noncommittal story swapping to interdependent joint work.

Fulton teachers' conceptions of teaching are rooted in joint work, through their history of collaboratively designing curriculum and their ongoing arrangements of teaching one another's homeroom students. The public nature of their practice leads to an implicit accountability between colleagues to strive for improved ways of meeting student needs. Examining assessment data is first and foremost a group activity among the Fulton team, structured into their grade-level team meetings. United under the philosophical umbrella of developmentally appropriate instruction, second- /third-grade Fulton teachers pledge to serve the "whole child," and see each student as an individual. Their joint work in switching students for literacy means that multiple teachers know a given student *as a learner*. Norms established over 4 years together as a team allow them to question one another about the progress of individual students, to expect one another to use a variety of observational and assessment data to describe that progress, and to pool their ideas on how to better meet the children's needs. Professionalism here means collective autonomy: acting together with freedom to debate and exercise expert judgment in a client-focused approach to student learning.

The second-/third-grade team members consistently express *collective* responsibility for *all* the students across their classes. This joint responsibility takes form, for example, when teachers explicitly agree that the classes for struggling students should be the smallest, and as a consequence teachers with the more advanced readers have larger classes. From an equity perspective, this arrangement allocates teaching resources according to student need. From a classroom management perspective, teachers generally believe that teaching more students in a smaller range is easier than teaching fewer students with a greater ability range. Further, the second- /third-grade team believes that having multiple teachers see each student provides "triangulated teacher judgment," which is more sound and accurate than the perspective of one teacher working alone.

At Hilltop, this level of joint work and joint responsibility is as yet only the principal's vision. Joint work entails revealing one's expectations for student learning, the routines one is comfortable with and those that feel risky, prized lessons and materials one has amassed over the years, as well as botched attempts at new strategies. In short, joint work puts into the public domain for scrutiny and debate myriad instructional decisions traditionally made autonomously and kept behind closed classroom doors. The second-grade Hilltop team works as much to break down these norms of privatism and autonomy as it does to learn to apply various data to instruction. The agenda set by school leadership challenges teachers to share student work as the means by which new norms of collaboration can flourish. Yet, in a profession that typically recognizes only novice teachers as legitimate help seekers (Little, 1990), the context for sharing student work matters a great deal. It matters whether signs of weak student work will be construed as inferior teaching or as a challenge that teachers will take on jointly.

The veteran Kay's trajectory—from avoiding joint scoring of student work to reluctantly attending the grade-level team meeting to contributing writing samples and agreeing to change her scores to be more consistent with the team's scoring—instantiates how collaboration and the use of student writing samples as data promote teachers' understanding of a common professional standard.

At the first meeting, Kay contributed no writing from her class, even though that had been the agenda, and seemed anxious that "the way my kids are writing today, they are all going to be [level] 1s [beginning]." At the second session, Kay brought the work samples from her class already scored and read none of her samples to the group until explicitly prompted by another teacher. The other teachers disputed the scores she gave, and Kay eventually changed some to align with their interpretation of the writing rubric. This does not signify that Kay completely altered her beliefs about what falls under legitimate group practice, but the change over time from avoidance to reluctant participation to accepting limited collective decision making suggests attitudinal changes consistent with the schoolwide changes the principal was instituting.

Trust Within Teams

The case studies suggest four dimensions of trust that help explain teachers' interactions and, ultimately, their level of joint engagement with specific kinds of data. The four dimensions of trust are that

- Other teachers have high standards;
- Other teachers won't think I'm incompetent;
- Others will participate/reciprocate in response to my engagement; and
- Problems I raise will be seen as collective problems.

These four dimensions create the bases to discuss student achievement results and student work. Without some belief that colleagues share standards, how do teachers discuss whether student work is adequate and whether assessment results reveal any problems? If teachers are not confident that they share concern about the same types of students, they may not agree on *whose* data to look at or whether the results are problematic for that group of students. If teachers risk being judged incompetent by their peers, perceive little engagement among other teachers, or are isolated when they bring up problems, they may be discouraged from sharing data analyses with their grade-level team.

Teachers on both the Fulton and Hilltop case study teams trusted that in comparing student work and assessment results, others would not view them as incompetent.

Trust That Other Teachers Have Similar High Standards

Fulton teachers convey in multiple ways a sense of trust in how well their colleagues meet the instructional needs of their students. They argue not only that the flexible grouping arrangement allows them to teach better because they have a narrower range of student needs in literacy class, but also that the students are better served by colleagues who are expert at meeting those needs. They volunteer one another for appropriate responsibilities on individual intervention plans for the most struggling students. When, under the Houghton-Mifflin adoption, they had no opportunity to score student writing samples together as a grade level—as they had in the past—they reported that they missed having a second professional judgment on the work and colleagues' suggestions on how to improve the work sample. Moreover, the way they exchange information about their homeroom students' progress in another's literacy class indicates that they trust the judgment that others make about their students' learning.

Hilltop teachers' beginning forays into exploring their performance standards for students did not reveal a lack of trust, nor did it particularly reflect trust that they share high standards for their students. Rather, they simply were awakening to the goal of developing common performance standards, as prompted by their principal.

Trust That Other Teachers Won't Think I'm Incompetent

This dimension of trust challenges norms of who may legitimately seek help in traditional teaching cultures. The risk of negative peer judgments acts as a disincentive for experienced teachers to seek support in response to data analysis. At Hilltop, both the novice and the experienced teachers seek advice from their colleagues. The veterans sought support mainly in the context of implementing the Houghton-Mifflin program for the first time. One, for example, did not know how to prepare her students for the writing assessment and accepted advice from another experienced and expert teacher on the team. Even the teacher whom others acknowledge as an expert literacy instructor lamented that the new program made her "feel like a new teacher again."

Fulton teachers routinely review their assessment data collaboratively with a focus on student needs and what they can do as a team, a pair, or individually to support students. In part, Fulton's inquiry work with the regional inquiry-based reform network gave teachers experience in examining data to adjust their instruction, "so people aren't scared to say, 'Well, look, this kid has a fluency rate of eight words per minute; what are we going to do?'" They argue that their "openness" allows them "to focus on the kids who really need the most help—and not be scared about that." As one teacher summarized, "[We] don't have that fear that [we're] going to get dinged because there's someone who's struggling in [our] class."

Trust That Others Will Participate/Reciprocate in Response to My Engagement

This third dimension of trust is essential to the logic of learning as a social enterprise (Bransford, Brown, & Cocking, 1999; Lave & Wenger, 1991).

Participants of a community need to trust that others will reciprocate in the learning process. Teachers need to trust that those with whom they share inadequate student work are willing to offer suggestions without impugning their professional adequacy.

The Fulton teachers exhibit this kind of trust during their grade-level team meetings. Each teacher believes that her colleagues care about her students as much as she does and, importantly, that other teachers can teach her students as well as she can. They "appreciate each other and respect one another and trust one another implicitly." Their discussions of individual students' strengths and weaknesses when grouping students and writing IIPs reveal this trust in one another's professional judgment.

At Hilltop, the principal is explicitly attempting to build an "adult learning community," and her strategy includes growing this specific kind of trust. She notes that when she arrived in 2001, teachers had strong social camaraderie, but instruction was about "valiant efforts individually," behind closed doors. "It was impolite!—it was against the culture—to talk to each other. . . . So the idea that we would talk and share data . . . ooh, oww!" She spearheaded a schoolwide discussion and book study about who their students were and what they as teachers could do, regardless of the disadvantages their students faced at home relative to more affluent children. This introspection seemed to forge a new level of trust among teachers, moving from individuals trying to do their best to team members engaged in the same goals and united by the same strategies.

Trust That Problems I Raise Will Be Seen as Collective Problems

Counter to the individualism characteristic of traditional conceptions of teaching, teachers at Fulton and Hilltop in particular trust that the problems they raise with their colleagues will be taken up as collective problems. The clearest example of collective problem solving comes from Fulton, where one second-/third-grade teacher said she felt she "is not the teacher [she] can be" with the student-switching arrangement under the Houghton-Mifflin adoption. The system affords the smallest class sizes for the most struggling students, so that the other teachers have more students. The teacher who raised the issue was overwhelmed by the larger numbers in her class, increased diversity in student ability, and difficulties of differentiating under the new HM program. The team took up the issue as a collective problem, even though the other teachers with large classes did not express the same level of frustration. Indeed, the team held several meetings to devise a compromise arrangement for the whole team, rather than view the issue as a problem of individual teacher skill.

The differences between Fulton and Hilltop suggest multiple pathways to developing the kinds of trust that facilitate collaborative data use. Hilltop started with structured data-related activities and built trust along the way. Fulton opened the school with high trust among a handpicked faculty united around a common vision of teaching, and slowly incorporated the use of data into its collaborative work.

Leadership

Trust is not the sole or a sufficient condition for stimulating collaborative uses of data. Essential too is leadership that sets purposes, articulates why using data matters, and provides strategic supports for teachers to learn about using data.

Both school and district leaders play agenda-setting roles. District leaders convey to teachers which data matter and the expectation that they use those data through curriculum and assessment policies as well as related practices. Such district messages, however, are heavily mediated by school leaders' agenda-setting and norm-building efforts.

Hilltop is a case of explicitly introducing data as a tool for learning about instruction and of structuring how teachers might develop the capacity to use such a tool. The principal's theory of improving instructional practice entails both teacher collaboration and examining data collaboratively. She and her leadership council set agendas and structured activities for second-grade team collaboration time, so that in this setting data are both what teachers reveal of their classrooms, as in war stories and examples of student work, as well as how they measure progress, as in assessment results. The concrete instruction-related activities undertaken during collaboration time are ensconced in other key routines and structures that institutionalize the conception of "teaching as the learning profession" (Darling-Hammond & Sykes, 1999). These other structures include the principal's "learning sessions" rather than staff meetings, faculty visits to a high-performing, high-poverty school, principal feedback based on her informal classroom observations, and regular reporting to the whole staff by each grade-level team on its collaborative work. The Hilltop principal also facilitates teachers' data use by using specialized roles such as instructional coaches and Title I teachers to fulfill data functions. Such functions include accessing data reports, interpreting and teaching teachers about data, providing instructional resources, and following up with teachers on intended classroom changes.

The Fulton principal has less need to establish a rationale for being data-driven because of the school's long-term participation in the regional inquiry-based reform network. Instead, the principal models data use in making schoolwide decisions, such as whether to change the school's multiage grouping of students. Teachers expect the principal to model such data use, which simultaneously reflects and replicates the school's inquiry norms.

Effects of District Policy

The Fulton and Hilltop teams' experiences in integrating various forms of data into their instruction-related work suggest that district curriculum and assessment policies can simultaneously enable and constrain teachers' data use.

The district typically determines *which formal data* are available to teachers. Oak Park policy mandates a specific set of literacy assessments, thus triggering the forms, abundance, and frequency of data used by the school system. Teachers are expected to attend to the results of the thrice-yearly district assessments, and this expectation is reinforced by the pacing guide that spells out the deadlines for each assessment, the student report card that lists the fluency score, and the requirement that literacy lead teachers facilitate "data meetings" with grade-level teams. In contrast to the standardized data from the state, which do not "really drill down," the district now provides assessments that allow the principal to "sit down with a staff so that a staff can look at [the data] and say, 'Oh! What's going on in *my* class?'" and allow a teacher to "sit down with [her] colleagues and say, 'Let's start to look.'" Indeed, the alignment of curriculum to assessment enhances usefulness insofar as teachers believe the tests measure a centrally important aspect of literacy development and—importantly—insofar as the HM program directly addresses the weaknesses revealed by the tests. The Fulton teachers' debate over the importance of fluency scores illustrates how teachers value and filter the available data through their own clinical lenses.

Paradoxically, however, the district's directive to use Houghton-Mifflin with fidelity circumscribes teachers' choices about how to act on the data. Can they use non-HM lessons if they find them more appropriate? Both Fulton and Hilltop teachers point to lost opportunities to respond instructionally to the assessment data because they are obligated to implement the Houghton-Mifflin curriculum. The HM materials more than fill the literacy block; both teams consciously gave up writing programs they considered successful despite their concern that the HM program underemphasizes writing.

The experiences at Fulton and Hilltop suggest that a certain amount of curricular flexibility and teacher discretion in adapting and incorporating instructional strategies and activities—as a matter of district curriculum *policy*—may better afford teachers the opportunity to respond to their analyses of student performance data.

District curriculum and assessment policies, then, influence organizational capacity to use data in several ways. The district makes available certain data that teachers otherwise would not possess. The alignment between curriculum and assessment can enhance the usefulness of certain data by providing curricular materials that match problems diagnosed in the assessments. However, overly restrictive curriculum policy limits teachers' abilities to respond to problems revealed in data analysis, by discouraging teachers from introducing materials outside of the adopted program or by maintaining a strict pacing guide.

CONCLUSIONS AND IMPLICATIONS

The Fulton and Hilltop case studies illustrate how grade-level team norms, school-level agenda setting and support for data-related functions, and district-level curriculum and assessment policies shape teachers' data practices. Grade-level team norms legitimize or squelch teachers' requests for help, displays of student work, joint analysis of student assessment data, and stories of lessons gone awry. That is, the norms either bolster or undermine the notion of using data for improvement by facilitating or frustrating teacher collaboration and professional learning. Such norms of interaction arise from teachers' conceptions of the profession, deeply ingrained in the local school culture but evolutionary under strong agenda setting. Agenda setting comprises deliberate and strategic activities to set the stage for teachers to use data. Agenda-setting functions establish rationales and expectations for teachers to use particular forms of data, model data use, and structure time to permit teachers to learn about using data within instructionally relevant collaboration. Leadership also provides capacity for key data-related functions.

Districts influence capacity through their curriculum and assessment policies. Those policies provide specific forms of data that teachers otherwise would not have, some of which teachers value. Teachers find district assessments useful when curriculum is topically aligned, when curriculum policy affords them flexibility to respond to the assessment data, and to the extent that their experience validates the assessment topics and results.

The organizational influences on teachers' use of data, then, arise from multiple levels. Moreover, agenda setting, collaborative norms, and organizational capacity are in all likelihood *individually insufficient* to result in teachers' broad use of data. Compelling arguments to use data and norms professing collaborative learning remain only good intentions unless capacity furnishes teachers with opportunities to use data, opportunities that match the particular, detailed way in which they think about their instruction.

Using data to improve instruction and overall school performance is a rational approach to the core mission of schools, teaching. However, the benefits of solving the technical problem—building data management systems and developing expertise in individuals—will be limited by the normative problem. How does using data fit with teachers' views of teaching? How does using data alter teachers' relationships with colleagues? What are the implicit organizational values around using data and around learning, and will teachers be supported in embracing those values? Normative change alone cannot establish concrete practices of using data. Building a rational system of data-driven instruction requires engaging nonrational aspects of the system: norms, values, and capacity situated in role definitions and hierarchy.

NOTES

1. These objections to large-scale, high-stakes standardized tests are neither new nor unusual (see, for example, Popham, 1995; Stiggins, 1997).

2. All district, school, and individual names are pseudonyms. The Center for Research on the Context of Teaching at Stanford University conducts the evaluation of the Bay Area School Reform Collaborative (BASRC). I am grateful to colleagues on the project team for their insights pertaining to teachers' data use generally. The team includes Pai-rou Chen, Celine Toomey Coggins, Heather Malin, Milbrey McLaughlin, Heidi Ramirez, Joan Talbert, and Aurora Wood.

3. The whole-language approach uses authentic texts, both fiction and nonfiction, as primary instructional materials and teaches decoding skills in context, without necessarily teaching phonemic awareness and phonics explicitly or systematically, as the California language arts framework demands (California Department of Education, 1999).

4. The Cycle of Inquiry follows a typical data-driven, decision-making model. It begins by identifying an area of focus on the basis of student achievement data, noting differential achievement between subgroups. The Cycle continues with two questions that narrow the student achievement concern and the teacher practice(s) that may ameliorate student performance. Subsequent steps set measurable goals for each question, drafting a plan to meet the goals, implementing the plan (including collecting prespecified data), and analyzing those data to answer the original two questions. The process comes full circle when participants refine their questions.

5. The school's philosophy of developmentally appropriate instruction is manifested in multiage groupings in each classroom for K–1, 2–3, 4–5, and 6–8.

6. These performance categories are promoted by the district's main professional development partner in reading, the Consortium on Reading Excellence (CORE). Intensive corresponds to below the 50th percentile on norm-referenced tests, or far below and below on the state's 5-point performance rubric (far below basic, below basic, basic, proficient, and advanced). Strategic is the 50th to 75th percentile, or basic. Benchmark is above the 75th percentile, or proficient and advanced.

7. The school leadership council includes the principal, the literacy coach, the reform coach, and several teacher representatives.

8. The knowledge management literature is devoted to uncovering how such knowledge can be captured, accessed, and queried across an organization (see, for example, Davenport & Prusak, 1998; Nickols, 2000; O'Dell & Grayson, 1998). I am grateful to Mark Schlager for dialogue on this point and for his insights contributing to the development of the ideas about war stories as data.

REFERENCES

Bay Area School Reform Collaborative. (n.d.). *BASRC cycle of inquiry*. Retrieved June 13, 2003, from http://www.basrc.org/

Bransford, J., Brown, A. L., & Cocking, R. R. (Eds.). (1999). *How people learn: Brain, mind, experience, and school*. Washington, DC: National Academy Press.

California Department of Education. (1999). *Reading/language arts framework for California public schools*. Sacramento: Author.

Darling-Hammond, L., & Sykes, G. (Eds.) (1999). *Teaching as the learning profession: Handbook of policy and practice*. San Francisco: Jossey-Bass.

Davenport, T. H., & Prusak, L. (1998). *Working knowledge: How organizations manage what they know*. Boston: Harvard Business School Press.

Lave, J., & Wenger, E. (1991). *Situated learning: Legitimate peripheral participation*. Cambridge: Cambridge University Press.

Little, J. W. (1990). The persistence of privacy: Autonomy and initiative in teachers' professional relations. *Teachers College Record, 91*(4), 509–536.

Lortie, D. C. (1975). *Schoolteacher: A sociological study*. Chicago: University of Chicago Press.

Nickols, F. (2000). The knowledge in knowledge management. In J. W. Cortada & J. A. Woods (Eds.), *The knowledge management yearbook, 2000–2001* (pp. 12–21). Boston: Butterworth Heinemann.

O'Dell, C., & Grayson, C. J., Jr. (1998). *If only we knew what we know: The transfer of internal knowledge and best practice*. New York: Free Press.

Popham, J. W. (1995). *Classroom assessment: What teachers need to know*. Needham Heights, MA: Allyn & Bacon.

Simons, H., Kushner, S., Jones, K., & James, D. (2003, December). From evidence-based practice to practice-based evidence: The idea of situated generalisation. *Research Papers in Education, 18*(4), 347–364.

Stiggins, R. (1997). *Student-centered classroom assessment* (2nd ed.). Upper Saddle River, NJ: Prentice-Hall.

PART III

Digital Resources: Technology to Facilitate Data-Driven Decision Making

Supporting the Art of Teaching in a Data-Rich, High-Performance Learning Environment

Valerie M. Crawford, Mark S. Schlager,
William R. Penuel & Yukie Toyama

Data-driven decision making (DDDM) has become part of the school account-ability and reform lexicon. The term commonly refers to policies and prac-tices involving the use of student achievement and other data (such as attendance, course-taking patterns and grades, and demographic data) to drive school improvement at the school, district, and state levels. In recent years, policymakers and administrators have come to view DDDM as having significant potential to improve education reform efforts and enhance stu-dent learning outcomes. The logic of DDDM is that analysis of data bearing on achievement and other related data will enable schools, districts, and states to identify areas needing improvement and to determine the degree of suc-cess or failure of actions taken to improve educational systems at various levels (Elmore & Rothman, 1999, cited in Massell, 2001).

DDDM clearly has an important role to play in school accountability and improvement. As practices of DDDM increasingly are implemented, commer-cial systems designed to support those practices are proliferating (Light, Honey, Heinze, Brunner, Wexler, Mandinach, & Fasca, 2005; Means, 2005; Palaich, Good, Stout, & Vickery, 2000). However, large-scale assessments have severe limitations as tools for teachers attempting to inform instruc-tion and instructional decision making, which can lead to inappropriate use of accountability data (Confrey & Makar, 2005). Often, large-scale assess-ments and the data they generate are not linked to classroom practices and outcomes (Herman & Gribbons, 2001), are not aligned with instructional objectives that are pursued in the classroom and embedded in the curricu-lum (Shepard, 2000; Stiggins, 2001b), do not cover sufficiently the domains tested to give a fair and valid picture of subject-matter learning (Confrey, chapter 3), and are not available to teachers in a time horizon that makes them useful in instructional decision making (Light et al., 2005). Consequently, data management and reporting systems that use large-scale assessment data are inadequate to help teachers and administrators understand and improve classroom-level instruction, curriculum enactment, and the effects of these on students' learning. Other data are needed, such as classroom-level, curriculum-aligned assessment and performance data whose content is well known to teachers and highly aligned with their instructional goals.

In chapter 3, Confrey argues that in the current era of accountability-based reform, state tests have been asked to perform different functions: monitoring schools' progress against a set of state-established benchmarks for student performance, certifying individual students' proficiency, and selecting students for different programs. We agree with Confrey that it is necessary to maintain a clear distinction between data used for administrative and school- and district-accountability purposes and data used for classroom-level instructional decision making. A growing body of research is documenting that classroom assessments embedded in the curriculum, and thus highly aligned with the instructional goals and curriculum enacted in the classroom, are more appropriate data sources for instructional decision making (e.g., Shepard, 2000; Stiggins, 2001b). We argue here that classroom-level instructional decision making requires classroom-level data suitable for diagnostic, real-time decisions regarding student learning and instruction. Enhancing data use in teachers' instructional decision making requires technical and social supports for collecting and interpreting data, as well as research on the type of classroom infrastructure that can support teachers' seamless integration of real-time data into their instructional routines.

This chapter reports on research that pursued the question: What would a classroom technology infrastructure look like that would make it *easy* for teachers to capture and analyze complex, nuanced information about students in *real time*, to inform their instructional decision making, and to individualize and optimize the classroom learning environment *while the learning process is still under way*? Our work is informed by arguments that student evaluation at the classroom level should serve primarily as assessment *for* learning rather than as assessment *of* learning (Shepard, 2000; Stiggins, 2001a).

In what follows, we first present some of the bases for our vision of a technology infrastructure for teaching and learning. Then we describe some key themes and findings from our early-phase design research investigating high school algebra teachers' instructional practices and work flow, to identify design requirements for a classroom technology infrastructure that improves instruction, diagnosis, work flow, and productivity, and enhances collaboration and communication among students and between students and the teacher. We also describe the conceptual framework for classroom technology design that emerged from this study. Finally, we discuss implications of this research and examine how application of this conceptual framework could inform the design of a classroom technology infrastructure for high-performance teaching and a learning environment that is data-rich for real-time decision making and feedback.

DESIGNING TECHNOLOGY FOR TEACHERS AS HIGH-PERFORMANCE PROFESSIONALS

Our approach to the data-rich classroom in which students and teachers have access to sophisticated content and services is aimed not at eliminating the need for teachers' professional judgment, as some fear, but, on the contrary, at providing teachers with the kind of technology tools and computing infrastructure available to other high-performance professionals, such as physicians and air-traffic controllers. This approach has the potential to help teachers optimize the learning processes that students engage in throughout the day and the year in ways that contribute to maximizing learning *outcomes*.

To unlock the potential of technology to support teachers' ability to engineer a powerful classroom learning environment, technologies that today are available largely as silos must be integrated into a coherent infrastructure that (1) supports all aspects of the teacher's performance of her job and (2) provides her and her students with powerful learning tools. Indeed, these two goals are intertwined—one of the teacher's key goals is to create a powerful environment that optimizes student learning, individually as well as collectively. To inform our analysis of the ways that classroom infrastructure designs can best support rather than hamper excellent teaching, we turned to the teaching literature for an understanding of what expert teachers know about their students' learning, how they know it, and what they do in the day-to-day context of teaching to help their students learn.

Teaching involves agility with a domain content, keeping students engaged, quickly assessing what students know and can do, diagnosing student misconceptions and instructional needs, and selecting alternative instructional strategies on the fly. This work is cognitively demanding. Teachers make decisions at a rapid rate, operating in conditions of high levels of simultaneity, with frequent interruptions. Teachers are responsible for ensuring that *all* students are *productively* engaged; determining when students' engagement with content, peers, and tools is not having the desired results; and deciding what to do to maintain or correct the course of action. Teaching increasingly is viewed as akin to the clinical professions, requiring acute judgment, continuous problem solving, progressive learning from unique cases, and the integration of many domains of knowledge and skill (Ball & Bass, 2000; Berliner, 1986, 1994; Hinds, 2002; Solomon & Morocco, 1999).

However, unlike other professionals who perform highly complex work that is consequential for society, such as physicians or air-traffic controllers, teachers do not have the data-rich, performance support, and information-feedback work environment that virtually all other high-performance professionals and many service professionals have at their disposal.

BUILDING A BETTER UNDERSTANDING
OF TEACHERS' TECHNOLOGY NEEDS:
A REQUIREMENTS ANALYSIS OF TEACHING ALGEBRA

Guided by an understanding of the state of the art in classroom assessment technology and a view of teachers' work as clinical, time pressured, and cognitively intensive, we began our empirical research aimed at developing design requirements for a classroom technology infrastructure that addresses teachers' job performance needs and creates a data-rich classroom in which easy-to-use information is readily available to guide instruction and improve and individualize learning while enhancing opportunities for collaboration and communication. Such a learning environment would support *high-performance* teaching, as well as enhancing students' active, metacognitive participation in learning.

Our initial focus was to describe and understand teachers' practices and then to begin to identify latent and manifest needs that could be addressed through technology. Our immediate goal was not actually to develop and test such a classroom technology—that undertaking is a long, multifaceted process—but rather to develop an analytical framework and design principles to inform later development and testing of a classroom technology infrastructure. The study we describe here thus represents early-phase design research with the modest goal of developing a framework to inform the design of an integrated solution that makes rich, complex, and multiple forms of data readily accessible to students and teachers.

The study focused on high school algebra teachers and classrooms. We selected algebra as a content area in part because this subject is a choke point in the academic pipeline for mathematics and science education, so that improvements to teaching and learning in this area have the potential to increase the flow through the math and science pipeline, and in part because relatively mature educational technologies (e.g., Cognitive Tutor) are available for this subject area.

The study was conducted over 7 months by a multidisciplinary team of researchers with backgrounds in mathematics teaching, student assessment, social cognition, and technology, and included extensive involvement of eight high school algebra teachers.

Methods

Our study used a multiple-case comparative design with methods drawn from technology design research as well as empirical methods from cognitive ethnography (e.g., Hutchins, 1995, 2000) and rapid ethnography (Holtzblatt & Beyer, 1996; Holtzblatt & Jones, 1992), using an adaptation of grounded theory methodological approach to theory elaboration (Glaser & Strauss, 1967; Strauss & Corbin, 1990). Cognitive ethnography emphasizes qualitative data collection and analysis to describe situated practice, with a focus on the tool-mediated nature of sociocognitive processes in work practices. Similarly, rapid ethnography entails qualitative methods to document work practices and activity structures, and relies on researchers and participants who represent differing perspectives on or within the practice or activity system under analysis. The term *rapid* applied to this approach reflects the relatively rapid cycles of data collection, analysis, design, and testing typically involved in technology design and development. Grounded theory is a data-rich, inductive, and comparative approach to theory elaboration that makes it appropriate for a case study design.

The grounded theory process cycled through three phases of data collection and analysis, each phase successively honing the research questions, foci of the data collection efforts, and analyses of the data: (1) exploratory research phase, (2) focused inquiry phase, and (3) validation phase. All six researchers on the research team were involved in all phases of the research activity.

Data collection instruments, activities, and analyses in the first and second phases had three main foci. The first was teachers' in-class and out-of-class work processes related to a list of critical instructional tasks (adapted from Shulman, 1987). These included creating assignments and assessments, evaluating students in class and out of class, interpreting and responding to students' ideas, and tracking students' assignments. The second was teachers' strategies for knowing what students know and providing feedback; and the third, teachers' work flow within the classroom. Work flow was tied primarily to artifacts, including student work assignments and information collected or documented about assignments and students' work. We also documented the daily routines of the algebra classroom, the general nature of classroom activity at different phases in the routine—whether primarily conceptual, procedural, or both—and the amount and format of students' classroom participation.

For data collection, the six researchers were assigned in pairs to an expert and a novice teacher. After each round of data collection, researchers analyzed and synthesized the qualitative data (field notes, interview notes, and transcripts) individually or in pairs. Next, all researchers met together to compare and hone analyses and refine the research questions. This process, typical of grounded theory, was followed through each phase of the study.

The research participants were eight high school algebra teachers in the San Francisco Bay Area. Four teachers were novices (defined as 3 or fewer years as a classroom teacher), and four were experienced (defined as 6 or more years of teaching). The technology they used was generally similar, consisting primarily of whiteboards or chalkboards and overhead projectors. None used intelligent-tutoring systems or other computer-based instruction. About half the teachers had students work in small groups regularly or daily, and half did not. About half the teachers made use of manipulatives (such as tiles) or other types of representations.

Algebra Classroom Routines

Algebra classroom routines are the activity structures that must be integrated into any successful performance-supporting technology, or else be replaced or transformed if new technologies introduce new goals for learning. We observed substantial similarity in routines across the eight teachers, with some important variations in key tasks and orientation to goals.

Typically, an algebra teacher begins class by giving students a small set of warm-up problems (on the whiteboard or chalkboard or on the overhead projector) to work through. While students are working (or expected to be working) on the warm-up problems, the teacher may take attendance or may move from desk to desk to check students' homework from the prior evening. If students are not held accountable by the teacher for showing her or him completed work on the warm-up problems, they sometimes may use this time to complete their homework, either by working problems or, as researchers observed at times, by copying another student's homework. The purpose of the teacher's homework check may be "compliance" (to see whether the student did the homework) or, less frequently, "performance" (whether the student understands the material and does the problems correctly); the process and pacing of this homework check typically reflect the differing goals. For example, if the goal is to check compliance, the teacher may mark the homework with a rubber stamp (all stamped homework is turned in at the end of the week or the unit for course credit). If the goal is to check performance, the teacher may save time by checking only the two problems she deems most difficult. If a performance check shows much student misunderstanding, she may review some procedures or concepts at the board. One teacher described this process as a "waste of time" because many students in her classes manage to copy homework answers either from their friends (before or during class) or from the answers on the board (instead of using them to self-assess their homework).

The teacher usually spends 5 to 15 minutes on the warm-up problems and homework review. Sometimes the warm-up problems relate to the next homework assignment; sometimes the teacher selects problems that review a topic germane to the day's new materials. During the warm-up problems, some teachers ask students to come up to the whiteboard to show their solutions, while other teachers put up the answers on the board and let students self-assess their work.

Next, the teacher introduces some new material, usually through lecture and demonstration on the board (or overhead projector), through guided problem solving—a process more interactive than lecture/demo—or through a simple demonstration of problem-solving procedures. Alternatively, rather than lead the class, the teacher may introduce a new set of problems for students to work out in small groups, and provide assistance as she or the groups judge help is required. The goal of this approach is to allow students to discover how the new material is different and to devise solutions while helping and motivating one another.

Typically, the remainder of class time is spent mostly on having students work through problems on the new material, so they can ask questions of peers or the teacher. Sometimes the next day's homework assignment is to complete the new problem set, which motivates students to use class time to complete the work, rather than talking with friends or addressing other coursework. If the homework assignment differs from the problem set, often the teacher announces the assignment before the end of class and allows students to use the remainder of class time to work on the homework.

Class concludes in a variety of ways. Sometimes students simply leave when the bell rings. Sometimes the teacher ends class with a brief wrap-up, summarizing a lesson, giving an overview of the evening's homework, or collecting student work done in class. Sometimes time simply runs out and a wrap-up does not take place.

Knowing What Students Know

One of a teacher's essential tasks is to determine what students know and what they are struggling with. Without this knowledge teachers cannot determine what instructional guidance or experiences will help students, nor can they evaluate students. We observed teachers using both formal and informal processes to determine what students know and can do, during and after class. For example, teachers often perform a quick, informal check of whether most students have understood the prior day's lesson to decide whether to move on to new material or engage further with the current content. Quick checks include reviewing homework at the beginning of class or asking "Any questions?" at the end of an explanation or lecture. Sometimes teachers need to examine an individual student's work closely to determine the source of an error or nature of a misunderstanding. Formal evaluations to ascertain what students know are typically quizzes or tests that take between 10 minutes and the entire class period. Besides helping teachers uncover what students know, formal evaluations are a mechanism to encourage or pressure students to master the target material.

We examined teachers' efforts to learn what students know not from the perspective of assessment theory, pedagogy, or accuracy of assessment information or inferences, but from the perspective of *work flow*, *workload*, *time effectiveness*, and *efficiency*. By *efficiency*, we mean the teacher's subjective perception of the value of information collected given the time and effort required from students and the teacher for various strategies.

Best Strategies for Determining What Students Know

In our first round of interviews, we asked teachers to describe their strategies for formal and informal assessment and to specify which delivered the most informative information about what students know and can do. We did not ask explicitly about the most time-effective strategies, assuming that whatever teachers reported actually using would be time-effective, given the overwhelming demands on their time. The teachers were evenly divided between considering formal assessments (e.g., a quiz) versus informal classroom observation and review of student work as more informative. Teachers who preferred quizzes indicated that the diagnosis was more systematic and the reliability of information was greater because students exerted more effort and the information was deeper. These teachers described quizzes as follows:

- I think the most helpful is the quizzes, simply because I can detect what they actually are understanding, the way they're understanding it, so that I can prepare them better for the big test.
- Unfortunately, it's the quizzes and the tests. I mean that's where they put in their most effort just because they know it's going to be graded; it's going to be recorded. It's a lot more formal to them so that's a better assessment for me to see what do you really know. The unfortunate part is it happens once every week or once every 2 weeks.
- We like a 5-minute quiz [at the beginning of class] just to check in on a skill to see where everybody is.

Teachers who preferred informal assessment during class time described a variety of informal evaluation strategies as useful.

- In most cases, the energy of the class is what can tell me. If in most cases, if they're all getting it, then it's very energetic. . . . Otherwise, the quieter the class is, the more difficult it is for me to read it.

- It's typically by the class discussion that happens. . . . And then I think that's substantiated or backed up by their quizzes and their tests, and the fact that a lot of them are actually attempting their homework.
- Well, I'm assessing them constantly in class by walking around.

These teachers said that by observing students work, they gleaned important information about student learning and got a "sense" of students' level of engagement with instructional materials.

Trade-offs in Strategies to Know What Students Know

One key finding about teachers' efforts to know what students know is that teachers view their strategies as a series of trade-offs between time and effort required to gain the information and quality and quantity of information. Nearly every teacher talked about the *trade-offs* necessary between formal and informal assessment. They generally seek and stick to strategies that are optimally *efficient*—that is, that produce the highest quality of information (depth plus breadth) possible within their tightly circumscribed time constraints and heavy workloads.

We found that the teachers used a variety of strategies to balance quality and sufficiency of information with time constraints to gain the information. Teachers varied in their appraisal of these necessary trade-offs to learn what students know. Some felt their information was only adequate, lacking richness or thoroughness for specific students or the class as a whole. Others felt their knowledge of individual students' skills, abilities, and understandings was accurate and rich.

Formal Assessment

Teachers in our study cited formal assessment as one of the most difficult aspects of teaching, along with classroom management and engaging all students in learning. Their description of the challenges of formal assessment emphasized the problem of time rather than of technique or professional skill or knowledge—the issues on which most research on classroom assessment focuses. We asked teachers to describe their processes for preparing, administering, scoring, and recording results from a formal assessment. The basic tasks in giving students a quiz are the following:

- Preparing the quiz or test, including selecting or creating the content of the items as well as creating and copying quiz papers;
- Administering the quiz or test during class time;
- Scoring the individual quiz or test;
- Entering scores into the grade book; and
- Returning papers to students during class.

Each task, other than class administration of the quiz, requires a significant amount of the teacher's out-of-class time. The actual test administration takes time away from instruction, so if the test feedback does not benefit learning, the test is not time-effective with respect to instruction (Stiggins, 2001b).

During interviews and focus groups, teachers made the following representative statements regarding grading and formal evaluation:

- Biggest pain? Grading, number one. So I'm writing over 100 comments and it probably takes me 2 hours a class. That's just a lot of time; I've got five classes. . . .
- The grading of papers is always time-consuming and hard to deal with, but a necessary part of assessing students.
- Making up new tests and quizzes for every unit that are different from last year's tests and quizzes. That is extremely time-consuming. Getting answers, making review sheets.

Teachers in our study used a variety of strategies to reduce the time and effort needed for each step of formal assessment. For example, a teacher sometimes may have students score one another's quizzes, or might have students write test questions and submit them for credit, then use their questions on the test. Sometimes teachers minimized the extent to which they provided written feedback on student papers to shorten the time required for marking.

This is a critical trade-off in formal assessment: the detail, quality, and quantity of feedback information provided to students about performance on the assessment, versus the time required to provide this detailed information. This trade-off emerged in our findings as a persistent issue. There are two sides to this issue: the amount and quality of information the teacher is able to provide to the student, and the amount and quality of feedback information the teacher herself is able to gain from grading or analysis of student work and the time required to do so.

Teachers expressed concern that the less information provided to students about their work, the less the assessment will benefit learning. Nearly every teacher in our study expressed the desire to make formal assessments valuable in the learning process, and nearly all lamented the time pressures that prevented them from providing more individualized feedback to students on their work.

Informal Assessment

Teachers in our study discussed informal assessment strategies and goals both in terms of understanding what students know and in terms of monitoring students' level of participation. However, some teachers felt that students' level of engagement with the activity was indicative of their level of understanding of the assignment, as in the case of the teacher who said she got a feel for the students' level of understanding based on the "energy level" of the classroom.

Informal evaluation during classroom activities was described by teachers primarily as monitoring completion of the work and its accuracy. The theme of trade-offs between time and quality of information (for students and teacher) was prevalent in teachers' discussions of this topic. When asked during interviews to describe their processes for formative assessment, teachers said:

- Go around the room checking. . . .
- See who's participating and who is not participating.
- It's one of my top priorities to be giving constant informal feedback. So you just can't do too much of it, and having the energy to keep it going.
- [I try] to look at their work, but you don't really have much time with any one kid or any one group because there are just so many of them. So many kids, so little time.

Assignment and review of homework also were described as important but highly problematic as an informal assessment strategy. In general, homework was viewed as necessary to give students practice with concepts and skills, but often inefficient and ineffective as an assessment tool, primarily because many students did not complete it. Moreover, with students copying one another's work, it was an unreliable indicator of their understanding and it was time-consuming to process. On the whole, the teachers perceived homework as difficult to grade and difficult to manage; further, they had problems motivating students to do it.

As with formal assessment, the critical trade-off in informal assessment is the amount and quality of feedback information provided to students versus the time required for the teacher to produce that information. Most teachers in our study felt that it was extremely important to provide as much feedback as possible to students, and the limits in their capacity to do so (in terms of time, resources, and tools) were a source of frustration to them. As one teacher said in an interview, "The biggest, absolute biggest pain in the neck is the daily problem sets. How I can assess them. Now, if I was a very thorough teacher, I'd probably spend 20 hours a day going through every individual problem set. I would like to really see all their work and be able to intervene at a much deeper level, but it's just, time won't allow it."

AN ANALYTICAL FRAMEWORK TO GUIDE DESIGN
OF CLASSROOM TECHNOLOGY INFRASTRUCTURE

Our research on teaching and learning activities, communication, and work flow in algebra classrooms moved our thinking about classroom activity and classroom technology infrastructure in the direction of systems theory (Checkland, 1981). Classrooms are learning *systems*, and systems have emergent properties that are not reducible to individual elements within the systems. A systems framework of the classroom will help designers of educational technologies and instructional interventions move beyond the one-off silo solution toward an integrated solution that builds capacity for teachers and learners.

Through the design requirements study described in this chapter, we came to believe that addressing the classroom as isolated lines of activity by 30 students and their teacher cannot unlock the potential of technology to enhance classroom learning. In particular, our findings regarding the challenges teachers face in processing (grading or marking) student work, and providing feedback in a time frame and form that truly can enhance students' learning, point to the necessity of a classroom technology infrastructure that augments teachers' capacity to construct and provide feedback by decreasing the time needed to process student work. In addition, our findings regarding the constraints that limit scrutiny of students' activity, work artifacts, and needs highlighted for us the need for increased channels of communication and flow of information, as well as for greater amounts of information, in readily usable form, for both teachers and students about classroom cognitive and social processes. The bandwidth for interaction and collaborative activity should be enhanced (Hamilton, 2004) so that students and teachers have increased channels of communication for providing information and feedback to one another. In a systems perspective, classroom communication channels are point-to-point or one-to-many but as a mesh network, potentially occurring simultaneously across all students at once, as well as synchronous and asynchronous.

Our systems perspective on the design of classroom educational technologies sees the power of technology as extending well beyond the current individual discrete-tool-based approach or even the metaphor of the "smart desktop" (Palaich et al., 2000). We posit a networked classroom technology infrastructure for data-rich teaching and learning with digital content, in which computer-supported classroom assessment is one of many services offered through a platform. Like Palaich and his colleagues, we see the teacher as a knowledge worker who desperately needs integration of the technology tools available to her. But beyond that, we envision something closer to a classroom platform for services (intelligent systems, digital resources, online activities, community tools, and so forth).

Through our analysis of teaching and learning in algebra classrooms, and the attendant issues of time, productivity, work flow, and engagement, we distilled a set of four analytical constructs, which we set in relation to one another within a framework that emphasizes their interrelatedness. Our framework posits a holistic view of the classroom as a highly integrated system of actors, tools, and content engaged in individual and social learning activities over time. This perspective accords with Hutchins's (2000) view that a cognitive system comprises all the actors within a setting, their interactions with one another, and the technical and cultural tools they interact with, not just the "head" of a single user interacting with a system tool. The analytical framework we developed is intended to inform design of a classroom infrastructure (network and tools). We believe it is generalizable to other activity settings in which actors use tools and collaborate in task activities.

The framework, shown in Figure 7.1, views the classroom as a space in which four dimensions, or layers, can be described. The goal of classroom technology design, from this perspective, is not to *maximize* the density (number) of events in each of these layers but to enable students and teachers to *optimize* the events for particular pedagogical or curricular objectives in a continuously changing learning context. Each element of this framework is described in turn.

Cognition

Student learning is characterized in the literature as a function of several cognitive, social, and affective factors, including student engagement, participation, time on task, regulation, feedback, and students' accountability for completion and quality of class work and homework. We use the term *cognitive density* to describe the aggregate level of students' engagement with learning materials and thinking, their progress in learning, their communication, and their use of time—that is, productive activity in the classroom at a given time. Increasing cognitive density is a general approach to improving learning and is independent of any specific pedagogical intervention. Cognitive density is a second-order effect of the interaction among more basic and measurable constructs: communicative, content, and temporal densities of the learning environment. Our framework suggests that giving teachers the ability to fine-tune, fluidly and continuously, the interaction of time, communication, and content will help them achieve and maintain optimal cognitive density across classroom routines.

Communication

Communication in the classroom can occur in speech, writing, or gesture, and can be digital or unmediated by technology. Messages can be sent in

Figure 7.1. Analytical Framework to Inform Technology Design for the Classroom as a Sociocognitive System

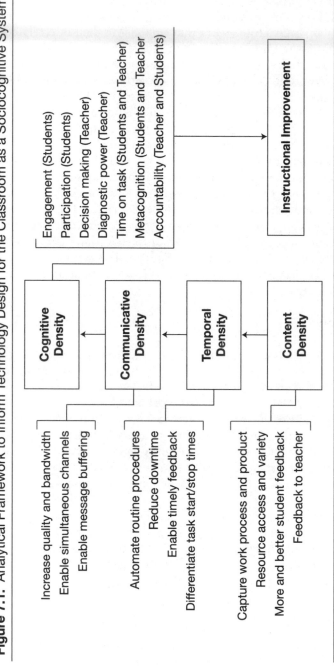

parallel or serially—one to one, one to many, many to one, many to many. Hamilton (2004) has described how technology can be used to increase the interaction bandwidth of a classroom. Imagine a networked classroom in which students have tablet PCs on which to accomplish their work. Interaction bandwidth is increased through screen-sharing capabilities and instant messaging, channels of communication that supplement the oral modality that typically predominates in the classroom. Furthermore, a message buffer, for example, of students' queries to the teacher, can allow the teacher to review multiple written messages simultaneously; then, seeing many students with the same question, she can send out a single appropriate reply simultaneously to each student with the same question. Alternatively, students could post questions to a central location, and students who know the answers could reply. Such configurations can dramatically expand the *communicative density* of the classroom. We speculate that when more communication occurs within the same time frame and students ask more questions and receive more help, students have greater time on task, which in turn increases the cognitive density of the classroom. Of course, we do not advocate uncontrolled and unmonitored "free-for-all" communication in the classroom, but rather the ability to tune the communication patterns and density to optimally support the desired activity (whether small-group, whole-class, or individual work).

Content

Content includes ready-made resources as well as artifacts generated by students or the teacher. It also includes students' solutions and other work produced by students and the teacher. Typically, students' interaction with content is heavily mediated by the teacher (Ball & Cohen, 1999). Even within the paradigm of reformed instruction, in which the teacher is encouraged to act more as guide than as transmitter of knowledge, students are fairly restricted in their access to instructional resources that could enhance differentiation of instruction and learner-centeredness of the learning environment.

If students had access to digital curriculum content and intelligent services (e.g., individualized instructional feedback) through a platform rather than as handouts or textbook pages, learning could be more effectively self-regulated and self-directed. Conceivably, students could access standards-aligned curriculum anytime and anywhere—from home or school. Students could complete and submit work and gain feedback immediately. They could access collaborators in the classroom, or anywhere in the world, through the network to complete learning activities cooperatively—or competitively, in game-based learning models. Information and data about student activities and accomplishments would be made available to the teacher automatically and integrated with her data-analysis and record-keeping software. Direct access by students and expanded access by teachers to appropriate, curriculum-aligned digital learning materials, as well as to feedback information about students' activities and results, greatly expands the *content density* of the classroom. Again, our view is not that more is necessarily better, but that content density can be increased and decreased to fit the situation.

Time

Temporal density is how much activity and communication occur in a given amount of time and is thus connected to communicative and content density. Time on task is the *sine qua non* of the organization of schools and classroom instruction. Other temporal issues in the classroom include class work flow and individual pace. Lower temporal density occurs when students wait for a turn to ask questions, or wait for the teacher to take roll or pass out materials. High temporal density occurs when all students are working and communicating. Automation of routine tasks is one simple example of how temporal density can be increased and downtime reduced.

In sum, our framework posits that each dimension or layer can have greater or less density at any point in time, and that the density of each layer is configurable with the aid of technology. Technology does not determine, but rather facilitates, configuration of the density of each layer. In addition, when the "space" is instrumented—that is, has a classroom network infrastructure with content and services with which students and the teacher interact—data about the configuration of each layer can be captured easily. These data (and syntheses of them) constitute feedback about the system, as well as about the actions and actors within it, which can be used in the moment by students in a self-regulatory manner and/or by teachers to achieve some instructional goal (e.g., to increase motivation, collaboration, or engagement with content). In Figure 7.1, the middle column lists the "layers" or elements within the classroom space. The left-hand column indicates some approaches by which each of these layers can be optimized through configuration of network settings and features. Finally, the right-hand column indicates the positive student and teacher outcomes that can result from optimal configuration of this space.

ENVISIONING TOMORROW'S DATA-RICH, HIGH-PERFORMANCE CLASSROOM

From the perspective of this framework, we begin to rethink classroom technology (or distributed online networks) as an integrated infrastructure with digital content and services that can greatly empower students and teachers in managing, personalizing, and adapting instructional resources, activities, interactions, and feedback in a way that enhances teachers' instructional practice as well as student learning experiences and achievement. This kind of configurability offers teachers and students many more possibilities for interacting with one another and with others outside the classroom. More important, the infrastructure can give teachers and students the information and feedback they need to optimize communication and collaboration, so that they occur among the right people at the right time, around the right content.

INFORMATION FEEDBACK AND FEED FORWARD

Teachers' considerable efforts to understand what students know, determine where they need help, and provide appropriate and timely feedback and intervention constitute an area of acute need. The timing of feedback is critical to its value in benefiting student learning (Bangert-Drowns, Kulik, Kulik, & Morgan, 1991). The time pressure to provide feedback was acute for some teachers in our study, and they used several strategies to render feedback more timely, as we saw earlier.

Given the realities of teachers' workloads, traditional classroom assessment and feedback methods are generally "too little, too late," with feedback coming in the days-long time cycles represented in Figure 7.2.

A classroom technology infrastructure has the potential to make rich information on learning, progress, and process (including engagement) available to students and teachers in real time. A platform approach in which teachers and students access content and services—which can include group learning activities, complex projects, and automatic scoring of simple and complex performances (Gibson, 2003; Quellmalz & Haertel, in press)— easily can provide instant feedback about multiple performances, events,

Figure 7.2. Time Lapses in Feedback to Students in Traditional Classrooms

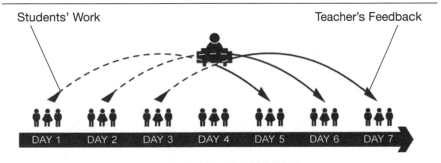

and processes to both teachers and students in real time, providing the rapid cycles of feedback represented in Figure 7.3. For example, as students work through a set of algebra problems during class, individually or in small groups, a teacher could have real-time, easy-to-read display of information about students' progress through the problem set, which problems they did correctly and incorrectly, as well as the ability to view students' work via screen sharing from her own tablet-type PC. Seeing incorrect strategies used frequently in students' work, the teacher could call the class's attention to the whiteboard for a demonstration of the correct solution steps. When students entered an incorrect solution into their tablet PCs, they could receive an automated response that says, for example, "That's not correct. Review your solution steps for the error." In this way, students' learning is regulated in real time, which has been shown to enhance learning (Black & Wiliam, 1998; Perrenoud, 1998; Wiliam, 2007). This feedback can motivate students and support teachers' ability to optimize lessons, learning interactions, and classroom processes.

In our vision of the networked classroom, the teacher is seen as the engineer of the overall learning environment, the orchestrator of learning activity in the classroom. Rich, complex information about not only students' learning activities but also their social interaction could be available to the teacher in real time to use in optimizing individual and social learning processes in the classroom.

The instrumented classroom we envision is quite different in scale, scope, and purpose from the technologies and assessments currently being advanced under the rubric of DDDM. Our platform would enable more diagnostic, real-time assessment for decision making on the fly. The kinds of assessment data yielded would not be limited to those that can be gathered from students working independently to complete multiple-choice tests. Instead, a multi-

Figure 7.3. Rapid Cycles of Feedback to Students in Classrooms with a Technology Infrastructure

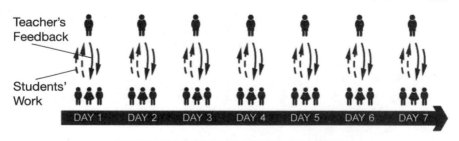

TECHNOLOGY WITH DIGITAL CONTENT

tude of complex skills, including students' abilities to collaborate with a diverse array of peers, could be assessed rapidly and easily. Further, and perhaps most important, such a platform recognizes the realities of classroom life and its demands for efficiency, while empowering the teacher to be an effective clinician, diagnosing individual student difficulties for the purpose of successfully reaching all students in the class.

This kind of classroom, furthermore, goes much further toward advancing the goal of creating assessments that are diagnostic and case-based, which, as Confrey in chapter 3 argues, is necessary for a fair and valid testing system. The kinds of individualization afforded by new networked technologies, including personalization of opportunities for collaborative learning from peers, enable teachers to act on diagnostic information on a case-by-case basis. Finally, the integration of data into longitudinal systems allows for both short-term and long-term use to guide instructional decision making in the moment or at the end of the week, unit, semester, or year. Such a vision may indeed be challenging to realize, but the importance of the need and the demonstrated promise of existing technologies suggest that the vision is realizable and that creation of data-rich classrooms for tomorrow is a worthy goal.

REFERENCES

Ball, D. L., & Bass, H. (2000). Interweaving content and pedagogy in teaching and learning to teach: Knowing and using mathematics. In J. Boaler (Ed.), *Multiple perspectives on mathematics* (pp. 83–104). Norwood, NJ: Ablex.

Ball, D. L., & Cohen, D. K. (1999). Developing practice, developing practitioners: Toward a practice-based theory of professional education. In L. Darling-Hammond & G. Sykes (Eds.), *Teaching as the learning profession: Handbook of policy and practice* (pp. 3–32). San Francisco: Jossey-Bass.

Bangert-Drowns, R. L., Kulik, C.-L. C., Kulik, J. A., & Morgan, M. T. (1991). The instructional effect of feedback in test-like events. *Review of Educational Research, 61*(2), 213–238.

Berliner, D. C. (1986). In pursuit of the expert pedagogue. *Educational Researcher, 15*, 5–13.

Berliner, D. C. (1994). Expertise: The wonder of exemplary performances. In J. N. Mangieri & C. C. Block (Eds.), *Creating powerful thinking in teachers and students* (pp. 163–186). Fort Worth, TX: Holt, Rinehart & Winston.

Black, P., & Wiliam, D. (1998). Assessment and classroom learning. *Assessment in Education, 5*(1), 7–74.

Checkland, P. (1981). *Systems theory, systems practice.* New York: Wiley.

Confrey, J., & Makar, K. M. (2005). Critiquing and improving the use of data from high-stakes tests with the aid of dynamic statistics software. In C. Dede, J. P. Honan, & L. C. Peters (Eds.), *Scaling up success: Lessons learned from technology-based educational improvement* (pp. 198–226). San Francisco: Jossey-Bass.

Elmore, R. F., & Rothman, R. (Eds.) (1999). *Testing, teaching, and learning: A guide for states and school districts*. Washington, DC: National Academy Press.

Gibson, D. (2003). Network-based assessment in education. *Contemporary Issues in Technology and Teacher Education, 3*(3), 310–323.

Glaser, B. G., & Strauss, A. L. (1967). *The discovery of grounded theory: Strategies for qualitative research*. Chicago: Aldine.

Hamilton, E. (2004). Agent and library augmented shared knowledge areas (ALASKA). *Proceedings of the International Conference on Multimodal Interfaces* (pp. 317–318).

Herman, J., & Gribbons, B. (2001). *Lessons learned in using data to support school inquiry and continuous improvement: Final report to the Stuart Foundation* (CSE Tech. Rep. 535). Center for the Study of Evaluation, University of California, Los Angeles.

Hinds, M. (2002). *Teaching as a clinical profession: A new challenge for education*. New York: Carnegie Corporation.

Holtzblatt, K., & Beyer, H. (1996, April). Contextual design: Using customer work models to drive systems design. *ACM CHI 96 Conference on Human Factors in Computing Systems* (pp. 373–374).

Holtzblatt, K., & Jones, S. (1992). Contextual inquiry: A participatory technique for systems design. In D. Schuler & A. Namioka (Eds.), *Participatory design: Perspectives on systems design* (pp. 177–210). Hillsdale, NJ: Erlbaum.

Hutchins, E. (1995). *Cognition in the wild*. Cambridge, MA: MIT Press.

Hutchins, E. (2000). The cognitive consequences of patterns of information flow. *Intellectica, 1*(30), 53–74.

Light, D., Honey, M., Heinze, J., Brunner, C., Wexler, D., Mandinach, E., & Fasca, C. (2005). *Linking data and learning: The Grow Network study (Summary Report)*. New York: EDC/Center for Children and Technology.

Massell, D. (2001). The theory and practice of using data to build capacity: State and local strategies and their effects. In S. H. Fuhrman (Ed.), *From the capitol to the classroom: Standards-based reform in the states* (pp. 148–169). Chicago: University of Chicago Press.

Means, B. (2005). *Evaluating the implementation of integrated student information and instructional management systems*. Paper prepared for the Policy and Program Studies Service, U.S. Department of Education. Menlo Park, CA: SRI International.

Palaich, R. M., Good, D. G., Stout, C., & Vickery, E. (2000). *Smart desktops for teachers*. Denver, CO: Education Commission of the States.

Perrenoud, P. (1998). From formative evaluation to a controlled regulation of learning: Towards a wider conceptual field. *Assessment in Education: Principles, Policy & Practice, 5*(1), 85–102.

Quellmalz, E. S., & Haertel, G. D. (in press). Assessing new literacies in science and mathematics. In D. J. Leu, Jr., J. Coiro, M. Knobel, & C. Lankshear (Eds.), *Handbook of research on new literacies*. Hillsdale, NJ: Erlbaum.

Shepard, L. (2000). The role of assessment in a learning culture. *Educational Researcher, 29*(7), 4–14.

Shulman, L. (1987). Knowledge and teaching: Foundations of the new reform. *Harvard Educational Review, 57*(1), 1–22.

Solomon, M., & Morocco, C. (1999). In M. Solomon (Ed.), *The diagnostic teacher: Constructing new approaches to professional development* (pp. 231–246). New York: Teachers College Press.

Stiggins, R. J. (2001a). *Student-involved classroom assessment* (3rd ed.). Upper Saddle River, NJ: Prentice Hall.

Stiggins, R. J. (2001b). The unfulfilled promise of classroom assessment. *Educational Measurement: Issues and Practice, 20*(3), 5–15.

Strauss, A. L., & Corbin, J. (1990). *Basics of qualitative research: Grounded theory procedures and techniques.* Newbury Park, CA: Sage.

Wiliam, D. (2007). Keeping learning on track: Formative assessment and the regulation of learning. In F. K. Lester, Jr. (Ed.), *Second handbook of mathematics teaching and learning* (pp. 1051–1098). Greenwich, CT: Information Age.

CHAPTER 8

Using Technology-Assisted Progress Monitoring to Drive Improved Student Outcomes

Naomi Hupert, Juliette Heinze,
Greg Gunn & John Stewart

In recent years much attention has been focused on the essential role that early reading instruction plays in later academic success. A wide range of studies reveal that students who are poor readers at the end of first grade rarely catch up to their grade-level peers (Francis, Shaywitz, Stuebing, Shaywitz, & Fletcher, 1996; Lyon, Fletcher, Shaywitz, Shaywitz, Torgesen, Wood, Schulte, & Olson, 2001; National Reading Panel, 2000; Shaywitz, Fletcher, Holahan, Schneider, Marchione, Stuebing, Francis, Pugh, & Shaywitz, 1999; Torgesen & Burgess, 1998). Research also shows that if those struggling readers are identified within the first few years of schooling and provided with targeted and intensive instruction, they are more likely to make the progress necessary to catch up with their peers who are reading on grade level (American Federation of Teachers, 2004). The need for early and ongoing assessments of students' reading skills is therefore vital.

Only recently has the education community really begun to consider the role that assessment plays in the process, to explore what teachers need in order to make use of assessment information, and to identify which types of assessments are most effective at supporting the development of students' reading skills. Progress monitoring is a form of ongoing assessment by which teachers regularly and systematically can monitor students' academic performance. Its purpose is to determine how well students, particularly those at risk of reading failure, are progressing toward meeting an identified goal. The impact of progress monitoring on student reading achievement has the potential to be great, and yet questions about whether progress monitoring makes a difference in teaching and learning persist. In this chapter, we discuss the effect that progress monitoring has on student achievement and teacher practice by reporting the findings of two studies. One study offers an in-depth look at how progress monitoring influences teacher practice based on qualitative data, including interviews and observations of teachers engaged in a statewide literacy initiative; and the other focuses on the analysis of a large data set to determine whether progress monitoring affects student outcomes as measured by the DIBELS (Dynamic Indicators of Basic Early Literacy Skills). Qualitative findings provide contextual information about the administration of progress monitoring in classroom settings and discuss teacher and student experiences as part of the progress-monitoring process. Quantitative findings indicate levels of impact for different frequencies of progress monitoring.

In both studies, teachers conducted progress monitoring using the DIBELS early literacy assessment on kindergarten through third-grade students. As a main component of the DIBELS, progress monitoring allows educators to check the progress of an individual student, determine whether the child is making adequate progress toward attaining grade-level proficiency, and ensure that those students who are receiving interventions are progressing on target (Good, Gruba, & Kaminski, 2001). In both cases, teachers administered the DIBELS progress monitoring to students one-on-one, using handheld computer software developed by an educational software company located in New York City, Wireless Generation. Teachers conducted progress monitoring in a variety of ways and at varying frequencies; nonetheless, both studies reveal that progress monitoring does appear to have a positive effect on student achievement and teacher practice.

Previous studies that examined the role of handheld computers in supporting teachers' use of assessment data to inform instructional decisions (Brunner & Honey, 2001; Heinze & Hupert, 2005; Hupert & Heinze, 2006; Penuel & Yarnall, 2005; Perry, 2003; Sharp, 2004; Sharp & Risko, 2003) suggest that teachers' use of handheld computers to support the collection of reading assessment data yields several positive effects. These effects align with key elements identified in recent research as necessary for teachers to be able to use student-level data to shift their own practice and meet student needs. According to research, for assessment data to be useful to teachers, they must be: (a) specific enough to show where students need help; (b) accessible in a timely manner so that teachers can act upon the information; and (c) comprehensible so they can be translated into practice (Popham, 1999; Schmoker, 2000). While simple, clear, colorful graphics help (Herman & Gribbons, 2001), presenting data in a way that is meaningful to teachers remains difficult (Ackley, 2001). Commercially published assessment data traditionally have arrived months, or even an entire school year, after teachers administered the test, and are delivered in a format that is static and not necessarily designed to meet the particular needs of teachers.

Yet as expectations for reading instruction and tailoring of instruction to student needs increase, so has the expectation that teachers will administer and make use of assessment data regularly to inform their classroom in-struction (Thorn, 2002). When asked about the experience of using handheld computers to collect assessment data, educators have responded that the use of handheld computers has had a positive impact on how they think about and make use of assessment data, and has the potential to alter what they do in their classrooms as they implement reading instruction on a daily basis. Findings from a multischool study on teachers' use of handheld computers to collect assessment data also indicate that the tools

- increase efficiency when administering an assessment;
- increase accuracy of the timed components of an assessment;
- decrease administrative tasks because the need for data entry is eliminated;
- improve access to data because assessment information is available immediately upon completion of an assessment;
- improve the relevance of the data as they reflect the most current state of student understanding and classroom teaching, and there-fore could be sensitive enough to show changes in student under-standing and classroom teaching (Heinze & Hupert, 2005; Hupert & Heinze, 2006).

These findings suggest that use of technology to support assessment activities may increase the likelihood that collected assessment data will become useful by providing teachers with immediate and relevant informa-tion about student progress. Yet many aspects of assessment—the data col-lection process, the analysis and representation of findings, the instructional decisions made based on these analyses—are undertaken without guidance from the research community. This chapter attempts to offer some guidance by addressing one aspect of this assessment process: progress monitoring. We examine progress monitoring and benchmark assessment data from a national sample of classrooms. Teachers in these classrooms are able to draw on the range of benefits offered by handheld computers and in this way have access to the key elements that researchers have deemed necessary in order to make effective use of assessment data. Given these optimal circumstances, we hope to answer the following questions:

- Does progress monitoring have a positive impact on student reading?
- Does the frequency of progress monitoring have an effect on student reading?
- What effects does progress monitoring have on teacher practice?

We attempt to answer these questions by drawing on interviews and obser-vations with classroom teachers as well as on analyses of the large set of progress-monitoring data collected over the course of the 2004–05 school year. We will discuss these findings further within the context of the classroom, where teachers are grappling with questions about how to make assessment data useful.

THE DIBELS ASSESSMENT ON A HANDHELD COMPUTER

The DIBELS assessment is an early literacy screening developed by Dr. Roland Good and a team of researchers at the University of Oregon (Good & Kaminski, 2002) to assess students' early literacy skills and identify those who are not on track for grade-level reading. The DIBELS targets a set of predictive literacy skills that research has shown are necessary for children to acquire if they are to become fluent and purposeful readers (Good, Simmons, Kame'enui, Kaminski, & Wallin, 2002; Good, Wallin, Simmons, Kame'enui, & Kaminski, 2002; Hintze, Ryan, & Stoner, 2003). The assessment is made up of a series of timed tasks and subtests that vary depending on the students' grade and the time of year administered. The subtests include: initial sound fluency (ISF), letter naming fluency (LNF), phoneme segmentation fluency (PSF), nonsense word fluency (NWF), and word use fluency (WUF). The assessment is administered during three benchmark periods throughout the school year—fall, winter, and spring.

During the 2004–05 school year an estimated 7,865 schools within 2,447 districts in 49 states and Canada used the DIBELS to assess over 1.7 million students, kindergarten through third grade. While originally designed to be administered on paper, the DIBELS is now among several reading assessments that have been developed for use on handheld computers. In 2003 an educational software company, Wireless Generation, collaborated with the DIBELS authors to develop a handheld version of the assessment. A teacher who is working in a school that uses handheld computers to collect student assessment data is able to view his or her roster of students, as it has already been input into the system prior to the assessment's administration. When preparing to assess a student, the system indicates which assessment subtests are appropriate for that student based on grade level, time of year, and, for progress monitoring, previous passages already administered. Teachers provide students with print copies of the assessment and are able to follow the students' reading, word-by-word, on the handheld screen (see Figure 8.1). Teachers use the handheld stylus to tap on the words read correctly, as well as to indicate the words missed.

The DIBELS assessment indicates students' risk for reading failure based on one or more subtests depending on the students' grade level. There are three risk categories: benchmark, or low risk because the student has met the benchmark for that grade; strategic, because the student requires strategic

Figure 8.1. Screen Shots on the Handhelds:
A Sample Class List and a DIBELS® Review

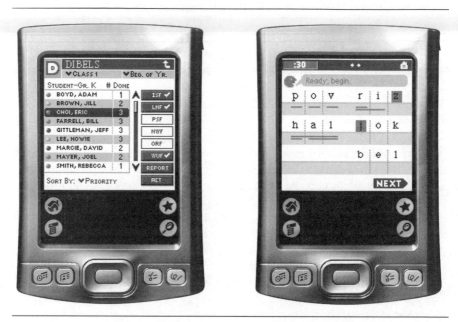

support to attain grade-level skill; and intensive, because the student requires intensive support to attain grade-level skill. Typically, students at the intensive level of risk have a 20% or less likelihood of reaching later reading goals without targeted intervention.

Once teachers administer an assessment or progress monitoring using the handheld, they immediately receive information about a student's risk category (see Figure 8.2; note the "running man," which denotes where the student is in terms of the different risk levels).

Teachers then can navigate to a screen that displays a graph, which reveals an individual student's progress or lack thereof, in relation to existing benchmarks. Teachers complete the data collection process when they upload the data at an electronic syncing station (a cradle for the handheld computer that connects to a desktop or laptop using a USB connection) after they have given each progress-monitoring or benchmark exam. Typically, school administrators designate a central computer station, located in the school's computer lab, reading resource room, or media center, where teachers can sync their data. Once the teacher uploads the data, anyone who has access to the password-protected web site can manipulate the data so they can view

Figure 8.2. A Student's Phoneme Segmentation Fluency Results

student-, classroom-, grade-, or school-level reports. (see Figure 8.3; the circles represent the benchmarks).

WHAT ADMINISTERING PROGRESS MONITORING LOOKS LIKE IN A CLASSROOM

The DIBELS progress monitoring consists of a short text that is leveled according to grade and time of year (beginning or end of year). A student reads the passage provided by the teacher and is timed for 1 minute. The number of words read correctly are recorded during that time. Good and Kaminski (2002) recommend goals, represented as the number of words read per minute, for students' reading to be considered on track to eventually read at grade level. For example, students in the spring of third grade must meet the minimal goal of reading 110 words per minute to be considered on track for reading at grade level, and will be considered in need of intensive support if they read below 70 words per minute on a specified grade-level text. Teachers note

Figure 8.3. Presentation of the Phoneme Segmentation Fluency Results for a Sample Student

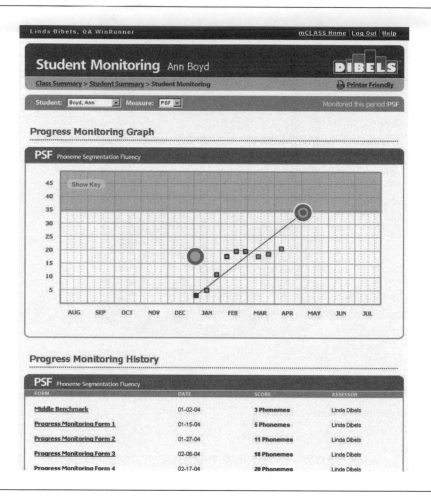

that one of the benefits the DIBELS has over other reading screenings is that it offers many leveled reading passages for each grade so that students can be progress-monitored frequently without having to reread passages previously used in other progress-monitoring sessions.

When using a handheld computer and software to collect progress-monitoring data, a teacher often will set up a station, or area, where she or he has students sit for a few minutes to complete the assessment task. The area often is located in a corner of a classroom, in a somewhat protected area, or is set up in a different room or location such as a quiet corner in a hallway, or a reading room. In most cases a teacher will progress monitor students one-on-one, while other students work independently at centers, or with a classroom aide. She will pull individual students out to administer progress monitoring over several days. In some cases a school interventionist or reading coach will administer progress monitoring while the teacher stays with the rest of the class.

During the assessment, the teacher presents the student with a DIBELS progress-monitoring booklet turned to a particular passage, selected by the teacher (based on the time of year, the student's grade level, and passages that that student previously read). The handheld computer screen displays the text to be read by the student. The teacher taps the screen to indicate that the student has begun to read, and the assessment software will freeze the screen at the end of 1 minute to indicate that time has expired. During that time, the teacher taps each of the words the student has read correctly. Once the minute has passed, the teacher will be prompted to place a marker on the handheld screen at the point in the text where the student stopped reading. Then the handheld screen will display a graphic indicating the number of words the student read in 1 minute, which is represented by an image of a running figure that stands on a continuum that starts as the color red, changes to yellow, and ends as green. In nearly all instances of progress monitoring, students immediately ask to see "where they are" on the screen after completing the reading. Teachers show students the screen with the running figure, and students see both what color they are ("I'm red") and what number they are ("I got 28 this time").

Once the administration is complete, teachers upload the new assessment data at a syncing station so that they then can view a student's progress over time by looking at a graph that plots the student's starting point (the number of words read in 1 minute at the beginning of the year) and can see the end point, or plot line, indicating the ideal progress for a particular student at a particular grade level. All progress-monitoring results then are plotted in relation to this aim line, and a teacher easily can see whether a student is making progress (following, or catching up to the expected aim line) or struggling (falling below, or failing to catch up to the aim line).

COLLECTION OF INTERVIEW AND OBSERVATION DATA FROM A READING FIRST EVALUATION

Over the course of 2 years, from 2003 to 2005, researchers conducted interviews with teachers, reading coaches, principals, and district-level administrators about the implementation of the DIBELS assessment and progress monitoring, as well as the use of handheld computers to support the collection and analysis of student reading assessment data. An analysis of these data reveals a range of interesting findings with regard to how teachers view assessment data, how and when they choose to make use of those data, and how they integrate the acts of collecting, viewing, and using the data in their classroom activities on a daily basis. Below we provide information based on data collected from interviews and observations conducted in a total of 17 districts and 34 schools. Researchers conducted 39 classroom observations in kindergarten through third-grade classrooms during the designated reading block, as well as interviews with 25 classroom teachers and 56 educators in other positions, including principals, reading coaches, superintendents, and district-level program coordinators. The data gathered from site visits to these schools provide contextual information, which can serve to inform our understanding of how progress monitoring is used by teachers to support their decisions about classroom instruction, especially decisions pertaining to individual student progress.

In interviews, teachers regularly report that they find the act of collecting data and receiving immediate feedback valuable. Many noted that the fast turnaround of information prevents data from being "dead on arrival" and improves its relevance for classroom decision making. Another point of interest is that progress monitoring appeared to increase students' involvement in their own academic progress. At some schools, students regularly plot their own progress on graphs or charts, which then are posted in reading rooms or classrooms. Teachers and administrators also noted the benefits of using the data to increase parent involvement. By using the DIBELS assessment data to introduce information about student progress to parents during parent–teacher conferences, and in schools where students are making strong gains in reading, teachers and administrators were better able to keep parents abreast of their child's progress, as well as share strategies that parents could use with their child in the home. Teachers indicated that interest in using student assessment data to engage parents has gained in popularity as educators exchange ideas across districts. In some cases, students even lead discussions with their parents about their own progress during parent–teacher conferences. Teachers report using their assessment and progress-monitoring data as way to introduce their reading goals and expected progress over the course of the year.

The emerging role that students are taking in the use of assessment and progress-monitoring data comes as somewhat of a surprise, particularly because it appears to be a result of ongoing progress monitoring taking place in so many locations. When progress monitoring was first introduced, interview data suggested skepticism among educators about an increase in time spent on assessments precipitating a corresponding decrease in time spent on instruction. Previous experiences with assessments led some teachers to question the appropriateness of assessments for such young children, and the overtesting of at-risk students. These concerns, however, quickly dissipated within our sample. We speculate that this was a result of the assessment's ease of administration (1 minute per student) and the data's relevance (the instant turnaround from assessment to data point along an individual aim line). Teachers also may be picking up on students' interest in their own progress as represented by their desire to view their progress on the handheld computer. These findings have led to more questions about the collection of assessment data as it relates to student outcomes, and in particular about the role that progress monitoring plays in supporting students' reading success and engagement in monitoring their reading growth.

PROGRESS MONITORING DATA SET

During the fall of 2004, approximately 10,000 teachers working in 31 states used handheld computers to collect and analyze data for approximately 200,000 students in pre-K through sixth grade. The data collected on these 200,000 students constitute our sample for this study. The data presented here have been collected by teachers, reading coaches, or others working at the classroom level in schools that have chosen to (a) adopt the use of the DIBELS assessment for early literacy, and (b) collect DIBELS assessment data using handheld computers. While the circumstances for data collection vary from school to school, district to district, and state to state, there are many commonalities that exist among all these locations. They are:

- All teachers, or others responsible for the collection of the DIBELS assessment data, participated in professional development events focused on the administration of the DIBELS assessment and aimed to support the DIBELS administration using a handheld computer.
- All teachers, or others responsible for collecting the DIBELS data, have access to a website where assessment data are shown and stored. This information is available in multiple visually enhanced formats that make use of graphics and color coding to highlight students at varying levels according to the DIBELS assessment.
- All teachers were exposed to the basic DIBELS recommendations about how often teachers should conduct progress monitoring. These guidelines suggest that students who are identified as performing at benchmark (on grade level) should be progress monitored least once every couple of months; students who are performing at the strategic level (requiring strategic support so that they can attain grade-level proficiency) should be progress monitored approximately once every 4 weeks; and students who are performing at the intensive level (needing intensive support to attain grade-level proficiency) should be progress monitored every 2 weeks. It should be noted that individual schools, districts, and states have requirements that may differ from

these, ranging from no requirement at all for progress monitoring, to weekly progress monitoring for the most at-risk students.

Analysis of Progress-Monitoring Data

To assess the impact of progress monitoring, we conducted multiple analyses using our sample of 200,000 students. The sample includes data on students for whom teachers conducted three benchmark assessments during the course of a single year. Students also received either no, minimal, or frequent progress monitoring. This data sample represents an extremely diverse array of district types, sizes, demographics, and instructional practices. However, it should be noted that this sample is somewhat self-selected in that a decision was made on either the school, district, or state level to purchase the DIBELS assessment system using Wireless Generation's mCLASS software to facilitate the administration of the DIBELS. Students' results from classrooms where teachers used paper and pencil to administer progress monitoring were not included in this analysis. To discover the impact that progress monitoring has on student reading outcomes as measured by the DIBELS, the data set was sorted into conditions according to the following variables:

1. student grade level: K, 1, 2, or 3;
2. time period of interest: beginning to middle of year or middle to end of year;
3. the number of progress-monitoring assessments administered during the period: none (no PM), 1–6 (infrequent PM, which would allow for approximately one progress monitoring every 4 weeks during a single semester), or 7 or more (frequent PM, which would allow for approximately one progress monitoring every 2 weeks during a single semester); and
4. the student's instructional support recommendation at the beginning of the period, as determined by the full DIBELS benchmark assessment: intensive (high risk), strategic (some risk), or benchmark (low risk).

Most of the analyzed conditions included an n of several thousand students or more.

The DIBELS measure used to assess gain in each grade and time period of interest was determined by the progress-monitoring guidelines published by the assessment's authors. For each student, a gain score was calculated by taking the difference between the student's raw scores on each measure at the beginning and at the end of the period. An effect size was calculated for each of the infrequent PM and frequent PM conditions by comparing its mean gain and standard deviation of gain with the mean gain and standard deviation of the corresponding no PM condition. To ascertain whether any meaningful differences exist between the results of students who receive varying amounts of progress monitoring, students' mean scores were compared with the standard deviations to determine the effect sizes. Table 8.1 shows the sample and effect sizes for each of the analyzed conditions.

Findings

The results of these analyses indicate that frequency of progress monitoring has a positive impact on student outcomes. Where fewer progress-monitoring administrations took place, smaller effect sizes were observed. Where larger numbers of progress-monitoring administrations took place, greater effect sizes were seen (see Figures 8.4a, 8.4b, and 8.4c; note that in Figure 8.4a high positive effect sizes are observed, especially in early grades, with frequent PM having greater effect and also that in Figure 8.4c even higher-performing students with higher amounts of PM show greater gains).

- The average number of progress-monitoring administrations per period in the infrequent PM conditions was 3 (a *monthly* progress-monitoring protocol would fall into these conditions). Small to moderate effect sizes were observed in all of these conditions, with the strongest effect sizes observed in kindergarten (ranging from 0.26 to 0.71).
- The average number of progress-monitoring administrations per period in the frequent PM conditions was 11 (a *weekly* progress-monitoring protocol would fall into these conditions). Moderate to large effect sizes were observed in almost all of these conditions, with the strongest effects observed in kindergarten and first grade (ranging from 0.40 to 1.25) and declining in the higher grades.
- In all cases, the frequent PM conditions had greater effect sizes than the corresponding infrequent PM conditions. This suggests that bringing the frequency of progress monitoring up to the levels suggested by the DIBELS authors—every 1 to 2 weeks for struggling readers— may yield a greater benefit to students than a less frequent approach.
- Comparable effect sizes were observed among the corresponding intensive, strategic, and benchmark categories. This important finding suggests that all students may benefit from some level of progress monitoring, even if they are showing good reading performance.

The differences in mean gains between the infrequent PM and no PM conditions, and between the frequent PM and the no PM conditions, were significant at the $p < .001$ level. These results reinforce, on a large scale, the existing research that progress monitoring has an impact on students' academic growth. More specifically, they imply that students who receive frequent progress monitoring are experiencing greater reading gains than those students who receive

Table 8.1. Analysis Results

Grade	Period of year	Assessment measure	Starting Support rec	No PM (PM count = 0) n	Mean Gain	Standard Deviation	Infrequent PM (0 < PM count < 7) n	Mean Gain	Standard Deviation	Effect Size	Frequent PM (PM count >= 7) n	Mean Gain	Standard Deviation	Effect Size
K	Beginning to Middle	Initial Sound Fluency	Intensive	6,850	9.5	10.9	6,807	13.7	11.4	0.38	1,277	17.0	11.8	0.66
K	Beginning to Middle	Initial Sound Fluency	Strategic	11,902	11.1	13.7	11,931	15.4	12.9	0.33	1,193	19.8	13.7	0.64
K	Beginning to Middle	Initial Sound Fluency	Benchmark	16,951	11.5	14.2	6,253	15.2	13.8	0.26	377	20.5	13.7	0.64
K	Middle to End	Phoneme Segmentation Fluency	Intensive	5,855	7.9	11.7	4,581	16.7	16.4	0.62	2,567	27.1	18.4	1.25
K	Middle to End	Phoneme Segmentation Fluency	Strategic	10,818	15.0	14.8	11,259	25.9	15.9	0.71	4,158	33.6	15.8	1.21
K	Middle to End	Phoneme Segmentation Fluency	Benchmark	19,186	15.4	13.0	11,350	22.3	13.3	0.52	2,659	27.7	13.7	0.92
1	Beginning to Middle	Nonsense Word Fluency	Intensive	7,020	17.5	16.6	4,678	24.5	15.8	0.43	1,644	29.6	15.7	0.75
1	Beginning to Middle	Nonsense Word Fluency	Strategic	7,526	22.5	17.0	6,847	27.8	15.7	0.33	1,665	33.9	17.2	0.67
1	Beginning to Middle	Nonsense Word Fluency	Benchmark	26,510	17.4	19.7	10,046	24.4	19.8	0.35	1,745	32.3	19.7	0.75
1	Middle to End	Oral Reading Fluency	Intensive	7,968	9.2	10.1	4,774	10.4	9.4	0.12	4,434	13.3	10.3	0.40
1	Middle to End	Oral Reading Fluency	Strategic	6,632	16.1	13.9	7,246	18.1	13.2	0.14	6,335	22.0	13.9	0.42
1	Middle to End	Oral Reading Fluency	Benchmark	22,072	20.6	16.4	10,435	24.4	16.4	0.23	3,956	30.0	17.1	0.56
2	Beginning to Middle	Oral Reading Fluency	Intensive	8484	13.1	13.0	5410	14.8	12.9	0.13	3058	19.1	13.0	0.46
2	Beginning to Middle	Oral Reading Fluency	Strategic	7731	23.5	14.3	7430	26.6	14.2	0.21	2617	31.4	14.0	0.55
2	Beginning to Middle	Oral Reading Fluency	Benchmark	21348	24.8	16.9	8107	28.2	16.9	0.21	1022	36.4	17.3	0.68
2	Middle to End	Oral Reading Fluency	Intensive	8414	11.3	13.0	8258	14.7	13.8	0.25	6034	18.0	14.0	0.50
2	Middle to End	Oral Reading Fluency	Strategic	4166	13.1	14.0	5142	16.5	14.1	0.24	2817	20.8	14.4	0.55
2	Middle to End	Oral Reading Fluency	Benchmark	22252	10.8	16.7	11424	14.7	17.0	0.23	2801	17.8	16.9	0.42
3	Beginning to Middle	Oral Reading Fluency	Intensive	10257	10.2	12.8	6778	11.8	13.0	0.13	3452	15.8	12.8	0.44
3	Beginning to Middle	Oral Reading Fluency	Strategic	9102	11.2	14.2	7511	13.5	14.9	0.16	2325	17.8	14.4	0.46
3	Beginning to Middle	Oral Reading Fluency	Benchmark	17757	12.0	17.7	6559	14.9	17.3	0.16	971	20.5	17.6	0.48
3	Middle to End	Oral Reading Fluency	Intensive	9121	17.0	16.2	9143	20.3	17.3	0.20	6126	22.4	16.7	0.33
3	Middle to End	Oral Reading Fluency	Strategic	6698	18.9	14.6	8158	21.9	15.2	0.20	4009	25.2	14.9	0.43
3	Middle to End	Oral Reading Fluency	Benchmark	15782	11.4	16.7	8207	14.1	16.6	0.16	2079	17.6	16.3	0.38

Figure 8.4a. Effect Size Charts

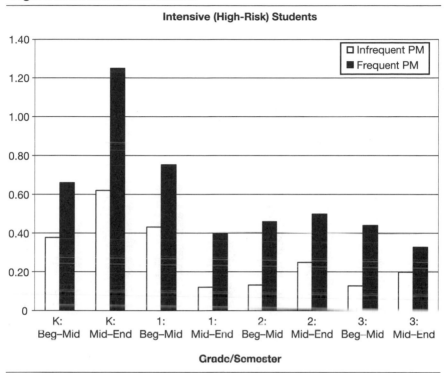

Intensive (High-Risk) Students

Grade/Semester

infrequent or no progress monitoring. It therefore appears that a positive relationship exists between more frequent progress monitoring and reading gains.

As educators and researchers, we recognize that the administration of an assessment, in isolation, is unlikely to change student reading outcomes. We can speculate that between the administration of the assessment and the student's change in reading outcome, something occurs that precipitates a change in reading. Moreover, we hypothesize based on these findings that whatever the "it" is that takes place between the assessment and the student outcome, increasing the frequency of the assessment makes the "it" more effective. This leads to questioning what takes place during and after progress monitoring. What kinds of interactions do teachers and their students have during this activity? And what do teachers and their students take away from this activity? Analyses of interviews and observations in a range of settings where progress monitoring occurs, provide perspective on what is happening during the progress-monitoring activity for both teachers and students.

Here we draw on classroom observations as well as the interviews with teachers and administrators about the use of assessment data to inform in-

Figure 8.4b. Effect Size Charts

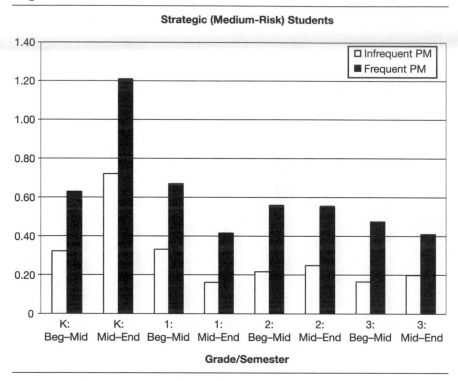

struction in order to further explore the relationship between progress monitoring and positive student reading outcomes. The data suggest that teachers follow the recommendations offered by the DIBELS developers for administering progress monitoring. Students identified as at benchmark on the DIBELS are progress monitored two or three times per semester, students identified as needing strategic support are progress monitored approximately once each month, and students identified as needing intensive support are progress monitored approximately once every 2 weeks. Within these recommendations variation exists from school to school, and even from classroom to classroom. Some teachers report feeling that progress monitoring is so valuable and so quick to administer that they regularly progress monitor all students, regardless of their support recommendation. Others feel that progress monitoring is so time-consuming that it takes away from instructional time, and hence administer it only to the most struggling readers in the class.

Several salient themes in regard to the benefits of progress monitoring emerged from the data collected. Progress monitoring can provide an opportunity for:

Figure 8.4c. Effect Size Charts

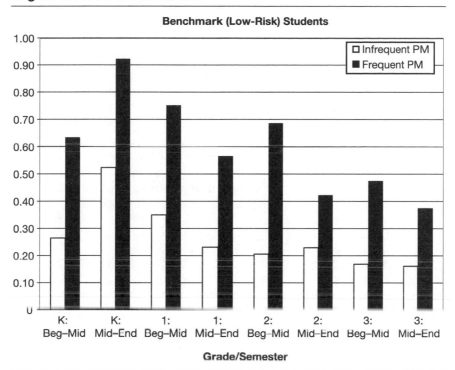

Benchmark (Low-Risk) Students

Grade/Semester

- a teacher and a student to sit quietly and read a connected text, with the teacher paying close attention to the student's reading;
- students to participate in the assessment process by viewing the outcome of the assessment immediately and noting progress or lack of progress; and
- a teacher to have access to clear grade-appropriate goals for students.

Each of these may seem like common events within the course of schooling, yet for many teachers and students the opportunity for these kinds of events is rare.

Time to Read Connected Text

With increased emphasis on the five big ideas in reading—phonemic awareness, phonics, vocabulary, fluency, comprehension (National Reading Panel, 2000)—and influence from the relatively successful Reading First Initiative, schools and teachers increasingly are focusing their reading instruction on the multiple discrete skills of reading to prepare students to become readers. Yet observations in multiple classrooms reveal that focusing on these skills alone may squeeze out the reading of connected texts. Students spend significant time reading decodable texts (designed to provide practice in a particular skill, such as reading a short "a" sound), but less time reading real texts. Teachers who have large classes and little, if any, classroom assistance do not have the chance to sit quietly with an individual student and listen to that student read. We therefore pose the question: Could the positive outcomes associated with frequent progress monitoring be a result of increased attention to and time spent reading connected texts, as well as a student spending increased time working one-on-one with a teacher? If so, more frequent progress monitoring would serve to yield both of these positive events. Still, it is difficult to expect that a single minute more spent on reading, even every 2 weeks, would have much impact on student outcomes. While this might represent a large percentage of the reading done by students needing intensive support, it is likely to be a very small percentage of the overall reading done by students who are already at benchmark.

Student Participation in Assessment

One of the greatest changes observed in classrooms where teachers introduced progress monitoring were teachers' and students' attitudes toward the data collected. In most cases, when it comes to assessment data, the teacher administers the assessment, submits the data to another entity (the state, the district), and then receives the results some time later. Usually, the results arrive after a student has left, or long after a particular skill or task was introduced. These data therefore are rendered useless and serve only accountability purposes. They are not designed to inform instruction in the classroom. The introduction of progress monitoring, particularly in conjunction with the handheld computer, has changed this considerably. Because teachers have immediate access to the data they collect, which are presented in a format that is readily accessible (so that it is immediately clear where a student "is"), these data can be incorporated into planning and discussions among teachers as they consider how to group students and provide targeted instruction.

In addition, teachers in different schools and districts in our study regularly include their students in viewing assessment data. In some settings, students reported their progress to their parents and families. In one particular instance, the parents of a child who told them about his results attended a parent–teacher conference wanting an explanation of what their child was discussing. This prompted the teacher to share progress-monitoring data with all of her students and their families. In other schools, teachers taught their students how to plot their own progress-monitoring data on charts and encouraged students to lead discussions about their reading progress using these charts during parent–teacher conferences. These are very different approaches to using data than previously existed in these settings before progress monitoring was introduced. Through the implementation of these approaches, students have become more empowered as individuals within the assessment process. They better understand what is being measured and what their goals are. More engaged in the process, students exhibit greater ownership over their own learning and perhaps feel a greater level of control over their ability to perform as readers.

Teacher Access to Grade-Appropriate Goals

The majority of teachers greatly appreciated the clarity and simplicity of the presentation of information associated with the progress-monitoring function. While very experienced teachers know what type of text, or fluency of reading, to expect from a student in a given grade, most teachers experience some trouble identifying exactly what a first, second, or third grader should be able to do as a reader at grade level. This problem is compounded in schools that serve large numbers of struggling readers. Teachers who have worked with struggling readers year after year can lose sight of what the expectations are of a student who is at grade level. For these teachers, regular access to information about where a student is in relation to expectations for his or her grade level is valuable. The use of progress monitoring ensures that teachers have a consistent and relatively accurate set of goals for their students and that expectations are consistent for all students. In addition, this information allows teachers to continually check on the impact that their classroom instruction is having in relation to reading at grade level.

Each of these three common elements in the administration of progress monitoring has the potential to play a role in increasing student outcomes on the DIBELS measure. While the chance to read connected text may not, on its own, have much impact, the opportunity for a student to receive individualized attention from his or her teacher is positive. In addition, opportunities for teachers and students to engage in conversations about student progress further their interactions and may encourage students to take ownership over their own academic achievement. At the same time, teachers must have access to accurate information about student reading levels in relation to end goals in order to determine progress and make judgments about appropriate and effective instruction. Without concrete goals in sight, teachers will struggle to identify whether a student is or is not making progress. Progress monitoring assists in the creation of clear goals and provides a consistent set of tools to track progress in reaching those goals.

Other factors should be considered when attempting to understand the relationship between progress monitoring and the student outcomes mentioned above. For example, the regular review and analysis of student progress might cause educators to more readily respond with more effective instruction that accelerates student growth. As noted above, this effect has been seen in other studies, including many that have monitored teacher behaviors in response to progress monitoring.

It is also important to note the possibility that there is a "testing effect" associated with progress monitoring, producing an increase in student scores with more frequent assessment. The less desirable type of testing effect, in which students end up memorizing test forms and items but do not actually learn to master the broader skill, most likely is eliminated because of the use of alternative text passages. The more desirable type of testing effect, in which repeated testing reinforces the student's skill and retention, may well be occurring here. This effect has been observed in many high-quality studies conducted in different domains of classroom instruction (Roediger & Karpicke, 2006).

FINAL COMMENTS

This analysis represents a broad, high-level view of the impact of progress monitoring. Studies that include more contextual information about the specific uses of progress-monitoring data (e.g., decision-making protocols and instructional choices) may yield more pertinent information about how to effectively implement progress monitoring to best benefit students. Nonetheless, these findings raise some interesting new questions. For instance, it has been widely accepted that progress monitoring and use of progress-monitoring data have important benefits for struggling readers, but these findings imply that there are important benefits for stronger readers as well. More research that investigates why and how this phenomenon occurs may prove quite valuable for schools trying to sustain strong reading growth for all students. Finally, educators continue to grapple with the question of how much progress monitoring is enough. This is an important question, as it is necessary to balance the time spent on assessment and using the data with the time spent on instruction. The findings presented in this study indicate a consistent correlation between frequency of progress monitoring and student reading performance, and support the implementation of progress monitoring at least at the levels recommended by the DIBELS authors. However, further investigation may suggest that, for optimal outcomes for all students, the recommended minimal frequency of progress monitoring should be raised.

REFERENCES

Ackley, D. (2001). Data analysis demystified. *Leadership*, *31*(2), 28–29, 37–38.

American Federation of Teachers. (Ed.). (2004). *Preventing early reading failure.* Washington, DC: Author.

Brunner, C., & Honey, M. (2001). *The consortium for technology in the preparation of teachers: Exploring the potential of handheld technology for preservice education.* New York: EDC Center for Children and Technology.

Francis, D. J., Shaywitz, S. E., Stuebing, K. K., Shaywitz, B. A., & Fletcher, J. M. (1996). Developmental lag versus deficit models of reading disability: A longitudinal, individual growth curves analysis. *Journal of Educational Psychology*, *88*(1), 3–17.

Good, R. H., Gruba, J., & Kaminski, R. A. (2001). Best practices in using Dynamic Indicators of Basic Early Literacy Skills (DIBELS) in an outcomes-driven model. In A. Thomas & J. Grimes (Eds.), *Best practices in school psychology IV* (pp. 679–700). Washington, DC: National Association of School Psychologists.

Good, R. H., & Kaminski, R. A. (2002). *DIBELS® oral reading fluency passages for first through third grades* (Tech. Rep. No. 10). Eugene: University of Oregon.

Good, R. H., Simmons, D. S., Kame'enui, E. J., Kaminski, R. A., & Wallin, J. (2002). *Summary of decision rules for intensive, strategic, and benchmark instructional recommendations in kindergarten through third grade* (Tech. Rep. No. 11). Eugene: University of Oregon.

Good, R. H., Wallin, J. U., Simmons, D. C., Kame'enui, E. J., & Kaminski, R. A. (2002). *System-wide percentile ranks for DIBELS benchmark assessment* (Tech. Rep. No. 9). Eugene: University of Oregon.

Heinze, C., & Hupert, N. (2005, October). *Results in the palms of their hands: Using handheld computers to support data-driven decision making in the classroom.* Paper presented at the Wingspread Conference on Linking Data and Learning, Racine, WI.

Herman, J., & Gribbons, B. (2001). *Lessons learned in using data to support school inquiry and continuous improvement: Final report to the Stuart Foundation* (CSE Tech. Rep. 535). Los Angeles: UCLA Center for the Study of Evaluation.

Hintze, J. M., Ryan, A. L., & Stoner, G. (2003). Concurrent validity and diagnostic accuracy of the Dynamic Indicators of Basic Early Literacy Skills (DIBELS) and the Comprehensive Test of Phonological Processing. *School Psychology Review*, *32*(4), 541–556.

Hupert, N., & Heinze, C. (2006). Results in the palms of their hands: Using handheld computers for data-driven decision making in the classroom. In M. van't Hooft & K. Swan (Eds.), *Ubiquitous computing in education: Invisible technology, visible impact* (pp. 211–229). Mahwah, NJ: Erlbaum.

Lyon, G. R., Fletcher, J. M., Shaywitz, S. E., Shaywitz, B. A., Torgesen, J. K., Wood, F. B., Schulte, A., & Olson, R. (2001). Rethinking learning disabilities. In C. E. Finn, Jr., R. A. J. Rotherham, & C. R. Hokanson, Jr. (Eds.), *Rethinking special education for a new century* (pp. 259–287). Washington, DC: Thomas B. Fordham Foundation and Progressive Policy Institute.

National Reading Panel. (2000). *Teaching children to read: An evidence-based assessment of the scientific research literature on reading and its implications for reading instruction.* Washington, DC: National Institute of Child Health and Human Development.

Penuel, W. R., & Yarnall, L. (2005). Designing handheld software to support classroom assessment: An analysis of conditions for teacher adoption. *The Journal of Technology, Learning, and Assessment, 3*(5), 50–70.

Perry, D. (2003). *Handheld computers (PDAs) in schools report.* Coventry, UK: British Educational Communications and Technology Agency (Becta), ICT Research.

Popham, W. J. (1999). Why standardized tests don't measure educational quality. *Educational Leadership, 56*(6), 8–15.

Roediger, H. L., & Karpicke, J. D. (2006, September). The power of testing memory: Basic research and implications for educational practice. *Perspectives on Psychological Science, 1*(3), 181–210.

Schmoker, M. (2000). The results we want. *Educational Leadership, 57*(5), 62–65.

Sharp, D. (2004). *Supporting teachers' data-driven instructional conversations: An environmental scan of Reading First and STEP literacy assessments, data visualizations, and assumptions about conversations that matter* (Report to the Information Infrastructure Project). Chicago: John D. and Catherine T. MacArthur Foundation.

Sharp, D., & Risko, V. (2003). *All in the palm of your hand: Lessons from one school's first steps with handheld technology for literacy assessments* (Report to the Information Infrastructure Project, Network on Teaching and Learning). Chicago: John D. and Catherine T. MacArthur Foundation.

Shaywitz, S. E., Fletcher, J. M., Holahan, J. M., Schneider, A. E., Marchione, K. E., Stuebing, K. K., Francis, D. J., Pugh, K. R., & Shaywitz, B. A. (1999). Persistence of dyslexia: The Connecticut longitudinal study at adolescence. *Pediatrics, 104*(6), 1351–1359.

Thorn, C. (2002). *Data use in the classroom: The challenges of implementing database decision-making at the school level.* Madison: University of Wisconsin, Wisconsin Center for Education Research.

Torgesen, J. K., & Burgess, S. R. (1998). Consistency of reading related phonological processes throughout early childhood: Evidence from longitudinal-correlational and instructional studies. In J. Metsala & L. Ehri (Eds.), *Word recognition in beginning reading* (pp. 161–188). Mahwah, NJ: Erlbaum.

CHAPTER 9

Incorporating Video in Instructional Strategies Designed to Improve Student Achievement: Thirteen VITAL

Ronald Thorpe & Margaret Honey

Among the wide array of voices calling for improvements in our nation's K–12 schools, there is fairly common agreement on the value of data and the need to use data to drive effective decision making. Not surprisingly, however, there is far less agreement around what data should be used and what decisions should and should not be made using them.

There is another issue connected to the call for data-driven decision making: It vaults over the basic fact that all people involved in schooling—from classroom teachers to state- and national-level policymakers—already use "data" to make decisions. One would be hard-pressed to find people in schools making decisions willy-nilly or using the equivalent of Chinese fortune cookies to guide the deployment of billions of dollars in preparing children for the future. Thus the more compelling and revealing dimensions of the topic have to do with: What data do educators use? How do they get the data? How do they use them?

This chapter describes an initiative, funded by the U.S. Department of Education's Ready to Teach program, that aligns instructional resources and strategies to data on student performance in math and English language arts (Grades 3 through 8) as measured on New York State's high-stakes tests. The goal of the initiative—known as VITAL (Video in Teaching and Learning)—is to help teachers connect content, instructional strategies, and the needs of individual students. It also connects instruction directly to assessment.

We begin with an old idea—the use of video in teaching and learning—but the design and implementation of VITAL move that idea toward innovative and intentional possibilities by aligning the video and related activities with specific instructional needs. The strategy looks at data in three specific ways: student scores on state-mandated, high-stakes tests; instructional strategies designed and vetted for use in helping students reach higher levels of achievement on the learning objectives cited in the tests; and video clips embedded in those instructional strategies and tested for their efficacy in improving student performance, whether a student is performing below or above proficiency. Also included in that third area are professional development protocols to help teachers use this combination of data.

Video, in forms from 16mm film to the newest DVD technology, has been part of classroom instruction for decades. Over the years the technology has improved markedly, but its associated pedagogy has been slow to change. With the advent of digital technologies and the ability to capture and deliver high-quality video materials whenever and in whatever form teachers and students need them, educators have the opportunity to explore more fully the role visual resources can play in the learning process. Compelling research affirms the connection between visual resources and increased learning. What remains is to discover what instructional needs are best served by video resources and what classroom practices result when the potential of these resources is realized.

Beginning in September 2005, Thirteen/WNET, along with its partners, the Grow Network/McGraw-Hill Company, the EDC Center for Children and Technology, and the research and evaluation firm Hezel Associates, embarked on a 3-year study designed to generate new usable knowledge about how video can be embedded into instructional strategies. The work is tied directly to teaching and learning as defined by New York State learning standards and measured by the high-stakes tests administered in math and English language arts for students in Grades 3 through 8.[1]

BACKGROUND

Film and video—and even for a brief period, television itself—have been part of America's classrooms since the middle of the 20th century. Anyone old enough to have been a student in the 1950s and 1960s remembers the 16mm projector, the characteristic sound of the take-up reel engaging, and the *flap-flap-flap* when the film came to an end. In between, there were many chances for hilarity: when the sound and image lost their synchrony, when things speeded up or slowed down, when an image slowly burned if the teacher dared to pause the film, or when the lights came back on and the teacher discovered the celluloid hopelessly entangled in a pile on the floor. Students found ample openings for mischief in the safety of those darkened classrooms, even as the teachers themselves found the chance for a brief rest from instruction or the chance to catch up on paperwork at the back of the room. Most of the time, the use of film in teaching and learning was a lesson in dreams deferred.

As miraculous as film was and is—giving teachers and students the chance to view moving images of life and nature as they really occurred or as they were created for the medium—it was also cumbersome. In addition, people knew too little about the cognitive advantages of the medium, trusting that the images themselves somehow would result in increased learning. Despite some valiant efforts on the part of teachers, the use of film always seemed to stand apart from what was being taught and learned rather than integrated seamlessly into the classroom environment. Still, even under such primitive and ill-conceived pedagogical applications, few students have ever forgotten the undulating Tacoma Narrows Bridge, the newsreels of World War II, and other classroom classics, even if they don't remember the point behind the films. Such is the power video has on the viewer.

Television itself burst onto the school scene with great promise in the late 1950s. Here was an inexpensive way to bring new learning to large numbers of children. But the impracticality of a broadcast schedule, combined with only a rudimentary understanding of how to use the medium in teaching and learning, soon pushed television out of day-to-day instruction and relegated it to allowing students to witness those major events that might occur during school hours (Eastern Standard Time, of course).

By the 1980s, the availability of VHS tapes eliminated some of the hassles of film. Even if no one knew how to get the VCR from flashing the ever-present 12:00, most teachers were comfortable putting a cassette into the machine and having the program play through a television set. But the pedagogical gaps persisted. There was still reliance on showing whole programs in darkened rooms, and the technology started to get a bad reputation when informed observers recognized teachers were using the tapes as a replacement for teaching rather than as an enhancement to learning. Furthermore, some of the most trusted programs, especially those with content that was better viewed by high school students, were coming from public broadcasting, and the format (either hour-long or series) simply did not work well within a traditional class period, or required more time to show than teachers could devote to the topic.

The move from analog to digital production and transmission of video, however, has brought new opportunities to the learning process. Teachers can use small pieces of video to help illustrate points and convey meaning—rather than tell complete stories—and these clips can be available to students and teachers literally whenever they need them via computers and various handheld devices. The technological barriers to integrating these materials into teaching and learning—combining them with traditional modes of lecture and text as well as more constructivist environments in which students are more actively involved in the learning process—have mostly disappeared, but the pedagogical barriers persist. What remains is the need for the fullest possible understanding of when video adds value to learning and how teachers and students can harness that value.

VITAL

As the nation continues its commitment to the No Child Left Behind (NCLB) legislation, teachers must know more about the needs of individual students in core subject areas, have tools to respond to those specific needs, and utilize those tools so that all students achieve to high levels based on state standards. The goal of VITAL is to create and distribute video resources designed to increase student performance in math and English language arts in Grades 3 through 8. These resources are being embedded in an electronically delivered analytical tool that shows teachers precise information about student performance levels measured against New York State standards. VITAL resources, including related professional development opportunities, initially are being distributed to teachers in New York State for math and English language arts. Eventually, these materials will be expanded to include additional content areas, and could be used for similar purposes in other states.

VITAL is being developed, distributed, and tested by four principal partners: Thirteen/WNET (Thirteen), the EDC Center for Children and Technology (CCT), the Grow Network/McGraw-Hill Company (Grow), and Hezel Associates (Hezel). The strength of this collaboration is compelling because of what each partner brings to the task, because of the connections among the partners, and because of work that is already well under way. The initiative is being supported by a 3-year Ready to Teach grant from the U.S. Department of Education, which requires a scientifically based randomized study, as well as substantial formative assessment to track its effectiveness.

The Grow Network's Online Analytical Tool

While all the partners are critical to the work being developed through VITAL, the work is largely dependent on the Grow Network because the VITAL resources are connected to and embedded in Grow's statewide reports. A company of educators and designers dedicated to a comprehensive approach to using assessment to improve instruction, Grow is committed to helping teachers reach toward the standards, and is motivated by concern about the harm that can be done by reporting data in a way that encourages "teaching to the test." Grow believes two requirements are necessary for a reporting system to foster instruction that is both informed by test data and grounded in the standards: (1) The categories of reporting, and the instructional materials they generate, must *deeply explain the standards that occasion the test;* and (2) the reported data and the recommendations made must work in complete concert to encourage the thoughtful use of data. The analytical tool—originally called the Grow Report but rebranded for use in New York State as nySTART (New York Statewide Testing and Accountability Reporting Tool)—is intended to give teachers a concise, balanced overview of class-wide priorities based on student performance on the state's high-stakes tests in math and English language arts (Grades 3 through 8). It also groups students in accordance with their learning needs and enables teachers to focus on the strengths and weaknesses of individual students. Each report is grounded in "categories of comprehension" that encourage teachers to act on the information they receive and to promote standards-based learning in their classrooms. These categories not only help to explain the standards, but also are derived from cognitive and learning sciences research about effective math and literacy learning. Grow did extensive work with its analytical tool in New York City schools, and the success of that work led to a contract with the New York State Department of Education to create a similar product, electronically delivered, for use statewide. This product was rolled out in the fall of 2006 and designed to capture the results of student performance on state tests administered at that time.

Thirteen—The Use of Video in Teaching and Learning

As a public television station, Thirteen has been producing the highest quality television since the early 1960s, before there even was a Public Broadcasting Service. Since 1989, its Education Department has been delivering professional development, primarily through the National Teacher Training Institute, designed to help teachers make effective use of video in teaching and learning. Substantial research confirms the value of video in helping learners develop deeper understanding, especially when combined with other modes of instruction such as text, lecture, and hands-on activities. Recent technological developments are making it easier to integrate video resources into classroom practice, moving beyond entire programs and focusing instead on selected clips.

Thirteen also has been the driving force behind the introduction of an educational video-on-demand service (EdVideo Online, or EVO) available free to all teachers and students in New York State. Use of that service, originally developed by United Learning and later bought by Discovery, has exceeded all expectations, with more than 3.5 million video clips viewed in the first 3 years (September 2002–August 2005). The service began with a searchable database of more than 2,600 full-length programs divided into more than 26,000 clips, and more resources are being added each year.

Based on the rapid rate of adoption by teachers—in all types of schools throughout New York State—and mountains of anecdotal testimony from teachers, it is clear that teachers consider EVO an important aid to instruction.

The distribution of clips, rather than whole programs, via the Internet is allowing teachers to capture much more of the potential that good video brings to teaching and learning. These clips, often 3 to 5 minutes in length, can become part of instruction, rather than replacing it, and they can be used more than once if students do not grasp the concept completely. They also are easy for the students themselves to use if they need additional review.

Even a cursory look at EVO, however, reveals that although it is certainly a step in the right direction, it has many of the same weaknesses found in most teaching and learning resources. EVO is based on a library model— that is, a vast collection of materials that a person must search through in hopes of finding just the right thing. It also is based on a one-size-fits-all format that emphasizes the delivery of generic content to a whole class rather than tailoring that content to the specific needs of individual students.

But what if a teacher didn't have to wade through a library of video clips to find what she needed? What if clips were preselected and tested for their effectiveness in moving students toward higher levels of performance in the specific content strands identified within the state standards? What if these clips and the related instructional guides were available to teachers online, embedded in reports that showed teachers how individual students were performing according to those strands? And what if teachers received professional development in how to use these resources effectively? VITAL is grounded in the promise implied in those questions.

In the 2005–06 school year, Thirteen, working with CCT, began to identify and test video clips that appear to help increase student performance in math and English language arts (Grades 3 and 4). These materials come primarily from Thirteen's animated series *Cyberchase* for math standards and from a variety of other programs for use in English language arts. Once found, the clips are embedded in nySTART. Eventually they also will be available to teachers as stand-alone resources through the State's Virtual Learning System, a Web-based site designed to house all instructional video for New York State schools, and on Thirteen's Web site. As mentioned earlier, nySTART reports will show teachers how their students are performing (below and above proficiency) according to content strands for New York State standards in math and English language arts. Embedded in those same reports will be links to VITAL resources, which will give teachers easy access to video materials and instructional strategies designed to help individual students move to higher performance levels.

Example

The following example provides more specificity about how and when the VITAL resources might be used by a teacher (see Figure 9.1).

There are five content strands in the New York State math standard: number sense, algebra, geometry, measurement, and statistics and probability. A fourth-grade teacher has online access to a report indicating how her students did on each of these content strands, with the percentages of students scoring below and above proficiency broken out by the standard. The teacher also has access to the results of individual students, providing an even more fine-grained view of what is needed to help students improve their performance.

In looking at the statistics and probability strand, the teacher notices that 45% of her students are performing below target range, 51% are performing within target range, and 37% are performing above target range. In order to help students improve their performance, the teacher must focus on the five "bands" of content included within this particular strand: collection of data, organization and display of data, analysis of data, predictions from data, and probability. While these bands define the content she must introduce to her students, her most important instructional decisions are those that address the needs of individual students to help them move toward proficiency and beyond. Under these conditions the data become a critical tool in decision making, and with them a teacher has a better chance of differentiating her instruction so that it results in gains by individual students.

While she is digesting the information available to her on nySTART, the teacher sees that next to each strand is a link to VITAL resources. She clicks, for example, on the statistics and probability link, where she finds a video clip from Thirteen's animated math series *Cyberchase*. Beneath a thumbnail image from the clip is a brief description of the clip and its purpose (in this case, to illustrate ways that two or more sets of objects can be combined), an indication of its length, and the choices of streaming the clip (for previewing purposes) or downloading the clip (directly onto her hard drive or burned onto a disc). The link also describes the math standard, the content strand, and the band with which the video clip is aligned. Finally, there are the instructional priorities (for below and above proficiency), with an instructional focus to be used with the video depending on the student's particular performance level. For example, a student scoring below proficiency might be asked to identify the two types of objects that characters in the clip use as they decide how to display and analyze their data, or to identify the number of possible combinations using one of the objects and to list each combination. A suggested focus for a student scoring above proficiency might be to identify the total number of possible combinations and to list each one, or to add two additional objects and identify the total number of resulting combinations.

This particular example offers a single video clip with different foci for students depending on their performance level. In other situations, completely different clips might be aligned with the different levels. But in every case, teachers will use data that rank a student's performance, in order to make decisions about instructional strategies designed to move that student's performance to a higher level. The video clips and strategies are preselected for her, and she has easy access to the resources, making differentiated instruction more likely.

CONTEXT AND RESEARCH BASE

Assessment, accountability, and standards have become the cornerstone of our new educational culture, with a special focus on students in greatest need—students from low-income families, students with special needs (special education students), and English-language learners.

Figure 9.1. Content Strands

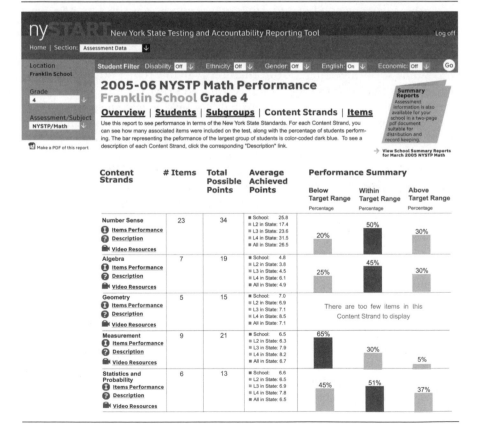

With this increased commitment to accountability, school systems now are required to use standardized assessments to capture academic performance data so that teachers and administrators can develop instructional strategies tailored to each student's learning needs. The success of this work depends on having (1) standardized assessments in all grade levels in core subject areas; and (2) teachers and administrators who are prepared to understand the data and use them to develop instruction that supports academic achievement.

New York State embraced the spirit and goals of NCLB through the development of statewide standards in all core subject areas and also through the development and administration of tests designed to measure student achievement according to those standards. With each step in the process, however, the education community, led by the Commissioner and the New York State Education Department, has learned more about the "gaps" that impede achieving the goal of moving all children onto the path toward proficiency.

One such gap has been in the system's capacity—from schools to districts to the state—to ensure that all critical partners (superintendents, principals, teachers, and parents) have access to data about student achievement that go beyond a raw score on a test. All tests on core subjects measure different areas of achievement. There are five content strands in the math standard in New York State, for example, and the strands are further divided into bands of more specific content. Running across the content strands are process strands. Two students with exactly the same scores on the Grade 3 math test could need vastly different strands to help them improve their performance level. All parties need to know what those next-level needs are and what instructional strategies are available to act effectively on the data.

New York State has taken an important step in addressing this need by contracting the Grow Network to create and deliver an analytical tool for teachers, parents, and school administrators across the state for students in Grades 3 through 8 (math and English language arts) and for all students in Grades 3 through 12 who qualify for the State's alternative assessment (special education). The Grow Reports (later renamed nySTART) were introduced and tested in New York City over a 5-year period, and their efficacy was corroborated through a 2-year study conducted by the EDC Center for Children and Technology (Light, Honey, Heinze, Brunner, Wexler, Mandinach, & Fasca, 2005).

In researching data-driven practices in New York City, CCT learned that teachers often experience a disconnect between the concepts described by the standards and the state tests for which they are accountable. Without appropriate tools and resources, teachers often feel they serve two masters: the *standardized test* for which they must prepare their students, and the *local standards* that determine their curriculum. The two are not always compatible and sometimes directly conflict. The alignment of the Grow resources with the test results helped teachers build a connection between their students' test results and the concepts and skills on which the standardized tests focus.

When standards call for discovery of complex concepts, for example, and the tests call for the mastery of specific content, teachers can feel caught in the middle. The rich conceptual work takes time away from the focused test preparation that directly affects student scores, but without time for more complex learning processes in which a greater variety of skills and strengths can be exhibited and practiced, students who are least successful continue to fall behind. By adding video content (and related materials) aligned with the specific New York State learning standards in English language arts and math in Grades 3 through 8, thus linking resources to both standards and test results, VITAL has the potential of helping teachers combine the "two masters."

Aligning curriculum, instruction, and standards is difficult (Pellegrino, Chudowsky, & Glaser, 2001). The work proposed through VITAL attempts to take proven instructional methods and combine them into a seamless alignment among these three functions, thereby increasing the likelihood that instruction will lead to increased achievement.

The Need for Data and the Efficacy of Grow Reports in Providing Data

When teachers have access to data describing the strengths and weaknesses of individual students, and when those data are aligned with research-based teaching strategies, teachers are able to respond to the needs of individual students in ways that result in higher student achievement. The Grow Network spent more than 5 years developing assessment reports that provide teachers with a clear picture of how their students did on the previous year's state tests in math and English language arts (Grades 3 through 8) within three basic categories: help with fundamentals (students scoring in Levels 1 and 2), additional instruction and practice (students scoring in Level 3), and advanced work (students scoring in Level 4). Based on how students performed on certain test questions, the Grow Report also provides teachers with strategies to help move the students to higher performance. A 2-year study of the Grow implementation in New York City (Pasnik & Keisch, 2004) found that:

- Data-driven decision making requires that appropriate data be turned into useful information that can contribute to making knowledgeable, informed decisions (Ackoff, 1989; Drucker, 1989). Digital technology has played a major part in making it possible for educators to interact with appropriate data that can be used to make more informed decisions. Specifically, the relative ease of use and sophistication of data-gathering, storage, and delivery systems have made data accessible in a meaningful format to whole sets of constituents whose access to data in the past was either nonexistent or presented in dense, unintelligible reports (Wayman, Stringfield, & Yakimowski, 2004).

- As a tool, the Grow Report tries to underscore ways in which test data can be used to inform instruction, not just accountability. It provides a format that builds a bridge between standards, testing results, and instructional strategies, as well as guides educators on constructing a rationale for differentiating instruction.

- As a resource that aligns test results with standards and instructional strategies, the Grow Report is highly successful in creating a navigational framework for educators. Grow Reports present data in a format from which teachers can draw information needed to support differentiating instruction and thinking about students' weaknesses as well as strengths. In this sense, Grow Reports help teachers navigate the tensions that exist in a high-stakes climate between the accountability model of schooling, where data from standardized tests drive assessment and define the standards, and a reform model, where diversity is considered in the curriculum and is defined by differentiated pedagogical practices tailored to the needs of individual students.

- Teachers use the testing data provided in Grow Reports to plan activities, lessons, and units. They sometimes use the data as a starting point for conversations with students, parents, specialists, and administrators. Mostly, teachers use test data to allocate their own resources: time, attention, practice, and homework.

Need for Improved Math

The need to improve mathematics instruction is well documented. The National Assessment of Educational Progress (NAEP) indicates that the United States is making steady progress in fourth- and eighth-grade mathematics. Between 1990 and 2000, the percentage of fourth graders at or above the proficient level doubled—proficient being the level deemed appropriate by the National Assessment Governing Board standards (U.S. Department of Education, 2005). However, as of 2003, only 32% of fourth graders and 29% of eighth graders were performing at a proficient level.

Although progress in mathematics achievement is occurring among all ethnic groups, it is not equal. NAEP data for 2003 show that while 43% of White fourth graders are performing at or above proficient, only 10% of Black fourth graders, 16% of Hispanic fourth graders, and 17% of American Indian students are performing at or above proficient. Even more striking are the percentages of fourth-grade students achieving below basic: White, 13%; Black, 46%; Hispanic, 38%, and American Indian, 36%.

Differences between achievement levels of eighth-grade students along ethnic lines are equally striking. In 2003, 37% of White eighth graders were at or above proficient, but the percentage for Black eighth graders was a mere 7%; for Hispanics the number climbs slightly, to 12%, and for American Indians, to 15%. The percentage of White students who achieved below basic was 13%. For Black eighth graders, the percentage was 61%; for Hispanics, 52%, and for American Indians, 48% (National Center for Education Statistics, NAEP, 2003 Mathematics Assessments).

Results from the 2003 Trends in International Mathematics and Science Study (TIMSS) show that mathematics performance among U.S. eighth-grade students is lower than that of 14 other countries (Mullis, Martin, Gonzalez, & Chrostowski, 2004).

Need for Improved English Language Arts Instruction

The need to improve achievement in English language arts is equally well documented. The latest results from the NAEP show that between 1998 and 2003, on the Reading and Writing Report Cards, the percentage of fourth-grade students at proficient in reading increased by only 2% (from 29% to 31%). Also, only 28% of fourth-grade students achieved the level proficient on the 2002 Writing Report Card.

In a 5-year period documented by the NAEP, eighth-grade students made no progress in reading: from 1998 to 2003, only 32% of students were at or above the proficient level. As with mathematics, there is a marked disparity between White and ethnically diverse students. As early as fourth grade, the percentage of White students at or above proficient in reading is noticeably higher than that of Black, Hispanic, or American Indian students. In 2003, 41% of White fourth graders were proficient, while only 13% of Black, 15% of Hispanic, and 16% of American Indian fourth graders were at or above proficient (National Center for Education Statistics, NAEP, 2003 Reading Assessments). Percentages of students below basic show a similar pattern.

The disparities increase for older children. In 2003, 41% of White eighth graders achieved at or above proficient in reading, while only 13% of Black, 15% of Hispanic, and 17% of Native American eighth graders achieved at or above proficient (U.S. Department of Education, NAEP, 2005). For these ethnic groups, far more eighth graders are below basic in reading and writing than are proficient.

At the middle school level, researchers have begun to identify the effectiveness of English language arts instruction that is an integral component of a comprehensive curriculum (Alvermann, 1998; Pearson, 1996). Most middle schools in the United States, however, offer little or no systematic reading program, and those that do, tend to offer it in the form of separate, corrective, or remedial classes rather than as programs integrated into the curriculum (Irvin, 1990). Remedial reading classes typically are focused on basic skills and have been criticized for not addressing the need to teach higher level comprehension skills (Greenleaf, Schoenbach, Cziko, & Mueller, 2001).

More than 8 million students in Grades 4 through 12 struggle with reading (U.S. Department of Education, 2003), and according to the *Reading Next* report commissioned by the Carnegie Corporation of New York (Biancarosa & Snow, 2004), as many as 70% of adolescent students "struggle in some manner and require differentiated instruction in areas where multiple circumstances conspire against students' chances for success, such as urban centers" (p. 8). In some urban centers as many as 80% of students are reading below their grade level.

The needs of students in Grades 4 through 8 who continue to struggle with reading and mathematics must be addressed so that they can meet the academic expectations of high school. Meeting the needs of this population requires changing how teachers approach their instruction across content areas and also demands attention to issues such as student engagement and motivation.

Video Materials Make a Difference

Recent research on the power of video as an instructional resource suggests that when appropriately matched with specific instructional goals, video materials help more students achieve at higher levels and tend to be more compelling to many more students than print-only resources. The Corporation for Public Broadcasting (CPB) released a report entitled *Television Goes to School: The Impact of Video on Student Learning in Formal Education* (2004). According to research studies, video stimulates class discussion, reinforces lectures and reading, provides a common base of knowledge among students, and helps teachers teach more effectively. Additionally, video has been found to be effective with special student groups, including the economically disadvantaged and the learning disabled (Grunwald Associates, 2002). With a demanding workload, limited resources, and high-stakes accountability testing, teachers value video when it is connected to curriculum (Fisch, 2004).

The CPB study found that instructional video was requested most often for math, even though "less than half of math teachers reported using video" (p. 11). A separate study conducted by Aiex (1988) also revealed the wide use of video to motivate writing and that "language arts teachers have successfully used film, news stories, even soap operas to organize writing activities for students at a variety of levels" (Corporation for Public Broadcasting, 2004, p. 13).

Although teachers have been slow to integrate computer-based tools into their classrooms, they appear to be comfortable using video resources, especially when the video is delivered over the Internet and is available in segments (rather than in whole programs) that are attached to lesson guides and other materials correlated to grade and content-specific state learning standards. These facts are supported by Thirteen's experience with teachers throughout New York State who have had access to a library of video resources through a free video-on-demand service (EVO). This service gives students and teachers access to Internet-based video and associated materials, and is one of the fastest growing uses of technology in schools. EVO usage by students and teachers in New York State doubled in each of its first 3 years, surpassing 3.5 million views (cumulative) during the 2004–05 school year (New York State Association of Public Broadcasting Stations, 2005).

Research not only indicates that teachers are comfortable using video, but also shows that video content improves student and teacher performance as well as changes student–teacher interaction in ways that facilitate student achievement. A randomized study conducted on *Unitedstreaming*'s video-on-demand service by an independent research firm found that student learning was substantially improved by exposure to content-related video clips (Boster, Meyer, Roberto, Lindsey, Smith, Strom, & Inge, 2004). The study, involving over 1,000 elementary and middle school students in three Virginia school districts, showed an average increase in academic achievement of 12.6% for students exposed to video content compared with students who received traditional instruction only.

Additional research studies of specific content that will be used in VITAL for elementary-level math content speak to the value of *Cyberchase*, the PBS award-winning children's show produced by Thirteen. MediaKidz Research & Consulting assessed the impact of Season 2 programs on mathematical problem-solving skills among a diverse group of 108 third- and fourth-grade students. Half watched 20 episodes of *Cyberchase* once a day, while the control group had no access to the video. Pre- and posttesting involved mathematical problem-solving tasks. Viewers outperformed nonviewers significantly on *all* measures of direct learning, *many* measures of near transfer, and *some* far-transfer measures tested weeks after viewing (Fisch, 2004).

National Teacher Training Institute

Thirteen's National Teacher Training Institute (NTTI) professional development model, which emphasizes collaborative, hands-on, technology-based learning through a "teachers teaching teachers" approach, has proven successful across grade levels and subject areas in communities across the country. Evaluations of the NTTI program have recognized its teaching and student achievements. In CPB's 2004 report *Television Goes to School*, NTTI is cited as one of the finest professional services in the field.

A 2004 evaluation of the project conducted by the Michael Cohen Group, LLC, reported that NTTI makes a "measurable impact both on teachers' and students' use of technology in the classroom" (Thirteen/WNET, 2004,

p. 2). Teachers at the five selected national affiliate sites reported significant increases in their comfort level with using technology in the classroom, a greater sense of confidence using technology in their daily teaching, and an increased use of technology in the presentation of daily lessons.

Students of teachers participating in NTTI activities benefited similarly. Students reported increased use of technological tools in the classroom, and an increased sense of competence using the Internet and video resources in their classwork, a result that was strong enough to improve their overall sense of self-confidence as well (Thirteen/WNET, 2004, p. 2).

Similarly, NTTI's internal evaluation—a three-step survey assessment designed by Teachers College, Columbia University—testifies to the strength and effectiveness of the program. According to the 2004–2005 project evaluations, completed by nearly 5,000 K–12 educators, 95% of NTTI participants reported that the project was an effective model for training teachers to use video in the classroom. Ninety-two percent of participants reported that they planned to use the knowledge and information gained at NTTI in their classrooms, and 94% rated their NTTI experience as effective in preparing them to integrate media into meaningful, standards-based lessons (Thirteen/WNET, 2005).

In order for teachers to utilize video to enhance student learning and achievement, they must be exposed to strategies and best practices in professional development sessions. *Television Goes to School* cites a 1988 study by Eckenrod and Rockman indicating that teachers exposed to instructional video resources tended to utilize videos and activities that were demonstrated as examples in training sessions, and far less likely to use materials that had not been demonstrated in training sessions.

CONCLUSION

The work outlined in this chapter promises to move educators toward a greater understanding of how data from standardized test results, combined with instructional strategies and powerful resources, can be used to inform decisions about classroom practice differentiated for individual students. Bridging the gap between assessment and instruction is at the very heart of data-driven decision making in schools. The nySTART reports give teachers the data of test results as road maps to future instruction not just for the lowest performing students but for all students. VITAL is being designed to connect video and related instructional activities to those data so teachers have easy access to strategies for helping students move to higher levels of proficiency. Based on the early and robust adoption of EdVideo Online among New York State teachers, research done specifically on that service, and the broader literature that supports the value of visual resources in advancing student learning, the VITAL partners hope to take video usage to the next natural step. Teachers have limited time for preparation and even less for instruction. Even though EdVideo Online, with its searchable database of segments, is a vast improvement over earlier technologies, it still requires each teacher to wander through a massive library of potential materials and then figure out how to integrate these materials with other classroom resources and match them to individual students. VITAL resources intend to cut right to that final point, providing teachers with resources already proven effective in improving student performance. By placing these segments and the related materials within the resources presented in nySTART reports—which themselves are already aligned with the demonstrated needs students must fulfill to move to the next step of mastery—Thirteen and its partners believe that the potential of video resources can be more fully realized, and that teachers will have an opportunity to use valuable data to make decisions about instruction for individual students based on their individual strengths and weaknesses.

NOTES

1. At the time this chapter was written, the initiative was halfway through its 3-year term. Final analysis of the results of the initiative will not be available until 2008.

REFERENCES

Ackoff, R. L. (1989). From data to wisdom. *Journal of Applied Systems Analysis, 16*, 3–9.

Aiex, N. K. (1988). Using film, video, and TV in the classroom. *ERIC Digest, 11*. Bloomington, IN: ERIC Clearinghouse on Reading and Communication Skills. (ERIC Document Reproduction Service No. ED300848)

Alvermann, D. (1998). The crisis in adolescent literacy: Is it real or imagined? *NASSP Bulletin, 82*(600), 4–9.

Biancarosa, G., & Snow, C. E. (2004.) *Reading next—a vision for action and research in middle and high school literacy: A report to Carnegie Corporation of New York*. Washington, DC: Alliance for Excellent Education.

Boster, F. J., Meyer, G. S., Roberto, A. J., Lindsey, L., Smith, R., Strom, R., & Inge, C. C. (2004, September). *A report on the effect of the unitedstreaming™ application on educational performance: The 2004 Los Angeles Unified School District mathematics evaluation*. [Cometrika, Inc., Baseline Research, LLC., & Longwood University]. Retrieved November 28, 2005, from http://unitedlearning .com/streaming/evaluation.cfm?id=315

Corporation for Public Broadcasting. (2004). *Television goes to school: The impact of video on student learning in formal education*. New York: EDC Center for Children and Technology.

Drucker, P. F. (1989). *The new realities: In government and politics/in economics and business/in society and world view.* New York: Harper & Row.

Fisch, S. M. (2004). *Children's learning from educational television: Sesame Street and beyond.* Mahwah, NJ: Erlbaum.

Greenleaf, C., Schoenbach, R., Cziko, C., & Mueller, F. (2001). Apprenticing adolescent readers to academic literacy. *Harvard Educational Review, 71*(1), 79–129.

Grunwald Associates. (2002, November). *Video and television use among K–12 teachers.* Survey results in PowerPoint format prepared for the Corporation for Public Broadcasting, Washington, DC.

Irvin, J. (1990). *Reading and the middle school student.* Needham Heights, MA: Allyn & Bacon.

Light, D., Honey, M., Heinze, J., Brunner, C., Wexler, D., Mandinach, E., & Fasca, C. (2005). *Linking data and learning: The Grow Network study* (Summary Report). New York: EDC Center for Children and Technology.

Mullis, I. V. S., Martin, M. O., Gonzalez, E. J., & Chrostowski, S. J. (2004). *TIMMS 2003 international mathematics report.* Chestnut Hill, MA: TIMSS & PIRLS International Study Center, Boston College.

New York State Association of Public Broadcasting Stations. (2005). *Video-on-demand usage data.* New York: Author.

Pasnik, S., & Keisch, D. (2004). *Teachers' domain evaluation report.* New York: EDC Center for Children and Technology.

Pearson, P. (1996). Reclaiming the center. In M. Graves, P. van den Broek, & B. M. Taylor (Eds.), *The first R: A right of all children* (pp. 259–274). New York: Teachers College Press.

Pellegrino, J. W., Chudowsky, N., & Glaser, R. (2001). *Knowing what students know: The science and design of educational assessment.* Washington, DC: National Academy Press.

Thirteen/WNET. (2004). *Impact assessment of the National Teacher Training Institute among participating teachers and their students* (Final Report). New York: Michael Cohen Group.

Thirteen/WNET. (2005). NTTI *evaluation* (Internal data). New York: Author.

U.S. Department of Education, Institute of Education Sciences, National Center for Education Statistics. (2003). *Nation's report card: Reading 2002.* Retrieved March 31, 2005, from http://nces.ed.gov/nationsreportcard/

U.S. Department of Education, Institute of Education Sciences, National Center for Education Statistics, National Assessment of Educational Progress (NAEP). (2005). *1992, 1994, 1998, 2000, 2002, and 2003 reading assessments.* Retrieved April 15, 2005, from http://nces.ed.gov/nationsreportcard/

Wayman, J. C., Stringfield, S., & Yakimowski, M. (2004). *Software enabling school improvement through analysis of student data* (CRESPAR Rep. No. 67). Baltimore: Johns Hopkins University, Center for Research on the Education of Students Placed at Risk. Retrieved April 15, 2005, from www.csos.jhw.edu/crespar/techreports/Report67.pdf

PART IV

Creating Data Cultures

CHAPTER 10

Supporting Equity Inquiry
with Student Data Computer Systems

Jeffrey C. Wayman, Katherine Conoly,
John Gasko & Sam Stringfield

The persistent challenge of fostering equality of educational achievement and outcomes for all students has been a topic of study for over 40 years (Coleman, Campbell, Hobson, McPartland, Mood, Weinfeld, & York, 1966; English, 2002; Jencks & Phillips, 1998; Rothstein, 2004; Stringfield & Land, 2002). Despite this attention, these authors and others have highlighted gaps in achievement that to this day remain associated with factors such as poverty, ethnicity, and disability.

The reauthorization of the Elementary and Secondary Education Act as the No Child Left Behind Act (NCLB) targeted over $11 billion in financial assistance to schools serving economically disadvantaged students.[1] In addition, NCLB established a blueprint for state education systems to follow in raising student achievement and required specific timelines, with an emphasis on closing achievement gaps for students from traditionally underserved groups. Specifically, this policy required states to set performance targets such that students from economically disadvantaged families, students with disabilities, students with limited English proficiency, and students from all major ethnic minority groups would achieve as well as their traditionally better-performing peers.

Accordingly, states have been required to revamp their student performance monitoring systems to provide transparency indicators of student achievement and progress. Specifically, states, districts, and schools now must report state achievement test data disaggregated by these defined subgroups and establish goals for attaining proficiency for every student by 2014.

Unfortunately, the NCLB legislation provided no mechanisms to facilitate the disaggregation and reporting of test data, nor were there supports for engaging in the important examination of each student's educational process. Consequently, this charge has proved to be a challenge for districts, many of which were already awash in student data but without efficient means for practical access. Paradoxically, many districts are now simultaneously data-rich and information-poor.

Coinciding with NCLB has been the advent of efficient computer technologies for aggregating, disaggregating, and examining student data (Wayman, Stringfield, & Yakimowski, 2004). Similar computer data systems have been used in business to manage and forecast business data, with increasing impact over the past 2 decades. In education, these technologies not only can help organize aggregated student data for NCLB reporting purposes, but more important, can offer unprecedented access to and assemblage of learning data at the individual student level. These educational data systems provide educators with support for thoughtful examination of individual student learning needs that can help close a variety of achievement gaps.

In this chapter, we discuss how student data systems can support an overarching goal of achieving educational equity. We begin with the literature surrounding educational equity, accountability, and the use of student data, followed by a brief discussion of student data systems. As an illustrative backdrop, we describe how the implementation and use of a student data system in the Corpus Christi, Texas, school district has helped some educators there examine educational equity. We conclude by outlining implications and directions for future research.

EDUCATIONAL EQUITY, ACCOUNTABILITY, AND THE USE OF STUDENT DATA

Educational equity means that each child is offered the opportunity and support to learn as much as he or she is capable of learning. Factors commonly associated with educational inequities include poverty, ethnicity, language proficiency, and special education status. However, many other factors may result in one child receiving less educational opportunity than others. Among these are homelessness, family mobility, availability of or access to resources, and resilience. Since the constellations of possible factors are as varied as the students themselves, one key to achieving educational equity lies in the ability of districts, schools, and educators to address the individual needs of each student, a crucial component of which is the efficient access and synthesis of information on individual students.

Through accountability policies, it is hoped that individual learning needs will be made apparent and then addressed through the process of explicitly monitoring the academic achievement of traditionally underserved and ignored groups. Few would argue the benefit of providing teachers, administrators, and other educators with rich learning information on individual students, but many are skeptical that current accountability policies are the mechanisms to facilitate the use of this information.

Many scholars are concerned that increased levels of accountability-related data actually may be detrimental to the goal of equitable education. Some have charged that accountability policies result in the surrender of sound pedagogical practice and substantive curriculum in favor of test preparation (McNeil & Valenzuela, 2001). Some caution that high-stakes accountability systems may not improve actual learning but may lead to unethical situations (Amrein & Berliner, 2002; Elmore, 2002; O'Day, 2002). Others argue that if schools and students are to be judged by equal accountability measures, they also must be granted equal access to equal resources that contribute to success, such as coherent curricula, qualified teachers, and safe schools (Fine, Bloom, & Chajet, 2003; Powers, 2004). Diamond and Spillane (2004) question whether accountability policies can reduce inequities because schools respond to these policies differentially: In their study, probationary schools, more likely to serve low-income and minority students, were less likely to respond in a fashion that stressed attention to pedagogy and individual student needs than were higher-performing schools.

We believe educators must extend their use of student data past the narrowest assessment and reporting mandates of accountability policies, toward the thoughtful, efficient use of a broad range of individual learning information on each student: data use in addition to accountability. In this sense, data use includes not only mandated formal assessments, but also a variety of data that may be collected on a child: formative assessments; writing samples over time; local assessments; learning history; family, demographic, and special program information; psychosocial measures; extracurricular participation; and many more items. Data used in this way not only provide the granularity necessary to assist in addressing individual learning needs, but also may address some of the equity concerns outlined by many scholars. Kim and Sunderman (2005), for instance, argue that multiple measures of student achievement may provide more accurate measures of school quality. Multiple measures would improve upon the one-size-fits-all model by providing for contextually relevant views of student success. While scholars such as Sloan (2004) have shown that the district focus on accountability policies can erode student–teacher relationships, it is not the presence of data that portends such deterioration; rather, it is the "macro" focus that results when educators conduct student data examination solely at the group level. Other studies suggest that examining *individual*-level student data actually can help improve views of and attitudes toward underachieving students: Massell (2001) finds that increased communication and knowledge provided by data may positively alter educator attitudes toward the school capabilities of some underperforming groups; and Armstrong and Anthes (2001) find that introducing teachers to using data can result in their heightened expectations of and attitudes toward at-risk students.

More generally, data use has been shown to be an efficient way to address a variety of individual student differences. Wayman and Stringfield (2006) describe how examining multiple forms of data in student learning histories helps teachers more efficiently and accurately choose students for admission into a gifted program. Data use in urban settings has been studied by Lachat and Smith (2005), who describe the benefits of data use in a high-poverty urban district, and by Brunner, Fasca, Heinze, Honey, Light, Mandinach, and Wexler (2005), who describe some teacher enthusiasm for the use of preformatted data reports in New York City. Symonds (2003) finds that schools effective at closing achievement gaps for varied groups of students are effective data users. Educator collaboration, often thought to be a key in pinpointing student learning differences, has been greatly enhanced and facilitated by data use, according to a number of studies (e.g., Copland, 2003; Halverson, Grigg, Prichett, & Thomas, 2005; Lachat & Smith, 2005; Wayman, Midgley, & Stringfield, 2006).

While the idea of using a broad range of student data to help understand individual student learning is attractive, it is easier said than done. Education for years has produced large amounts of student data, but these data typically have been stored in ways that render them inaccessible to most practitioners. This situation has changed recently with the advent of computer systems with user-friendly interfaces allowing rapid, easy access to student data for teachers and other education professionals (Wayman et al., 2004). We argue that examination of individual student learning data is virtually impossible without involving efficient student data storage, retrieval, and presentation systems. Even successful data-use initiatives conducted without technology have entailed an undue amount of effort and necessarily have been limited in scope (Kerr, Marsh, Ikemoto, Darilek, & Barney, 2006; Stringfield, Reynolds, & Schaffer, 2001; Supovitz & Klein, 2003). In the following section, we briefly describe the current state of such student data systems.

STUDENT DATA SYSTEMS

Aggregation of data at the district or school level helps highlight possible areas of concern for educational equity. However, equity issues in education cannot be addressed solely by aggregating data for groups of students. Educators must move beyond—or "drill down" into—these aggregations to identify the needs of specific students. Historically, this has been difficult for educators, in no small part because school data traditionally have been stored in ways that were nearly inaccessible to practical educators. Fortunately, this situation is changing with the advent of a burgeoning number of computer systems being marketed for the purpose of efficiently delivering student data to educators. Unfortunately, no system provides comprehensive access to solutions to educational problems, so districts must choose between many types of data systems.

Wayman (2005) describes three common types of data systems that deliver student data to educators: (1) student information systems (SISs) that provide real-time accounting of daily school functions (e.g., attendance, schedules); (2) assessment systems that rapidly organize and analyze frequent benchmark assessments; and (3) data warehousing systems that provide access to historical data of all types and link disparate databases.

As described by Wayman (2005), these functions often do not intersect, and as a consequence data systems typically are not structured to perform all of these functions at once. More and more, commercial vendors are looking to provide solutions that combine features from varied areas, but this is still not common. School personnel often must choose between or piece together varied types of data systems under the following limitations.[2]

Student information systems provide a wide array of daily functions that potentially can improve the work flow of a school and district by managing previously time-intensive detail work such as attendance, grade reports, enrollment, and course scheduling. Increasingly, SISs are being built to also facilitate communication between home and school, offering parents a portal into various information sites regarding their children. SISs usually are not designed to provide easy analysis or access to these data beyond the current school year (data from previous years typically are archived and thus not instantly available) and rarely are designed to facilitate assessment, examine longitudinal data, or examine significant numbers of variables at once.

Assessment systems potentially offer powerful facilitation of periodic, systemic assessment of student learning. Often using commercially provided and researched assessments, these systems can enable school personnel to administer, grade, and organize assessments, as well as examine these assessments to illuminate current strengths and deficiencies. These systems also may offer varied forms of instructional management; one of the more popular functions is assessments that are aligned with and linked to state standards and curriculum supports. Assessment systems typically are not designed to provide access to assessment data over time because of the high volume of data they generate. Moreover, assessment systems typically do not link these data to other forms of data, such as SIS data, historical student data (e.g., demographic information), other learning assessments, or state assessments.

Data warehousing systems draw together and offer seamless access to disparate forms of data. A district data warehouse may contain such items as state and local assessment results, student learning histories, teacher information, and demographic information such as absences and free lunch or special education status. Data warehouses place nearly all available data on a student at the fingertips of a teacher, administrator, or staff member, thus offering a powerful tool to analyze a variety of learning phenomena in tandem.[3] Because of their size, data warehouses are not designed to be dynamic, but instead require periodic uploading or "refreshing" of the data. As a result, data warehouses do not perform functions such as frequent assessment or SIS functions—these are performed on other systems and loaded into the warehouse.

In most systems, data are accessed through user-friendly data presentation interfaces that offer two types of access: preformatted reports and query tools. Preformatted reports are previously compiled summaries of data that are available for viewing or printing with one click and require no specifications, alterations, or input from the user. Query tools allow ad hoc data specification, permitting the user to browse data or to construct customized reports. Query tools are more common and more powerful in data warehouse software than in other types of systems.

The data presentation interfaces offered by most commercial vendors are easy to learn and use, employing familiar Web-form elements such as check boxes and pull-down menus. Through these user-friendly systems, data are accessible to all educators at all levels of technical expertise: Most users who can check the weather online or shop on the Internet can quickly learn how to access student data using these interfaces.

While the instant diagnosis of learning needs provided by assessment systems is important, some authors (Mieles & Foley, 2005; Wayman et al., 2004) have suggested that the power offered by data warehouses—the ability to examine simultaneously a number of learning measures over a student's career, including real-time assessment—is critical to full and efficient use of student data for educational improvement.

It is our position that for districts to address equity issues effectively, classroom teachers must have warehouse access to relevant and timely data, accompanied by the sorts of user-friendly features described above. The Corpus Christi Independent School District exemplified this position when it implemented its student data systems, as described below.

CORPUS CHRISTI INDEPENDENT SCHOOL DISTRICT AND STUDENT DATA SYSTEMS

In this section, we describe the Corpus Christi Independent School District, equity issues in the district, and the district's student data systems.

The District

The Corpus Christi Independent School District (CCISD) is located in southeastern Texas, on the Gulf of Mexico. During the 2006–07 school year, CCISD was serving approximately 40,000 students in 40 elementary schools, 12 middle schools, 5 high schools, and 5 special campuses (e.g., an alternative high school, an early childhood development center). A large portion of these students are poor, with 64% classified as economically disadvantaged. Seventy-four percent of CCISD students are Latino, 18% are non-Latino White, 6% are African-American, 2% are Asian, and less than 1% are American Indian (percentages do not add not add up to 100 because of rounding). Seven percent of CCISD students are classified as limited English proficient.

The equity challenges faced by CCISD are not unlike those of other urban districts. Data provided on CCISD students by the State of Texas show that non-Latino White students generally have outperformed African-American and Latino students over the previous 4 years on both the reading and mathematics portions of the Texas Assessment of Knowledge and Skills (TAKS). Table 10.1 shows the percentage of students meeting the minimum standard for reading, disaggregated by ethnicity and economic status. Table 10.2 shows similar data for mathematics.

Additionally, many in the district believe that Latino students in CCISD are not being prepared for college. Table 10.3 shows that Latino students are less likely to take the SAT or ACT than are African-American or non-Latino White students.

The District's Student Data Systems

The CCISD uses multiple data systems and software programs to access student performance data both at the individual student level and at the aggregate

Table 10.1. Percentage of Students Meeting Standard on Reading TAKS

	2003	2004	2005	2006
All	77	79	81	87
African-American	70	72	76	84
Latino	74	76	80	85
Non-Latino White	88	90	91	94
Not Economically Disadvantaged	85	86	86	92
Economically Disadvantaged	70	73	77	83

Table 10.2. Percentage of Students Meeting Standard on
Mathematics TAKS

	2003	2004	2005	2006
All	61	60	64	69
African-American	50	49	55	62
Latino	56	55	60	65
Non-Latino White	78	76	80	83
Not Economically Disadvantaged	69	68	72	76
Economically Disadvantaged	54	53	58	64

level. The district historically has used student performance data to guide
continuous improvement planning and customized student interventions. For
years, its primary student data system was a commercially available student
information system, Pentamation, that handled student demographic information, enrollment and attendance data, grades, and transcript history. CCISD
technical personnel historically supplemented the Pentamation SIS with locally developed applications to serve specific data needs.

Recognizing the ongoing limitation of these systems and in response to
a curriculum audit, CCISD administration decided to acquire a student data
system that would offer curriculum support and provide all educators efficient access to student data for instructional improvement, as well as facilitate equity inquiry by offering broad inquiry at the student level.

After exploring commercially available systems, in January 2004, CCISD
purchased SchoolNet.[4] This commercially available instructional management system was deemed a good fit not only because it provided a data
warehouse to pull together the variety of disparate data sources in CCISD,

Table 10.3. Percentage of Students Taking SAT/ACT (by
Graduating Class)*

	2003	2004	2005
All	60.5	65.7	70.6
African-American	73	77	79.8
Latino	52.3	57.2	61.9
Non-Latino White	70.7	75.2	80.1

* Data unavailable for 2006 and for Economically Disadvantaged students.

but also because teachers and administrators found the interface intuitively easy to navigate, and it enabled granular "drill-down" analyses that take a user from district or school summaries down to the student level. SchoolNet also provided the required district curriculum support, along with the capacity for teachers to easily access curriculum and develop lesson plans.

SchoolNet offers a variety of modules; CCISD purchased three: (1) the Account module for data warehousing, integration, and access; (2) the Align module to facilitate curriculum storage and information access; and (3) the Assess module to offer administration and processing of periodic formative and benchmark evaluations. The Account and Align modules were implemented at the start of the 2004–05 school year; the Assess module was implemented at the start of the 2005–06 school year. A detailed description of CCISD's implementation of SchoolNet is given in Wayman and Conoly (2006).

The district continues to use Pentamation as the primary SIS, feeding data from Pentamation into SchoolNet. Additionally, certain data functions, such as those for discipline and special education, are still handled through systems separate from SchoolNet. Disciplinary data are handled through Pentamation; district personnel intentionally separated these from SchoolNet to avoid possible bias in teacher perceptions of certain students. Special education data are handled through a district-developed system called the Special Education Manager (SEM), because CCISD personnel report that SchoolNet is unable to process the individual education plans required for special education students.

EQUITY INQUIRY IN CORPUS CHRISTI

Here we present three examples illustrating how student data technology can support inquiry toward educational equity. Their common theme is that student data systems can provide detailed learning information on each individual student in the school or district as well as offer a rapid response that matches action with diagnosis. Neither of these capacities is typically available without an efficient, district-wide system.

The three examples include a range of issues in educational equity: special education, student transience, and minority-student achievement. They hardly exhaust the potential uses of data warehousing and reporting software; rather, they indicate how a data system can support the type of granular examination needed to facilitate education for underserved students.

Central Office Examination of Group Representation in Special Education

In the state of Texas, there are increasing efforts by policymakers and educators to expose special education students to mainstream classes and curriculum.

This is partially due to a belief that "mainstreaming" special education students advances their learning, but it is also due to NCLB mandates. Despite the popularity of mainstreaming, prior to NCLB districts were allowed to exempt a large number of special education students from accountability calculations. Current NCLB mandates limit the number of students taking an alternative state learning assessment, so many Texas school districts are reducing the number of students served in special education by increased intervention for special education students placed in general education.

As a consequence, special education in CCISD no longer is viewed as a place to harbor struggling learners, but as a service to those students. Supported by its student data systems, CCISD is aggressively examining every special education student. Data from SchoolNet, the SEM, and district-developed discipline reports have indicated three particular areas in need of attention:

- Students in the special education program overwhelmingly participate in federally funded free and reduced-price meal programs.
- African-American students are overrepresented in CCISD's special education program.
- Special education students are overrepresented in disciplinary programs such as in-school suspension or a disciplinary alternative education program.

As a result of these inquiries, central office staff have begun weekly monitoring of special education referral rates, which has allowed central and campus administrators to monitor, support, and quickly intervene when appropriate. Each week, the Executive Director for Instructional Support holds a special education cabinet meeting, during which data are examined with an eye toward updating the status of each special education student and implementing individual changes where needed. Data used include:

- Number of students currently in special education
- Aggregation of special education students by equity group (e.g., ethnicity, lunch status)
- Number and names of students newly referred to special education
- Aggregation of new referrals by equity group
- Disciplinary reports on special education students
- Identification of students ready for dismissal from special education.

This inquiry sets in motion a number of events involving personal contact between the central office and school staff regarding individual students. The Coordinator for Assessment Services contacts the diagnostician or licensed school psychologist in a particular school to ensure that students of poverty, limited English proficiency, or ethnic minority (particularly African-American students) are not being placed into special education due to linguistic, cultural, or social experiences not indicative of learning problems. The Executive Director for Instructional Support personally calls principals to discuss specific students and data trends, to brainstorm interventions, and to provide on-site supports. The School Services Director supervising individual principals also is notified of data and needs for corrective action, which then are documented in the campus continuous improvement plan. Various members of the cabinet are charged with informing school diagnosticians or licensed school psychologists about appropriate data as well as offering supports and interventions.

District administrators report that an effort focusing so specifically on students and campuses was previously impossible, but now is quite practical due to the development of CCISD's student data systems. Prior to the implementation of these systems, detailed special education reports were difficult to assemble, resulting in slow dissemination; further, they were not always available for each individual student. Having special education reports instantly available at the student, school, or district level allows weekly cabinet meetings that result in a tailored diagnosis and intervention specific to each individual student. Problems that were weeks or months in diagnosing—if at all—now are considered in a matter of days, resulting in timely and appropriate student interventions. Additionally, mining locally available data has enabled CCISD to explore special education issues by poverty status, information not available through the state databases.

Examination of Transient Students in an Elementary School

Evans Elementary School, situated near a number of shelters for homeless or displaced families, enrolls all the elementary-school-aged children from these shelters, so much of its student population is highly transient. Data available through the State of Texas show campus mobility averaging 43% from 2003 to 2005. Campus administrators report this figure may reach as high as 90% of students in a given year, many of whom transfer in and out of Evans a number of times throughout the year. Some Evans students may attend as many as 10 schools in CCISD in a given year.

Despite this challenge, Evans now has attained the status of "recognized" by the State of Texas (70% of students in all subgroups passed state achievement tests). Cissy Reynolds-Perez, principal at Evans for 5 years until the 2006–07 school year, attributes much of this success to the ability to follow these students through SchoolNet.

Before SchoolNet, it was difficult to obtain a learning history of a student who enrolled (or re-enrolled) in Evans. The student's cumulative folder could take days or weeks to physically arrive in the Evans office, and when it did, it was often incomplete. During this time, the student would be attending classes, but the teachers would have little to go on except intuition regarding his or her individual learning needs. This frustrating process, undoubtedly familiar to most educators who deal with student turnover, is compounded in schools such as Evans that deal with students who may stay for only a matter of days or weeks. Perez-Reynolds summed up this frustration, saying, "Just when we would get their information, the student would leave."

Reynolds-Perez reports that the district-wide implementation of SchoolNet was a great help because Evans educators were able to access a student's learning history immediately upon enrollment. Through SchoolNet, all students' learning histories follow them as they transfer from one school to the next. Reynolds-Perez said when students enrolled or returned, "We would find their reading level or whatever, find out what their history was, and start attacking those skills right away, because we didn't have much time." She also noted the impact on educators who read in student histories the vast number of schools some students had attended over the course of a school year.

This rapid information also offered opportunities for efficient communication with former teachers of recently enrolled Evans students. Often, Evans educators would email the student's former teachers with questions about particular skills; having comprehensive data available so quickly not only generated more specific questions, but allowed former teachers to answer while their experience with the student was fresh in their minds.

Keeping Up with Underrepresented Minority Students

In Garcia Elementary School, several opportunities exist to address educational equity issues. Nearly half of its 400 students are classified by the state as "at risk," approximately 90% are "economically disadvantaged," and almost a third are of limited English proficiency. Dr. Patricia Castillo has been principal of Garcia Elementary for 7 years, and like most principals, she wants to educate every child and to keep her school as highly rated as possible. When she first came to Garcia Elementary, the school had no capacity to efficiently examine student data and often lost higher accountability ratings because of the performance of one or two subgroups. She said, "Without a data system in place, I couldn't go child by child, subgroup by subgroup. I have learned that every single child has to be looked at and that data analysis is the only way we're going to be able to identify every single child. Otherwise, we're sunk."

In the 2005–06 school year, 28 Garcia Elementary students were African-American, two short of NCLB recognition as a "subgroup" requiring reporting and accountability scrutiny. Garcia wanted to be prepared in case Garcia's

African-American population reached this 30-student subgroup threshold, so she and her staff instituted a year-long examination of each individual African-American student in the school. This effort was enabled and enhanced by the thorough information and rapid turnaround of benchmark testing data provided by SchoolNet.

To address the learning needs of these students, Castillo and the teachers used SchoolNet to examine benchmark tests given schoolwide, identifying where students were not passing in a particular benchmark and identifying needed skills by objective. Garcia educators worked with the parents of these students, clearly outlining for them the objectives where their child was weak and identifying skills and methods for work at home. Garcia Elementary employs retired teachers as tutors, so relevant objectives were addressed further during tutoring sessions for these students.

The progress of closely examining individual student progress was not foreign to the teachers of African-American students. Since the inception of SchoolNet, Garcia Elementary staff have given each teacher a notebook outlining the learning needs of students and classifying students by subgroup. Additionally, Castillo has implemented a structure for examining data— Garcia faculty meet every other week to examine data and collaborate about supportive resources and strategies.

Efforts at Garcia Elementary to help African-American students have achieved success, as measured by state test scores. Ninety-nine percent of African-American students in Grades 3 through 5 met the standard score on the reading and mathematics TAKS exams, with the exception of fifth-grade reading, where 92% of African-American students met the standard. With the exception of third-grade reading, all of these percentages represent a 2-year increase of at least 11%, with both fifth-grade reading and math passing rates up over 50% in this period.

USING DATA SYSTEMS TO ADDRESS EDUCATIONAL EQUITY: FUTURE DIRECTIONS AND IMPLICATIONS

Data Systems and the Individual Student

To address issues of educational equity, it is necessary to diagnose and respond to the learning needs of each student individually. Accountability mandates such as NCLB have been helpful in identifying student groups in need, but such policies rarely provide support for delving deep to help individual students.

Addressing individual needs necessitates the use of all available information on a student. Noguera (1995) describes an inservice activity asking teachers how to prepare to teach in a foreign country; they generally responded with activities to help them become familiar with the students, their background, and their culture. Unfortunately, in our own country, many teachers lack such information about their own students, especially students from histori- cally underachieving groups. There is a variety of student information that can help educators know more about individual students and their learning needs, including formative and summative achievement tests, learning his- tories, grades, student background, and many other elements. When this information is joined with educator experience, observation, and resource support, a powerful learning environment is created for the student.

It is encouraging that computer data systems have made such informa- tion available in unprecedented breadth and detail, and at prices that increas- ingly are viewed as affordable. Schools and districts have always possessed a wide variety of student data, but only with the advent of these systems have timely student data and information become a new resource for all educa- tors aiming to tackle stubborn educational equity issues. Still, efficient, dis- trict-wide implementation and use of a student data system remain new and uncommon to most districts—especially as used to close achievement gaps— so it is important to learn from districts that have already invested resources in these systems.

One goal of NCLB is to motivate local educators, through reporting and highlighting the achievement of various groups, to address individual learn- ing needs, to "leave no child behind." In the examples provided here, we saw educators who certainly were motivated by the desire to help each student succeed, but also were motivated by external pressure for particular groups to achieve at certain levels.

An excellent illustration of these dual motivations comes from Dr. Castillo's group of 28 African-American students. Although these children were a small minority in her school, Dr. Castillo initiated a successful plan to ensure the success of each individual in order to ensure that the group suc- ceeded. Dr. Castillo may well have tracked these students without NCLB motivation, but doing so in such depth without a data system such as CCISD's would have entailed superhuman effort. Even with NCLB pressures, similar groups of students surely are being left behind in schools across America that do not enjoy the supports provided by CCISD's data system; it is unlikely that many educators in these schools are prepared to move from identification of group needs toward examining each individual student based solely on ag- gregated data as mandated by NCLB. Consequently, it is our position that successes as described in Garcia Elementary are nearly impossible without the efficient data system support enjoyed by CCISD educators. We believe accountability policies would be strengthened by addressing such supports.

In discussing the importance of rapid, efficient use of data, Wayman and colleagues (2004) assert that each day in which data go unused is a lost op- portunity to better diagnose and educate children. Nowhere is this more apparent than in the vigilant watch kept on the transient students of Evans Elementary School. Reynolds-Perez and her staff understood that many of these students would not stay long at Evans, yet they also understood that even one efficient day or week of education might make a difference for the students. If, in fact, a student transferred 10 times in one year (not uncommon in the district), these days of efficiency might add up to a month or more of educational value added for this student over what he or she would have received without such vigilance. Attention of this sort is not possible without the quick information flow provided by the data system.

While Evans serves an area near numerous shelters, the student transience of this school is similar to that of many schools in large urban districts. We hold that data warehouses that facilitate information flow could be overwhelmingly useful for large urban districts with transient student populations.

Even a successful implementation such as CCISD's ran afoul of numerous problems. For instance, district leaders reported some frustration that SchoolNet was unable to handle some of the special education plans necessitated by federal mandate. We also should note that the "feel-good" stories presented here are from exemplary users of the system; while on the increase, such stories are not yet common throughout the district.

One concern highlighted by these examples is the scalability of leadership for data use. Studies describing the importance of leadership in effective inquiry (Copland, 2003; Wayman & Stringfield, 2006) suggest that effective data use is highly dependent on leadership. If so, how can leaders be prepared to take action as described here? And how can enough leaders be developed to fill schools and districts nationwide? In our opinion, the issue of leadership remains a pressing and unsolved problem in achieving equitable education in all schools.

Pedagogically, what is happening in CCISD and other districts utilizing student data systems is not new. Effective education has, and always will be, about diagnosing individual learning needs and responding accordingly. However, the capacity provided by student data systems to rapidly diagnose and respond to learning needs is unprecedented. In envisioning a technologically enabled school system, Wayman and colleagues (2004) note that even if educators in such a system are not better prepared pedagogically, they are empowered to be significantly more efficient and effective educational professionals. Such is the case for any educator supported by these systems.

Optimal Student Data Systems to Support Equity Inquiry

As noted by Wayman (2005), there is not yet a "killer app" that performs all student data functions. Schools and districts that want full function must combine multiple systems that perform a number of functions; our recom-

mendations are summarized below. The capabilities on this list are important not only when the focus is specifically on educational equity, but more
generally, when the focus is on attention to individual student learning needs.
Note that by "system," we refer to the overall system a district has created
by linking together multiple systems that provide various functions.

1. The system must support longitudinal student data, spanning the
   entire range of a student's career. To address inequities, educators
   need a full picture of a student's background and learning; such a
   picture is not imparted by data from the current year or even just
   recent years.
2. The system must provide seamless access to a broad variety of types
   of data typically stored in disparate systems, such as disciplinary data,
   assessment data, student demographics, and grades. This access must
   be seamless to the user, offering the ability to examine varied types
   of data concomitantly. Currently, this function is served most closely
   by data warehousing.
3. The system must offer a user-friendly query tool that allows users to
   browse student data easily with a minimum of training. Such tools
   are necessary to involve educators in needed examination of individual student data. Although such data can change opinions and
   attitudes about student learning, educators seldom are drawn to them
   if examination requires undue effort.
4. The system must offer a comprehensive, but preformatted, student
   history. Its contents are similar to the cumulative folder available in
   school records, but this history allows educators to access a student's
   learning and background profile with one click.
5. The system must easily accommodate student mobility within a district and, where possible, outside of a district. Learning records—
   and subsequent learning strategies—of transient student should be
   immediately available. In efficient data systems, changing the school
   associated with a student should leave his or her other records intact.
6. The system must allow rapid refreshing of relevant data. While historical elements are important, a student's learning situation can
   change rapidly, and educators need to be informed quickly of new
   assessments, formative assessments, and other changes such as disciplinary actions, changes in family situation, and other conditions
   that impact education.
7. The system must offer broad drill-down capacity. Accountability
   policies mandate examination of student groups, whose data should
   be available from the system. Additionally, it is critical that educators be able to peel back layers of these groups through a series of
   clicks to gain more granular data down to the student level.

8. The system must provide data to relevant parties in real time. The system may provide some data to parents while restricting their access to data on other parents' children. The system may provide data to teachers on their current or former students, while restricting some data on other teachers' students. The system may provide data to principals, while restricting some data on specific students in other schools, and so on. (Similarly, an online credit card statement may allow a user up-to-the-minute data on his or her card, but block access to data on a neighbor's card.)

9. The system must be accessible from outside the school, enabling educators, who frequently work from home or elsewhere, to access data on individual students from outside the "brick and mortar" of school walls.

10. The system must offer access to appropriate stores of information that help educators tailor responses to the data they see. The system must offer support such as curriculum, standards, resources, and discussion boards.

CONCLUSION

Throughout recorded history, educators have struggled with how best to apply scarce resources to educate as many students as possible, including their most precious resource, time. Given the nature of the educational enterprise, this is likely to be an ongoing struggle.

Recently, potentially powerful new tools have been developed that enable educators to efficiently access learning information on their students. Specifically, user-friendly tools that deliver vast amounts of student information allow educators to diagnose and react to student learning needs more rapidly and efficiently than ever before. Widespread adoption of these tools in districts and schools, coupled with efficient training on their effective use, may well hold promise for increasing the number of learning needs educators are able to address in a given day, week, or year. We have highlighted methods and supports that can lead to more attention given to more needy children and, in turn, the creation of more opportunity.

NOTES

1. Note that in most states, NCLB/Title I funds only partially compensate for large differences in overall school funding, driven by inequities in local land values and taxation policies.

2. Often, a district may piece together one or more systems and add nondata elements such as curriculum resources, access to state standards, or communication modules, broadly calling their system an "instructional management system."

3. Many are surprised to learn that linking various forms of student data for examination has heretofore not been common in schools. Prior to the advent of data warehousing, the seemingly trivial task of exploring relationships such as student achievement and ethnicity, or student achievement and teacher characteristics, was accomplished only after intensive labor by district or school staff to combine the data needed for analysis.

4. In providing this example, the authors do not endorse the product SchoolNet over other available products reviewed in Wayman and colleagues (2004). Rather, our purpose is to allow readers to see the advantages of any of several data warehousing and presentation software packages through a specific example.

REFERENCES

Amrein, A., & Berliner, D. (2002). High-stakes testing, uncertainty, and student learning. *Education Policy Analysis Archives, 10*(18). Retrieved December 1, 2006, from http://epaa.asu.edu/epaa/v10n18/

Armstrong, J., & Anthes, K. (2001). How data can help. *American School Board Journal, 188*(11), 38–41.

Brunner, C., Fasca, C., Heinze, J., Honey, M., Light, D., Mandinach, E., & Wexler, D. (2005). Linking data and learning: The Grow Network study. *Journal of Education for Students Placed at Risk, 10*(3), 241–267.

Coleman, J. S., Campbell, E. Q., Hobson, C. J., McPartland, J., Mood, A. M., Weinfeld, F. D., & York, R. L. (1966). *Equality of educational opportunity.* Washington, DC: U.S. Department of Health, Education, and Welfare.

Copland, M. A. (2003). Leadership of inquiry: Building and sustaining capacity for school improvement. *Educational Evaluation and Policy Analysis, 25,* 375–395.

Diamond, J., & Spillane, J. (2004). High stakes accountability in urban elementary schools: Challenging or reproducing inequality? *Teachers College Record, 106*(12), 2392–2397.

Elmore, R. (2002, April). *Stakes for whom?* Paper presented at the annual meeting of the American Educational Research Association, New Orleans.

English, W. F. (2002). On the intractability of the achievement gap in urban schools and the discursive practice of continuing racial discrimination. *Education and Urban Society, 34*(3), 298–311.

Fine, M., Bloom, J., & Chajet, L. (2003). Betrayal: Accountability from the bottom. *Voices in Urban Education, 1,* 12–23.

Halverson, R., Grigg, G., Prichett, R., & Thomas, C. (2005, September). *The new instructional leadership: Creating data-driven instructional systems in schools* (WCER Working Paper 2005-9). Wisconsin Center for Education Research, University of Wisconsin-Madison. Available from http://www.wcer.wisc.edu/publications/workingPapers/Working_Paper_No_2005_9.pdf

Jencks, C., & Phillips, M. (1998). *The black–white test score gap*. Washington, DC: Brookings Institution Press.

Kerr, K. A., Marsh, J. A., Ikemoto, G. S., Darilek, H., & Barney, H. (2006). Strategies to promote data use for instructional improvement: Actions, outcomes, and lessons from three urban districts. *American Journal of Education, 112*(4), 496–520.

Kim, J. S., & Sunderman, G. L. (2005). Measuring academic proficiency under the No Child Left Behind Act: Implications for educational equity. *Educational Researcher, 34*(8), 3–13.

Lachat, M. A., & Smith, S. (2005). Practices that support data use in urban high schools. *Journal of Education for Students Placed at Risk, 10*(3), 333–349.

Massell, D. (2001). The theory and practice of using data to build capacity: State and local strategies and their effects. In S. H. Fuhrman (Ed.), *From the capitol to the classroom: Standards-based reform in the states* (pp. 148–169). Chicago: University of Chicago Press.

McNeil, L., & Valenzuela, A. (2001). The harmful impact of the TAAS system of testing in Texas: Beneath the policy rhetoric. In G. Orfield & M. Kornhaber (Eds.), *Raising standards or raising barriers: Inequality and high-stakes testing in public education* (pp. 127–151). New York: Century Foundation Press.

Mieles, T., & Foley, E. (2005). *Data warehousing: Preliminary findings from a study of implementing districts*. Philadelphia: Annenberg Institute for School Reform.

Noguera, P. A. (1995). Preventing and producing violence: A critical analysis of responses to school violence. *Harvard Educational Review, 65*(2), 189–212.

O'Day, J. A. (2002). Complexity, accountability, and school improvement. *Harvard Educational Review, 72*(3), 293–329.

Powers, J. M. (2004). High stakes accountability and equity: Using evidence from California's Public Schools Accountability Act to address the issues in Williams v. State of California. *American Educational Research Journal, 41*(4), 763–795.

Rothstein, R. (2004). *Class and schools: Using social, economic, and educational reform to close the black-white achievement gap*. Washington, DC: Economic Policy Institute.

Sloan, K. (2004). Playing to the logic of the Texas accountability system: How focusing on "ratings"—not children—undermines equality and equity. In A. Valenzuela (Ed.), *Leaving children behind: How "Texas-style" accountability fails Latino youth* (pp. 153–178). New York: State University of New York Press.

Stringfield, S., & Land, D. (Eds.). (2002). *Educating at-risk students*. Chicago: National Society for the Study of Education.

Stringfield, S., Reynolds, D., & Schaffer, E. (2001, January). *Fifth-year results from the High Reliability Schools project*. Symposium presented at the meeting of the International Congress for School Effectiveness and Improvement, Toronto.

Supovitz, J., & Klein, V. (2003). *Mapping a course for improved student learning: How innovative schools systematically use student performance data to guide improvement*. Philadelphia: Consortium for Policy Research in Education.

Symonds, K. W. (2003). *After the test: How schools are using data to close the achievement gap*. San Francisco: Bay Area School Reform Collaborative.

Wayman, J. C. (2005). Involving teachers in data-driven decision making: Using computer data systems to support teacher inquiry and reflection. *Journal of Education for Students Placed at Risk, 10*(3), 295–308.

Wayman, J. C., & Conoly, K. (2006). Managing curriculum: Rapid implementation and sustainability of a districtwide data initiative. *ERS Spectrum, 24*(2), 4–8.

Wayman, J. C., Midgley, S., & Stringfield, S. (2006). Leadership for data-based decision making: Collaborative data teams. In A. Danzig, K. Borman, B. Jones, & B. Wright (Eds.), *New models of professional development for learner centered leadership* (pp. 189–206). Mahwah, NJ: Erlbaum.

Wayman, J. C., & Stringfield, S. (2006). Technology-supported involvement of entire faculties in examination of student data for instructional improvement. *American Journal of Education, 112*(4), 549–571.

Wayman, J. C., Stringfield, S., & Yakimowski, M. (2004). *Software enabling school improvement through analysis of student data* (CRESPAR Tech. Rep. No. 67). Baltimore: Johns Hopkins University. Retrieved on December 1, 2006, from http://www.csos.jhu.edu/crespar/techReports/Report67.pdf

The Challenge of Adoption in Implementing Comprehensive Data-Driven, Decision-Making Solutions

Jonathan Bertfield & Michael Merrill

Saying you want to become a data-driven management culture is one thing; actually fulfilling that vision is another. Districts looking to implement a culture of data-driven management quickly discover this distinction, and the best ones actively plan for the inevitable resistances that accompany such a dramatic shift in teaching and administering. Of course, many districts are motivated to pursue this course by a traumatic event. The precipitating crisis can take many forms: a prolonged failure that results in a state takeover, or an external audit that determines that the district is wholly out of line with where it should be, to mention but two. These types of real-world situations can motivate a district to evaluate many things, including the very foundations of its pedagogical practice. The successful districts, of course, greet such news as a challenge, an opportunity for dramatic improvement.

Two such districts—the School District of Philadelphia (taken over by the state of Pennsylvania) and Corpus Christi Independent School District (which received the bad news from an audit that its district curriculum was in poor shape)—can serve as exemplary models. Despite differences in size, geography, demographics, and history, the leadership of both districts proactively and consciously reached out to the district as a learning community, appealing to the ultimate desire assumed to be shared by all: to work together in each grade and at every administrative level to achieve greater academic results not only for the district as a whole, but also for each individual child within it. And in both we can see some similarly shared foci, steps on the way to the ultimate goal.

- *Acceptance*: The initial "changing of minds," the mental realignment required by a paradigm shift;

- *Embracing*: The resulting changes in the actual behavior of administrators and instructors; and
- *Institutionalization*: The subsequent maintenance of both of these psychological and behavioral changes as data-driven management works its way into the everyday fabric of district culture.

While following these same steps, our two districts chose different general approaches: Corpus Christi emphasized upfront evangelism across the board, while Philadelphia accepted what one practitioner there calls "benevolent consensus," allowing that certain minds would be changed only with time and experience. However, both districts consciously understood the importance of adoption and met the anticipated resistance with resolve.

This chapter delineates how these two districts, both relatively large urban districts with mobile student and teacher populations but different in many other aspects, made their way through these steps in their own manner and with their own results. We examine how the change management techniques used by these districts can be aligned with the best practices outlined in the work of Kotter (1995). In particular, we sketch how the districts implemented and used SchoolNet, a suite of data management applications (reporting tools for administrators, professional development management tools for teachers, and benchmark testing for students) that together constitute a platform of what is becoming known in the world of educational technology as an "instructional management solution" (IMS). The results of that change are still in the making, but revealing glimpses of Corpus Christi's rate of adoptions, and of Philadelphia's recent gains in student achievement, hint at what they might be.

DEFINING DATA MANAGEMENT AND IMSs

To understand the possibilities for data management today, it is important to note that there are two interlocking requirements.

1. Instructor and administrator acceptance and use of data-driven decision making; and
2. Technologies that facilitate the timely and consistent use of data for that purpose.

In this chapter, we discuss the use of data within the context of IMSs; more particularly, we focus on two districts that have implemented SchoolNet as their IMS. SchoolNet pulls together and displays a vast range of instructional data; ideally, as SchoolNet (and systems like it) grow and expand, they will display all data considered relevant to instruction. While SchoolNet is a suite of Web-based applications, other types of IMSs might be client-server-based or be cobbled together from a host of disparate applications. Some might even be homegrown, custom-made applications, likely accreted over years within a district. Finally, we can see a proto-IMS at work in what is likely still the norm in many districts: the systematic passing around of spreadsheets and paper as a district filters information up and down the administrative chain.

No matter what the technology used, however, at least as important in achieving educational goals is the acceptance of and dedication to data management by teachers and administrators in a district. While we firmly believe technology that is well designed by its creators, and well suited to the district adopting it, can facilitate proper data management, such a technology on its own cannot make the difference. Whether looking to respond constructively to an exigent crisis such as those noted at the outset of this chapter, or pursuing an IMS under less trying circumstances, a district cannot simply drop a new IMS into the instructional realm and expect immediate results. Rather, experience shows that adoption must be driven through the stages of accepting, embracing, and institutionalization sketched above.

Data management is not new to the classroom setting, of course. Good teachers have been using student feedback and responses to drive their instruction for as long as there has been good teaching. One can even see the Socratic dialogue itself, with its iterative processes of synthesizing participants' responses, as a form of data management—albeit one that in the written form that has been passed down to us seems less dynamic than a modern instructor might hope for. But today's IMSs provide data for use by educators and administrators that go far beyond what has been widely available even within the careers of our youngest teachers.

Student performance data provide the cornerstone of IMSs in Corpus Christi, Philadelphia, and other districts; specifically, they include both current and historical scores on assessments, and data from supplemental and intervention programs, grades, and teacher notes. The IMSs also include current and historical views of other student-related items such as program enrollment, socioeconomic detail, attendance, and disciplinary data. Data are made available to various levels of instruction as needed: A teacher sees the data on her students; a principal, on those students within a school; a superintendent, across the district. SchoolNet's Account module, for reporting and analysis, is an example of a powerful aggregator and disaggregator of data: Sections, classes, grades, schools, and subdistricts all roll up to allow for convenient access of data no matter what one's role; and if, say, a superintendent wishes, she can "drill down" from the uppermost level to a detailed view of any student within her district.

Within an IMS, the curricula, instructional materials, and lesson plans also qualify as meaningful data points used to refine, track, and improve instructional activity. In SchoolNet's curriculum management module, for example, an instructor can see results for the latest benchmark tests, find those students who did not meet proficiency for a particular standard, and search for reteaching materials to use to bring these students up to speed—all without leaving a Web browser.

An effective IMS also should assume that teachers are important assets who must be managed and deployed effectively. In today's IMS, teacher data include the number of lesson plans a teacher has created and the lessons she has planned and administered, as well as the performance of students under her charge. In addition, teacher data also cover a teacher's employment and attendance record, current and historical credentials, and professional development credits and activity. A system like SchoolNet can help administrators measure the efficacy of professional development in terms of actual improvements in student achievement.

With time, of course, as districts become ever more dedicated to and proficient with the new techniques of data management, the universe of data that seem relevant to the instructional process is likely to grow. It is not hard to imagine a day when financial data (where and when funds are spent in a district) and even the vagaries of the physical plant (too hot? too cold?) will be directly correlated to student achievement—even that of individual students on individual standards.

But while we are still on the path to that future ideal, we can watch as our chosen districts—and by extension a host of other districts that recently have implemented SchoolNet or other IMSs—define their own particular "flavor" of IMS. While the IMSs themselves may be more or less flexible in the way they handle, say, particular data fields for special programs for different districts, more interesting in fact in this context is that every district has its own distinct spin on the implementation, adoption, and even eventual use of an IMS. When implementing SchoolNet, a district may choose to purchase or roll out modules in a particular order according to its needs: One district may wish to start with benchmark testing, while another will feel that making its summative testing results available across a district is the most important initial step in its efforts to improve student achievement.

As a district becomes more deeply involved with its IMS and more dedicated across the board to data management, not only does its culture shape the IMS and its users perforce, but a sense of what would constitute best practice becomes clearer. The IMS acts as a "platform" that gives all users across a district access to data, to materials, and to instructional and administrative planning tools. A potential future—one that SchoolNet, for example, actively pursues—would be one in which the platform facilitated a network that allowed those users to share data and to learn and deploy best practices between districts connected to the network—again, of course, with the shared goal of ultimately improving student achievement.

WHAT DIFFERENTIATES DATA MANAGEMENT
SOLUTIONS FROM OTHER INNOVATIONS?

An instructional management solution brings with it tremendous potential to impact the daily lives of educators and students. To the inexperienced observer, the IMS in and of itself may seem to be the answer to many of the most intractable problems public school districts face today. Over the years, however, various "silver bullet" solutions offering similar levels of promise have come and gone. As Schmoker (2004) notes, "The record is clear that these failed, unnecessarily complex reforms have had only the most negligible impact on what should be our core concern: The quality of teaching students receive" (p. 424). It comes as no surprise, then, to the scholar of school reform, or to the on-the-ground participant over whom these waves of reforms have washed, that resistance, active or passive, greets what many might suspect to be just the next "flavor of the year." With each new education reform movement seemingly focused by default on fixing the problems caused by the previous regime, rather than providing immediate responses to the underlying core problems, justifiable skepticism (if not cynicism) easily can become the norm.

Districts we have seen that have successfully started down the path to implementing an IMS such as SchoolNet have accepted the negative ramifications of the silver bullet effect upfront and taken proactive measures to deal with them. However, as we have already noted, data management should not be seen as the "new thing," but rather an elaboration on what good teachers have always done. Districts with ambitions for successfully implementing an IMS have emphasized this *continuity* with past practice rather than playing up its *revolutionary* aspects.

Unlike a silver bullet innovation, data management does not promise a single magic elixir to solve a district's problems; rather, it provides a means for setting goals and measuring progress toward them. Instead of promoting one way of teaching, it facilitates the use of many forms of pedagogy; it creates a paradigm shift that, given the right leadership, allows a district to closely examine virtually all of its instructional practices. Questions asked by a district implementing an IMS range widely across the instructional space.

- What is a curriculum?
- How do we use assessments?
- How do we encourage best practices?
- How do we communicate with one another as a community of learners?

Of course, such broad and deep questions require a superintendent to take a strong leading role—and probably expend significant political capital—but simply asking questions this broad provides a useful side effect: By crossing functional boundaries, these questions force cross-disciplinary groups to form, either ad hoc or by design. Remarkably, many of the early project meetings that are part of the SchoolNet rollout process constitute the first instance of collaborative work meetings in a district. Teams from Curriculum and Assessment collaborate to work out which data points the IMS should display for test results. Teams from elementary, middle, and high school need to collaborate to develop common rubrics and nomenclature, as do representatives of the district office and building-level administrators. Cheerleaders arise throughout the district, from various levels, and out of a variety of functional groups— from what are otherwise separate "silos"—the IMS begins to look like something much more than "just another" IT solution.

CHANGE MANAGEMENT

None of the district managers we focus on in this chapter explicitly referred to themselves as change agents. Yet if we look at their actual activities, we discover that they have expended significant energy on aspects of what has become known as "change management." This process of challenging the status quo has not been solely an intellectual pursuit for these districts. Rather, the goal has been to go beyond changing the way educators in the district *think* and bring about a significant shift in the way they *behave*.

Even if districts are not consciously employing the theory, strategies, and tactics of the expansive and ever-growing field of change management, we believe that an analysis of their practical efforts can be illuminating in terms of some basic change management concepts. The work of Kotter is particularly relevant here and provides a framework through which we can view the work of our two districts. In his article (1995) "Leading Change: Why Transformation Efforts Fail" (later expanded into book form), he provides a structure for successful change, in what he sees as a fairly linear order.

1. Establishing a Sense of Urgency;
2. Forming a Powerful Guiding Coalition;
3. Creating a Vision;
4. Communicating the Vision;
5. Empowering Others to Act on the Vision;
6. Planning for and Creating Short-Term Wins;
7. Consolidating Improvements and Producing Still More Change; and
8. Institutionalizing New Approaches.

While avoiding a dogmatic interpretation of the literature, one that might obscure the particularities of the change process within school districts, we see a number of elements at work in Corpus Christi and Philadelphia that align with Kotter's keys to successful change management.

Establishing a Sense of Urgency

Failure to build an appropriate sense of urgency within an organization undergoing change is one of the key failings highlighted by Kotter (1995). He describes a number of examples where heads of corporations fabricated crises in order to get the attention of their teams. Driven by a sense of urgency—receivership in Philadelphia, a challenging curriculum audit in Corpus Christi—both districts had the imperative to change thrust upon them. We could say they had nowhere to go but up. In both Philadelphia and Corpus Christi, the leadership teams were helped, in a sense, by the widespread understanding of the seriousness of their situation. While consensus around the appropriate solution seemed some way off, the reality that things had to change was clear to everyone.

For Corpus Christi this pivotal moment came after the Texas Association of School Administrators conducted a district-wide curriculum audit to evaluate the instructional coherence and alignment in the district. The auditors came to a harsh conclusion, but one readily accepted by most of the district's educators. The curriculum was neither coherent nor well aligned.

Inevitably, as the eighth largest school district in the United States, the stakes associated with Philadelphia's nadir were going to be even greater than those of a medium-sized district in southern Texas. The seriousness of a state takeover—the largest takeover of its kind to that point—was compounded by a $217 million deficit, and further exacerbated by the reform commission's transfer of 45 low-performing schools to the control of the privately run Edison Schools.

Interestingly, both districts saw their situations as an opportunity, a call to action that required a new, and at the time undefined, approach that would serve as the engine driving the district to higher performance. But how to funnel the reformative energy resulting from this recognition?

Forming a Coalition

From the start, both districts recognized the need to build a powerful coalition across a wide range of constituents. In Corpus Christi, Dr. Katherine Conoly was appointed by the district Superintendent to lead the effort to identify a technology-based curriculum management tool. Dr. Conoly's experience with similar efforts made clear to her the need to build a cross-departmental team that would be able to drive any new initiatives out across the district. With this in mind, Dr. Conoly formed an inclusive steering committee with members from a broad range of functional areas: teachers, curriculum and instruction, technology, assessment, special education, sub-populations, and union representatives. According to Dr. Conoly, "Having widespread input at the onset greatly improved our chances of selecting a system that met everyone's needs." The committee was charged by the district leadership with developing a plan to unite all curricula, whether written, taught, or learned: the written curriculum prepared by the district, the materials taught in the classroom, and the learning actually absorbed by the student. In converging around this goal of building a "one-stop shop" for curriculum, lesson design, and student data, the team began to move away from an approach conventional in the district, one that, in Dr. Conoly's account, was "very reflective, but not very reactive."

With the first step of building a broad coalition of support across the district under way, Dr. Conoly worked to cement the consensus by ensuring that the district's senior leadership used the coalition's messaging in calculated public displays. At its most basic level, this meant ensuring that all communications, such as a series of promotional videos presented to faculty members and district-wide mailings referencing the IMS project, were endorsed or co-signed by the Assistant Superintendent's office. At a deeper level, Dr. Conoly also ensured that the IMS training was part of a Superintendent's Leadership Conference—attended by all school principals—and lobbied successfully to have principals use their regular meetings with teachers as an opportunity for sharing ideas about the IMS and, more important, for reviewing the data generated by the system.

Philadelphia's approach was quite different. In light of a district culture still working its way out of a decentralized model, the district leadership felt that rather than build consensus before significant action was attempted, they instead should move quickly to show quick results. To focus on building consensus too early, they felt, could lead to a trap in which reflection would overcome action. The team's approach was to avoid the heavy evangelism we saw in Corpus Christi; instead the team allowed the products to "do their own marketing." In the words of two management experts, Pascale and Sternin (2005), "People are much more likely to act their way into a new way of thinking than to think their way into a new way of acting" (p. 80). To that end, the district assigned its Educational Technology team to push the program forward with a limited degree of broad consensus.

Two factors helped build a coalition of support for the project in Philadelphia. First, the district tied the rollout of the IMS to computer hardware upgrades. As new regions upgraded their hardware systems, they were able to get access to the IMS tools; the IMS thus benefited from the normal enthusiasm teachers and administrators expressed for their new computers. Second, Philadelphia used a technique we already saw at work in Corpus Christi—leveraging the authority of the district leadership. Paul Vallas, the Superintendent, and Dr. Greg Thornton, the new Chief Academic Officer, both stated publicly that the IMS was a key tool in their strategy to improve student achievement across the district.

Creating a Vision

Markedly, in creating an initial vision, the first step for both of these districts was imagining the final goal—even if only schematically. Upfront, both Philadelphia and Corpus Christi acknowledged that the shift to a data-driven environment would take time. What is more, they were both well aware that the very nature of their organizations was poorly suited to supporting an innovation that required a long-term commitment. We discussed earlier how the educational community's well-founded cynicism toward innovations poses a strong challenge to all new approaches, but that resistance was far from the only one.

The school leaders recognized that their tenure and the tenure of the senior administrative colleagues around them would be relatively transitory. In Philadelphia, in 5 years, there had been four CIOs (Chief Information Officers) prior to the current one. Corpus Christi had four assistant superintendents for instruction in the first year of implementing the IMS. This instability presented significant challenges since each official brought a different focus—one saw himself as an innovator, another sought to maintain the status quo, while others adopted a micromanager role. (Remarkably, across the nation this type of volatility is the norm, as evidenced by a 2002 study that found that 64% of school board presidents reported turnover of three or more superintendents in the past 10 years [Glass, 2002].)New leadership in any organization brings with it the invigorating potential for fresh thinking and what can be, for many, a healthy disassociation from the actions of previous incumbents. Of course, that disassociation, in and of itself, does not distinguish between successful and failed programs. As new leaders arrive with a clear mandate for change, their ability to bring existing successful initiatives to a grinding halt is a stark reality. Thus the impact of this kind of revolving door on the ability of a school district to follow through on innovations has been well documented, and a fact not lost on our subjects.

At the classroom level, the impact of consistently poor levels of retention was stark. For large urban districts, retaining new teachers is an ongoing struggle; Philadelphia, for example, adds 1,000 new teachers each year, while only 40% of teachers stay past their fourth year.

The goal in both districts, therefore, has been to enshrine the instructional management solution firmly as the central hub of the district, both on the strategic-planning level, as it builds the curriculum and plans for student growth, and on the tactical level, as it accesses data and individualizes instruction. For Vince DeTolla, Director of Educational Technology in Philadelphia, the focus from the start has been to make the IMS "foundational."

Dr. Conoly drew her terms from the work of Fullan (1991) and others, look-ing at "sustainability" as the goal. The challenge for both DeTolla and Conoly was to create enough momentum behind the initiative so that despite the employment volatility in the classroom and district, the culture of data would survive, thrive, and grow. To borrow the phrase often used in international politics, how can the leadership create "facts on the ground," real-world, working examples, to help build a stable reality in their districts?

In Corpus Christi, the IMS team sought to introduce a wide range of training opportunities to support the implementation, specifically to counter the transitional nature of the district leadership.

The arrival of Dr. Thornton as the new Chief Academic Officer, at the start of the 2004–05 school year, was the first big test for Philadelphia. Dr. Thornton hit the ground running and has continued to drive hard at imple-menting the IMS and extending its reach. It is possible to conclude that Phila-delphia "got lucky": Dr. Thornton had been a champion of using data in his previous position in Montgomery County, Maryland, and needed no con-vincing of the value of the IMS. We would contend, however, that Dr. Thornton was able to build successfully upon a vision already in place, using his own insights to support that existent model.

Communicating the Vision

While *acceptance* is only the first step on the way to full adoption, changing minds requires determined effort. Our chosen districts showed great creativity in the face of this challenge. In Corpus Christi, Dr. Conoly and her team deployed a range of techniques designed to smooth the transition of the IMS into the district; they explicitly saw this as a marketing effort. This initiative began with developing initial awareness of the IMS. Long before it was imple-mented, colored flyers distributed in staff members' salary envelopes an-nounced the imminent arrival of a "dynamic new data system." The flyers, employing a movie theme, highlighted various modules of the SchoolNet applications as "coming attractions." In the second phase of the marketing initiative, Conoly's team moved beyond the initial, generalized introduction of an IMS to showing specific benefits of the system. New flyers featured sample reports, revealing another layer of the rationale for the data project and giving district staff the opportunity to raise issues in a nonconfrontational atmosphere.

With the benefits clearly described, the third phase of the marketing initiative sought to build excitement and enthusiasm for the IMS. Dr. Conoly's team returned to the movie theme with a series of humorous movie paro-dies. The videos were entertaining—presenting self-consciously slapstick parodies of *Star Wars* and Mickey Spillane movies—but nonetheless conveyed serious and meaningful messages about the IMS and its intended goals. The district sought to show that it respected its audience and wanted to give educators plenty of warning that change was coming. The district was focusing intently on what Fullan (1991) describes as the "practicality ethic," where anyone on the receiving end of a change effort, and especially teachers who fear the impact of change on their daily lives and the lives of their students, questions the drivers behind the change and assesses the impact and reward he or she considers to be likely as a result of the change. By opening a dialogue early and confidently, the district gave its intended user audience the chance to absorb the new reality and raise issues, while simultaneously giving itself the best chance to succeed.

The steering committee extended its media evangelism by filming a more serious video clip designed to reinforce the message that the introduction of an instructional management solution wasn't just another short-term initiative; it had the support of a broad base of stakeholders and as such was poised to be a permanent fixture in the district. This video featured the Superintendent of Schools as well as the head of the American Teachers Union in Texas, both of whom expressed high expectations for the new solution.

For the leadership teams in both districts, professional development has been a key ingredient in establishing change. While the evangelism and internal marketing programs were effective at raising awareness and building enthusiasm among educators, more work will be needed to allow the IMS to permeate the inner workings of the district, a process Dr. Conoly has called the "re-culturization" of the district. In Corpus Christi, application training was realized through a train-the-trainer model. By the start of the rollout, 88 certified trainers were in place across the district. Five hundred district staff were trained at the Superintendent's Leadership Conference, and over 2,500 teachers and principals were trained by the end of the first week of school. In Philadelphia, training has been given to thousands of teachers across the district using both special hands-on workshops and regular professional development activity.

Empowering Others to Act on the Vision

Kotter (1995) notes that empowering others to act on the vision is essential to change. Research has shown that an excellent way to effect change in districts is to foster "professional learning communities." Schmoker (1994) and Dufour (Dufour & Eaker, 1998) have spelled out what professional learning communities are and how to build them. Schmoker talks about the need to "replace complex, long-term plans with simpler plans that focus on actual teaching lessons and units created in true 'learning communities'" (1994, online). In Corpus Christi, teachers now use the IMS to create lesson plans based on preconfigured templates. These plans are reviewed by a panel of master teachers; those approved are cleared for the district-wide database of lesson plans and made available to all teachers in the district through SchoolNet's application. In the first year of the rollout, teachers created over 9,000 lesson plans, of which 80% are now available for daily use by teachers.

Allowing the community to develop best practices is also evident in the way Corpus Christi rolled out a benchmark assessment program in the second phase of the project. The basic premise of a benchmark assessment program is the delivery of periodic, standards-based tests to a consistent body of students, usually with all students in a grade taking the same assessment. At the detailed implementation level, there are a multitude of opportunities for a district to mold the substance of such a program: Who writes the test items? What standards are used to drive those items? How often are tests delivered? How are the resultant data used? A group of teachers from the district spent 5 months examining best practices and reporting back to the larger steering committee on these and other questions. From Dr. Conoly's perspective, this review of best practices was an opportunity for renewal and reform: "Everything is now up for re-examination . . . and it's an energizing process." We mentioned earlier the use of principals' meetings and superintendents' summits as opportunities to share ideas and review data. In these meetings, teachers and principals use SchoolNet's reports on student achievement as the basis for collaborative discussion. In return, they both take away better methods with which to produce better data and better results, all of which they bring to the next such meeting . . . and the virtuous cycle goes on.

The ultimate goal for struggling districts in general and our focus districts in particular is to effect positive change; to move away from patterns of system-wide management and individual behavior that have failed in the past. As we discuss above, the development of professional learning communities has been used as one of the most significant tools in encouraging that change. The implementation of an IMS, with its attendant need for deliberate and long-term implementation, was both a driver and a beneficiary of the extension of the professional learning communities beyond the level of the individual school in both Corpus Christi and Philadelphia.

One of Fullan's (2005) many writings on this issue discusses the concept of professional learning communities "writ large" and the impact that can have on an educational system: "District cultures improve when schools learn from each other, and when districts learn from one another" (p. 221). Corpus Christi has taken the lead in a cross-district user group focused solely on the use of SchoolNet's instructional management system. Called Texas SchoolNet Users Group (TSNUG), this group, as would be expected, seeks to understand how best to use data to increase academic achievement. Group members meet quarterly to share best practices and to learn from one another's successes and failures. TSNUG members have begun to discuss how they might share lesson plans and assessment-item banks across district boundaries. For Fullan, this type of shared learning is not only welcome but critical to the implementation of change.

In order to empower members of the organization undergoing change and engage them as members of a professional learning community, Philadelphia has established key performance indicators and a well-defined process supporting them. Dr. Fran Newberg, the project manager for the IMS program, describes the development of a culture, driven by Dr. Thornton, that focuses on "management by fact"; metrics are a key component in delivering facts to manage by. The leadership team was expanded beyond the educational technology group referenced earlier, to include regional superintendents and a representative selection of school principals. The final constituents of this team were representatives from the technology vendors and the University of Pennsylvania's Fels Institute of Government, who were responsible for rolling out the indicators as part of their Schoolstat program. This team worked over a number of months to identify a collection of key performance indicators that administrators would be required to use, such as the level of student and teacher attendance, reading levels, and suspension and serious incident data. Personnel at all levels of the district—principals at the school-building level, regional superintendents, and even the Chief Academic Officer's team at district headquarters—track their progress and discuss the success or failure of initiatives with reference to the same indicators. Using the same metrics allows a common language to develop among principals and regional managers, and also allows the district leadership to effectively compare data points across the district. For Dr. Newberg, this measure continues the departure from the radical decentralization of the district's previous leadership: "We have moved away from the paradigm of schools as independent entities."

Another value of using shared indicators is the focus on analyzing rather than retrieving data. No one expects principals and others to be creative about which report to bring to a particular meeting. Again, this approach is not about introducing a reflective process; rather, it is about getting the right data and knowing how to interpret them. As Dr. Newberg notes, many of the staff in Philadelphia are "data-driven people," yet their ability to act on those impulses was hampered by two factors. First, there was lack of access to the data—all requests for reports had to go through the office of assessment, which, although happy to supply the data, couldn't possibly provide reports to every teacher and principal in the district. Second, there was no shared understanding of what data to gather, or how to analyze those data. As the IMS and the other data initiatives in the district become established, both these barriers have been pulled down.

As Philadelphia trains its regional and principal-level staff to become more proficient with the data, the goal is for that expertise to trickle down to the teaching staff through principals' meetings at the building level, thus deepening the data culture across the district.

Planning for and Creating Short-Term Wins

Kotter (1995) notes that "planning for visible performance improvements" and subsequently "recognizing and rewarding" those who facilitated those improvements are essential for building momentum for change (p. 61). As discussed earlier, neither district rushed the deployment timetable. Corpus Christi sought a short-term win with the online lesson plans. A previously cumbersome process was reinvented using the IMS, and almost every teacher in the district was provided the opportunity to use the application with limited risk and in highly positive circumstances. Because use of the IMS tool was mandated for lesson-plan creation, a large percentage of teachers soon had lesson plans they could use, built into the system, formatted around a common rubric, and able to be shared with others.

For Philadelphia, getting the curriculum online was the first opportunity to tap into the core concerns of teachers. This allowed the project team to establish a rapid beachhead, convincing users that the system would help them in their daily lives, rather than simply changing their routine or, worse, simply adding to their workload. Vince DeTolla credits much of the deployment's success to the "pull" nature of the initiative. Teachers didn't need to be sold on the IMS because the in-person professional development accompanying the rollout gave them an opportunity to see its immediate impact on their instructional and administrative activities.

In both districts, we have seen how understanding the need for quick wins translated into a patient, staggered rollout of the suite of applications. Corpus Christi began with Align, SchoolNet's curriculum management module, and Account, SchoolNet's reporting and analysis module, both of which were elements of the IMS focused on managing the delivery and performance of the district's new curriculum. Only after a full year of developing the curriculum and building support and training for the program did the district move to adopt Assess, the suite's benchmark assessment component.

Within this staggered rollout, the team in Corpus Christi established a series of attainable goals for each user within the district. Teachers and administrators were given five targets to gauge their proficiency with the SchoolNet suite. The targets were conservative, straightforward uses of the program such as generating a specific type of report and accessing the state standards. These were simple enough to avoid overwhelmingly complex language or requiring users to become experts, but meaningful enough to imbue each user with a real sense of achievement: Once mastering the task, they know how to use the system at some level. These tasks also passed the relevance test; they were rooted in the everyday realities of the urban teacher, specifically, the daily need to access the standards efficiently and effectively.

Philadelphia used its previously established "cohort groups" to stagger the rollout across the district. Essentially groupings of schools based on common criteria such as hardware upgrades and performance levels, the cohorts allowed the large district to function as a group of small districts managed by a common entity, with the goal of maximizing efficiency. An initial deployment across several cohort groups was followed in the second year by a larger rollout, with the entire district coming online only in the third year. Looking ahead, the district has begun rolling out a parent communication initiative that will provide families access to online and printed reports of student data. In addition, the district now has built enough educator comfort with online tools that it plans to phase out the printed version of the curriculum within the next 12 to 18 months.

With each new phase of the adoption initiative, both districts have added depth to the use of data, thereby allowing users at each level to build their own comfort with the system; in turn, newly "converted" users support new users as they embrace the system. Thus, Philadelphia's initial cohorts served as mentors to the wider community of teachers and administrators. Those trained educators in turn will be able to support the issues and growing pains associated with rolling out access to the broader community.

Consolidating Improvements/Institutionalizing New Approaches

Fullan (2005) defines the success of a school leader in terms of not just student achievement, but also "how many good leaders he or she leaves behind who can go even further" (p. 220). It is clear to us that the leadership teams at both these districts have grasped this insight and applied it to much of their thinking. To further promote the longevity of the data management initiatives, the districts have begun working with SchoolNet to establish a "Data Coach" program. This program answers the "Now what?" challenge that using data leads to; once users understand the basics of *how* to use the tool, they ask *what* to do with it to increase student achievement. Now that practitioners have started to incorporate a new set of tools into their daily practice, how do they become users with an increasingly sophisticated perspective on the potential of the data? The short-term goal of Data Coach is to unpack the true potential of the data at their disposal and give graduates the knowledge and focus to extract the right data and the most effective reports out of the system. The longer-term target is tightly focused on developing instructional capacity within the district faculty and, in doing so, ensuring the continuity of the data initiative beyond the tenure of its primary evangelists.

In his eight-tiered "schedule" of steps toward improvement, Kotter (1995) breaks out a cycle of consolidating improvements from the later process of institutionalizing change; because our districts are still in the early parts of what has proven to be a multiyear effort, most of our evidence shows that these stages have not yet become differentiated. After the initial phases of accepting and embracing the IMS, the leadership teams focused on consolidating improvements with an eye toward institutionalizing the vision across the district. The Data Coach program, for example, seeks to build a trained, knowledgeable cadre whose expertise and assumed continual use of the IMS will help sustain the pressure for ongoing and expanding implementation of data-driven instruction.

Another example of institutionalization is the districts' planned engagement of the broader community. Philadelphia will roll out parent access to online and offline reporting across the district over the next 12 months. This rollout is intended to build on the broad, passionate support group of parents who will, it is hoped, continue to advocate for an informed and data-oriented learning community of which they can be a part.

PROGRESS?

Monson (2002) wisely advises his readers to be skeptical about new innovations claiming to drive change across educational systems, exhorting us not to use buzzwords such as "data-driven decision making": "We shouldn't say we are doing something unless we are really doing it and preferably doing it well" (p. 25). Given this caveat, it seems wholly appropriate to question the simplistic notion of an easy and necessary correlation between deploying an IMS and higher test scores for all students. We can see very clearly, however, that using data as a central pivot in the district forces changes in attitude, behavior, and instructional practice. Working in a managed instructional environment transforms the notion of a curriculum by facilitating its immediate distribution and by allowing its creators to track its usage and effectiveness.

By providing for the creation of a varied database of lesson plans, an IMS transforms the notion of the individual lesson plan because it allows educators across a district to benefit from the experience and expertise of a master teacher—while, if appropriate, at the same time tapping into the creativity and fresh thinking of a first-year teacher. Assessment reports become opportunities for immediate action as opposed to historical reflection well detached from the moment 6 months earlier when a student filled in a bubble sheet. A student's record is no longer owned by the secretarial pool with access guarded by layers of bureaucracy, but can be shared in real time the instant the student appears in a new school.

Adoption across a district, of course, is crucial to these sorts of transformations. A Temple University report (Jurgensen, 2005) notes that most Philadelphia principals encourage the use of SchoolNet, and many insist on its use for reviewing item analysis and benchmark data. Corpus Christi has seen significant levels of adoption. One measure of the district's success is the widespread use of the lesson plan creation tools that helped lead the district toward its goal of a coherent and aligned curriculum. In addition to the authoring and storing of thousands of lesson plans in SchoolNet, a majority of teachers and principals have built custom student performance reports in SchoolNet for parent conferences and academic planning.

But will adoption of an IMS, and its attendant ideology of data-driven instruction, and even the major transformations sketched above, actually lead to improvements in student achievement? Clearly these are early days in the history of this particular data-focused innovation. That said, both districts featured here have shown that a well-deployed and well-managed adoption of an IMS can have significant impact on student achievement. The gains in student achievement since Philadelphia adopted SchoolNet's IMS were documented recently in an article by the district's CIO, Patricia Renzulli (2005), who describes an aggressive reform program centered on a comprehensive technology solution. As the biggest impact, she points to some very real gains in performance scores, with the number of schools meeting adequate yearly progress nearly tripling, from 58 to 160, and several areas of significant efficiency gains, including the speed of turning around assessment data and reducing the impact of student mobility.

REFERENCES

Dufour, R., & Eaker, R. E. (1998). *Professional learning communities at work: Best practices for enhancing student achievement*. Bloomington, IN: National Educational Service.

Fullan, M. G. (1991). The teacher. In M. G. Fullan (Ed.), *The new meaning of educational change* (pp. 117–143). New York: Teachers College Press.

Fullan, M. G. (2005). Professional communities writ large. In R. Dufour, R. Eaker, & R. Dufour (Eds.), *On common ground: The power of professional learning communities* (pp. 209–223). Bloomington, IN: Solution Tree.

Glass, T. E. (2002, May). *School board presidents and their view of the superintendency*. Memphis, TN: University of Memphis.

Jurgensen, E. (2005). *Report on the Philadelphia School District's implementation of SchoolNet*. Philadelphia: Temple University.

Kotter, J. P. (1995, March-April). Leading change: Why transformation efforts fail. *Harvard Business Review, 73*(2), 59–67.

Monson, R. J. (2002, December). Using data differently. *School Administrator, 59,* 24–28.

Pascale, R. T., & Sternin, J. (2005, May). Your company's secret change agents. *Harvard Business Review, 83*(5), 73–81.

Renzulli, P. (2005, July). Testing the limits of one-stop data access. *THE Journal.* Retrieved September 2005, from http://www.thejournal.com/artcles/17335

Schmoker, M. (2004, February). Tipping point: From feckless reform to substantive instructional improvement. *Phi Delta Kappan, 85*(6), 424–432. Retrieved October 8, 2007, from http://www.pdkintl.org/kappan/k0402sch.htm

CHAPTER 12

The Evolution of a Homegrown Data Warehouse: TUSDstats

Lisa Long, Luz M. Rivas,
Daniel Light & Ellen B. Mandinach

School districts attempting to use data for decision making have found it difficult to analyze different types of data (e.g., assessment, demographics, attendance) without data being stored in a central location (Militello, 2005). Often, data are stored in ways that make them inaccessible to educators, making schools data-rich but information-poor (Stringfield, Wayman, & Yakimowski-Srebnick, 2005). Data warehouses recently have been at the forefront of technology applications as ways for districts to store data effectively while making information accessible to educators. Data warehouses integrate multiple sources of data that often are stored in disparate forms into one electronic repository allowing for the examination of relationships across a variety of domains (Wayman, 2005). Systems typically provide query and reporting tools that allow users to run preformatted and/or custom reports (Stein, 2003). Homegrown or commercially developed warehouses offer potential solutions to help educators efficiently mine and interrogate data from which they can make informed decisions.

The decision to invest in a data warehouse is complex. One of the first decisions districts must make when planning to implement a warehouse is whether to develop a homegrown system or buy a commercial product developed specifically for the K–12 market (for product reviews, see Stein, 2003, or Wayman, Stringfield, & Yakimowski, 2004). According to Stringfield and colleagues (2005), districts should consider the following when deciding whether to build or buy: their assessment of data needs, available resources, time to implement, and cost. Districts should consider whether they have the skills to create a data warehouse and whether they can develop internal expertise for managing, maintaining, and improving a locally developed system (Stein, 2003).

There are advantages and disadvantages to both choices. Districts may have the internal resources, such as skilled technical staff and network infrastructure, to develop and maintain a homegrown data warehouse. Even with these resources, however, a homegrown warehouse takes years to develop and implement fully. Commercial vendors usually have practical experience and specialized staff that allow them to get a system established faster than district staff can, usually putting a functional system in place in a few months (Stringfield et al., 2005). Districts must weigh the trade-offs between the seemingly lower cost of a slowly developed local system and the seemingly higher cost but more rapid implementation of a commercial product (Stringfield et al., 2005) to determine the best fit for their particular circumstances and objectives.

Although student management systems and school and district data systems began to emerge as early as the 1960s and 1970s, pioneering districts such as the Broward County Public Schools (Spielvogel & Pasnik, 1999) and the Cleveland Municipal School District (Consortium for School Networking, 2005) saw the pressing need to consolidate data into one central location beginning in the mid-1990s. At this time, commercial warehousing options for schools were quite rare. The pioneering districts developed their own data warehouses from scratch. By developing data and technological expertise and/or seeking assistance from outside consultants, these districts were able to create their own data management solutions. These visionary districts invested ahead and were prepared for some of the assessment accountability requirements of the No Child Left Behind Act (2001).

This chapter describes the evolution of TUSDstats, a data warehouse developed by the Tucson Unified School District (TUSD). Like Broward, Cleveland, and others, TUSD developed a data warehouse before packaged options proliferated and prior to the No Child Left Behind Act (NCLB). Beginning with the creation of a student information system and moving to the development of a Web-based data warehouse, TUSD built its own solutions to manage the large amounts of data it collects. Through this process, the district has built internal capacity to develop, implement, and support its technology systems. TUSDstats is designed to give administrators, educators, parents, and the public access to a variety of educational data collected by the district. We examine the warehouse's design using a framework developed by Light, Wexler, and Heinze (2004) and elaborated in a project funded by the National Science Foundation (Mandinach, Honey, Light, & Brunner, chapter 2; Mandinach, Honey, Light, Heinze, & Rivas, 2005). While technology forms an important part of a district's data management and analysis, Stein (2003) notes that "an organizational understanding of the appropriate use of data is equally, if not more, important" (p. 4). This chapter also provides examples of how TUSD is using data at the district, building, and classroom levels, linking it to the conceptual framework for data-driven decision making created by Mandinach and colleagues (chapter 2).

HOW DATA TECHNOLOGIES SHAPE
THE TRANSFORMATION PROCESS

The management information systems (MIS) literature (Ackley, 2001; Ackoff, 1989; Drucker, 1989) contends that the design of decision-support systems affects the process by which raw data are transformed into usable knowledge. At a minimum, data tools help collect and organize data, but most tools also support the summarization and analysis of data. However, all software has built-in assumptions that shape the final product (Lehman, 1990) and in relation to data-decision systems, these assumptions affect utility (Sarmiento, n.d.; Wayman et al., 2004). Even such basic decisions as how to aggregate raw numbers and the design of reports shape the flow of information. For example, data warehouse technologies are a first step in collecting and organizing data. But the way a data warehouse collects data (e.g., whether test scores are associated with demographic data or not) and structures the database (e.g., whether the basic unit is the student, teacher, or class) influences the next steps in the process. Reporting and retrieval technologies shape the potential for organizing and summarizing data into information. Seemingly simple choices like the interface and visual presentation can make the information more understandable to the user.

Building from the literature on data-driven decision making and MIS, we identified six factors that illuminate how a data-support system affects the user's process of understanding and using data in an educational context (Light et al., 2004). These dimensions encompass tool functionality, data collection, data entry, and organization, as well as how the tool enables the user to interact with the data. Each dimension identifies key traits, or clusters of traits, that shape how educators use the tool (see Mandinach et al., 2005, for examples of variations along these dimensions). There is no value implied by being higher or lower on any given dimension. They are:

1. *Access and ease of use.* This dimension encompasses the degree to which the tool is easy to use. The tool can vary from being intuitive to requiring extensive training. Access is defined not only by the existence of sufficient infrastructure, but also by whether the design allows different levels of access within the data warehouse to different users. Given the sensitive nature of data in the education system, access issues are complicated by issues of privacy and accountability (e.g., teachers have access to their own students' records, but not

broad access, whereas principals have access to data across class-rooms within their schools).

2. *Length of feedback loop.* The feedback loop stretches from data collection to reporting. The utility of the tool is mediated by the util-ity of the data at the time of user access. Some data are time sensi-tive and have declining value. Other data may not be as time sensitive or may become more valuable within a longitudinal perspective (Gorry & Scott-Morton, 1971). For example, a student's single stan-dardized test score may not be useful data a year later, but it becomes an interesting data point in a sequence of 5 years of test performance.

3. *Comprehensibility of the data.* The tool can help support the user's understanding of the data. Various reporting strategies, such as graphical representations, supporting data, and grouping and aggre-gating data, can help the user make inferences from the data. The tool can include additional data, such as explanations or background information, to help the user better understand the implications of the data. Comprehensibility embodies a tension between supporting interpretation of the data versus dictating an understanding of them.

4. *Manipulation of the data.* Data tools vary in the extent to which users can query the database or manipulate the data. The flexibility of the tool impacts the types of queries that can be made that can help the user to solve different problems with the data. Flexibility also allows the user to manipulate the data in such a way that the tool can handle different problems (Arnott, 1998). For example, the tool may allow a user to aggregate data at multiple levels, such as the individual, the classroom, or the grade. Such flexibility can be helpful to the user, as opposed to a tool that does not permit upward or downward aggregation by all users.

5. *Utility and quality of the data.* Schools can enter literally thousands of variables into a data system. The utility of the data refers to the extent to which the data provided to educators align with their needs and objectives. Quality encompasses the scope and accuracy of data provided and how well they correspond to the types of decisions envisioned (Feldman & March, 1988; Gorry & Scott-Morton, 1971).

6. *Links to instruction.* This dimension, specific to educational decision-support systems, refers to the system's capacity to bridge informa-tion (either physically or conceptually) with practice.

It is important to keep in mind that these dimensions interact with one another in both positive and negative ways. For example, creating a tool that allows the user to do complex manipulations of the data most likely would decrease ease of use by creating a more complex tool, which also would af-fect the level of analytical knowledge needed for a user to understand the results. Or creating a more accessible data tool may require omitting private data from the system.

In this chapter we examine the data collected in Tucson in terms of three frameworks created in the course of our research. First, the chapter examines TUSDstats in terms of the six functional dimensions in our structural framework. Some of these dimensions are more applicable to data warehouses, and relevance may vary depending on the type of user. We then transform the data, as part of an evaluation framework, into a systems map depicting the relative importance of various factors that contribute to the data culture created within TUSD. Finally, we link the data to the components of the conceptual framework (Mandinach et al., chapter 2).

METHODOLOGY

The findings in this chapter are based on data collected for a 3-year study, funded by the National Science Foundation, designed to create an evaluation framework for data-driven decision making (see Mandinach et al., chapter 2). As part of this project, researchers collected data from six school districts using three different technology tools for data-driven decision making. TUSD was selected because of its pioneering contributions to and history with data warehousing.

To learn about the warehouse design as well as data use at all levels of the district, we conducted interviews with district administrators, instructional technology staff, information technology staff, researchers, school administrators, and teachers. A sample of six schools (two elementary, two middle, and two high schools) was selected for building-level interviews. A total of 65 individuals were interviewed: district administrators (including the superintendent and assistant superintendent) and staff ($n = 10$), building-level administrators ($n = 7$), teachers ($n = 41$), and other school staff ($n = 5$).

TUCSON UNIFIED SCHOOL DISTRICT

Profile and Demographics

TUSD is a midsized urban school district located in Tucson, Arizona. Currently, TUSD is the second-largest school district in the state, serving a student population of over 60,000. The district employs 3,700 teachers, 3,600 support staff, and 200 administrators. The ethnic makeup of students is 51% Hispanic, 35% Caucasian, 7% African-American, 4% Native American, and 3% Asian-American. Although the student population is diverse, individual schools tend to have more homogeneous populations, ranging from 99% Hispanic within some schools to 99% Caucasian in others. The district serves approximately 18,000 Title I students, the largest number in the state.

TUSD has 110 schools. During the 2004–05 school year, 14 schools did not make adequate yearly progress (AYP) as defined by NCLB. Several of the district's schools are underenrolled due to students leaving for charter schools. Within TUSD's boundaries there are 52 charter schools, and all of the underenrolled schools are geographically close to charters.

TUSD is governed by a five-member board elected by the public. In the past, the district lacked stable leadership in terms of its superintendent. A former superintendent was brought back from retirement and named interim superintendent. The board later extended his contract, and as of the 2006–07 academic year, he is still at TUSD. A search will be conducted for a permanent replacement in 2008.

Federal and State Demands for Data

In addition to the accountability and reporting demands of NCLB, TUSD must comply with the State of Arizona's mandates. State policies explicitly require districts and schools to use data for school improvement planning and processes. Arizona LEARNS (Leading Education Through Accountability and Results Notification System) is the Arizona Department of Education's school accountability system (see http://www.ade.state.az.us/azlearns). Unlike NCLB, Arizona LEARNS measures school performance over a 3-year period (see Table 12.1). Measures include whether the school met AYP, results of the state-mandated test—Arizona's Instrument to Measure Standards (AIMS)—and graduation/dropout rates. Based on the results of these measurements, schools are identified and labeled as excelling, highly performing, performing, or underperforming.

Another state policy, Proposition 301, also implements specific educational accountability measures. Proposition 301, passed by voters in November 2000, authorizes a 0.6% sales tax increase to support education. As part of this proposition, to receive state funding, each district must submit electronic data on a school-by-school basis, including student-level data, to the Arizona Department of Education. Districts also are required to submit daily attendance electronically to the state.

Some of the funds collected from Proposition 301 are targeted to enhance teacher salaries based on performance. Each district develops its own performance-based pay plan. In TUSD, school councils—elected representative groups of parents, teachers, school staff, and community members—in collaboration with the principal, develop and approve a school improvement plan, as well as three site goals for increasing student achievement. If a school attains at least two of the three goals, faculty earn a stipend. Site goals must

Table 12.1. Comparison of Arizona's Accountability Systems

NCLB	Arizona LEARNS
Required by federal law	Required by state law
One-year snapshot of student performance	Longitudinal examination of student performance
Components of evaluation: AIMS scores Percent of students assessed Attendance/graduation rates	Components of evaluation: AIMS scores Measure of academic progress (MAP) Graduation/dropout rates Adequate yearly progress (AYP)
Labels schools depending on whether AYP is met (yes/no)	Labels schools on a graded scale: Failing to meet academic standards Underperforming Performing Highly performing Excelling

Source: Arizona Department of Education, www.ade.state.az.us

be based on analysis of data and must prioritize areas in which the school has the greatest need for improvement. Specifically, goals must measure student growth, clearly identify the group(s) of students to be measured, and include baseline data of where students began and how much progress they will make by the end of the school year. Additionally, schools must identify the data source and/or measurement to be used for assessing improvement. An example of an acceptable goal is "All third-grade students will improve from 42% to 47% in reading achievement as measured by AIMS."

Data Management Systems in the District

The district has a history of developing its own data management systems. In 1990, the TUSD Governing Board charged the district to develop, administer, and maintain a student information system to standardize and unify student records. In response, the Technology and Telecommunications Systems (TTS) Department staff developed Sonora, a student information system, implemented in 1993. Sonora was accessible through a wide-area network within the district. During the 2000–01 school year, TTS released Mojave, a Web-based student information system, accessible through the Internet. Mojave can be accessed by all district personnel and is used mainly by school staff, including principals, teachers, and support staff. The district requires teachers to enter grades and daily attendance using Mojave.

In the spring of 1998, the district began plans to construct a data warehouse. At this time, only a limited number of commercially available software options existed for collecting and analyzing K–12 educational data. The district had little choice but to build its own data warehouse specifically to suit its needs. District leaders assembled a team within the Accountability and Research (A and R) Department to build the data warehouse. According to the developers, the project was kept alive by not trying to design every part of the system at once. Rather, staff conducted a needs assessment to determine what type of data stakeholders needed and then built one system module at a time. The warehouse initially was implemented as an Intranet site accessible only to TUSD employees on district computers. It later evolved to a web-based data warehouse now known as TUSDstats.

TUSDstats

TUSDstats (http://tusdstats.tusd.k12.az.us) combines data from several sources, with most of the data coming from the district's student information system, Mojave. TUSDstats (see Figure 12.1) contains four main categories of school and district data (assessment data, demographic data, school profiles and ratings, and information about special programs), student-level data, and several other related links (what's new, student-level information, resources, on-line testing, stats chat, handouts, and frequently asked questions).

The assessment data section contains data from AIMS, Terra Nova, writing prompts, Core Curriculum Standards Assessment (CCSA), past tests (Stanford 9, SAT, and ACT), and student grades. The demographic data section includes data on attendance, mobility, suspensions, enrollment, stability, and dropouts. The section on school profile and ratings includes data on state and federal mandates, such as AYP; school quality surveys; percentage of students tested; school profiles; and the STAAR Measure (Student Achievement Accountability for Results), which is a combined measure of AIMS, CCSA, and the Stanford 9. It also includes a graphing tool that enables users to represent a variety of assessment and demographic data in different ways, and at different levels of aggregation, and to view the data longitudinally. The special programs data site includes information on a variety of activities and programs, such as GATE, Title I, exceptional children, desegregation, math placement, the family resource and wellness center, language assessment services data, senior surveys, the Spanish exit test, and school improvement plans.

Access and Ease of Use. As a web-based resource, TUSDstats is easily accessible to users through the Internet. While large amounts of data are accessible to the public without requiring a log in, individual student data are password protected and accessible only to authorized users. Several data-

Figure 12.1. Main Page of the TUSDStats Website

access levels require authentication. At the district level, central administrators have access to site-specific information at schools with which they are associated. School administrators have access to their school's teacher- and student-level data. Principals can view individual student and all class and grade aggregations for their school. Teachers have access to student-level information and class aggregations for their current and past classes. Teachers also are able to view AIMS results for their students at the concept level (e.g., number sense). The warehouse also provides access to parents, who can create their own account and view their child's test scores, grades, attendance, and teacher's contact information. When parents log in, they also receive bulletin board messages from their child's school.

Length of Feedback Loop. The feedback loop varies for different types of data. Data such as attendance are updated daily. State assessments administered during the spring are available the following fall. Quarterly writing assessment results are entered into TUSDstats by teachers, making the data immediately accessible. Other data such as school profiles and rankings are updated annually.

Comprehensibility of the Data. TUSDstats organizes summary data into tables and graphs showing aggregate assessment scores (see Figure 12.2). The multiple forms of graphical representations are intended to make the data readily understandable to different users. TUSDstats also includes in-

Figure 12.2. Screen Shot of Data-Presentation Modes from TUSDStats

2004–05 Quarter 1 Writing Scores for 2005–06 class(es) of SAMPLE ELEMENTARY

Name	Grade	Ethnicity	I&C	Org	Voice	WordC	SentF	Conv	Total	Avg	Mastery
SA-E	5	Hispanic	3	2	2	2	3	2	14	2.3	Below
KB	5	Nat. Am.	1	1	1	1	1	1	6	1.0	Below
JB-F	5	Hispanic	4	4	4	5	4	4	25	4.2	Meets
MB	5	Hispanic	3	4	3	3	4	4	21	3.5	Approaches
ID	5	Hispanic	4	4	4	4	4	4	24	4.0	Meets
AE	5	Hispanic	4	3	3	3	3	3	19	3.2	Approaches
OFM	5	Hispanic	1	1	1	1	1	1	6	1.0	Below
YG	5	Anglo	4	4	4	3	4	4	23	3.8	Meets

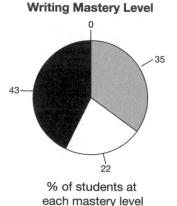

Writing Mastery Level

0

35

43

22

% of students at each mastery level

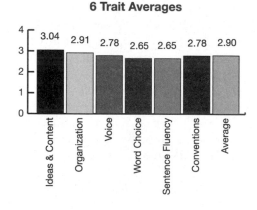

6 Trait Averages

3.04 2.91 2.78 2.65 2.65 2.78 2.90

Ideas & Content, Organization, Voice, Word Choice, Sentence Fluency, Conventions, Average

formation about, resources for, and definitions of key measurements (e.g., reliability, validity, criterion-referenced testing), as well as instructional topics about which teachers should be knowledgeable. The resources section of TUSDstats contains links to explanations of statistical terms (e.g., central tendency, dispersion), lesson-planning assistance, information about the many tests and accountability measures students must take, and descriptions of the state standards. These resources are written for maximum comprehensibility on the part of practitioners. They provide simple examples to help the naive user understand the fundamental concepts needed to interpret student performance data. All definitions are written using simple terminology.

Manipulation of the Data. TUSDstats contains predesigned queries and web-based reports. Users can run queries and reports by selecting criteria from features such as pull-down menus and check boxes. Users can select queries based on aggregate data and using criteria such as ethnicity, grade level, and school year. TUSDstats does not provide users with an advanced query tool. If users want a query not available on TUSDstats, they need to request it from the A and R Department. If a number of people ask for the same query, A and R staff may decide to add it to the options in TUSDstats, thereby customizing the warehouse to the needs of its users.

Utility and Quality of the Data. TUSDstats integrates school and student achievement data, offering administrators, teachers, and parents access to a variety of educational data. The warehouse is organized into sections that include assessment, demographic, and school profile data. Table 12.2 shows the data available within TUSDstats. Assessment data include test scores for district-developed assessments, state-mandated tests, and national assessment such as SAT/ACT scores. Course grades are available for middle and high schools. Demographic information includes attendance records, student enrollment by ethnic background and gender, mobility rates for schools, and dropout rates for middle and high schools. School profiles are available for all schools and include student achievement as well as student and school demographics. Additionally, school accountability ratings such as AYP can be looked up for each school.

Links to Instruction. The student data screen of TUSDstats contains a number of data sources, including direct links to the quarterly prompts and other assessment data. The quarterly prompts are administered by teachers for diagnostic purposes, and the results are intended to be readily amenable for use as an instructional tool in the classroom. Teachers can search the warehouse, examine test scores, and then link to a section that provides suggested instructional steps based on student performance. Several types of

Table 12.2. TUSDstats: Organization of Data

Assessment Data	School Profile and Rankings	Demographic Data	Special Programs
State-mandated, norm-referenced, and criterion-based tests in reading, writing, and math	District-level measures to proficiency of goals	Attendance	Gifted and Talented
	State and federal rankings	Enrollment	Exceptional Education
		Mobility	
District assessments	School profile	Stability	Title I
	School quality survey results	Suspensions	Language Assessment
SAT/ACT scores		Dropouts	
Writing prompt scores	Percentage of students tested		Desegregation
			Senior Survey
			Math Placement
Grades for middle and high schools			
Scores for elementary schools			

direct links between assessment data and instructional supports are included in TUSDstats's resources pages, among them a lesson-plan builder that enables teachers to use the assessment data to craft appropriate lessons, based on student needs.

Use of the Data Warehouse

Although TUSD has had data management systems in place for over 10 years, and collecting and using data have always played a prominent role throughout the district, with the implementation of NCLB, data use at all levels in the district increased substantially. In this section we discuss the use of data by district administrators, building administrators, and classroom teachers.

District-Level Use of Data

Administrators refer to the district as being "data-driven and people-powered." With the proliferation of accountability mandates, the district recognizes the need for administrators and educators who are skilled in using data appropriately, as well as access to and use of data on which to base decisions. The district hopes that data accessed through TUSDstats will help educators focus on improving student achievement. Administrators use TUSDstats to view aggregate school data and identify low-performing schools.

They also use data to identify district-wide issues such as why students are leaving the district to attend charter schools.

Charting the Impact of Charter Schools. In the 2003–04 academic year, over 8,300 students who live within TUSD boundaries left the district to attend charters. Losing these students reduced TUSD's annual revenue by $40,000,000. Subsequently, the district received a $40,000 grant from the National Education Association to study why parents withdraw their children from the district and to make recommendations to the TUSD Board. The data warehouse is being used to track when students leave and return to TUSD, with fairly complex cohort analyses conducted to identify trends. The analyses indicate that parents withdraw their children after elementary school and before middle school, feeling that a charter will provide more individualized attention than is possible in TUSD's middle schools. However, many parents become disenchanted with the charters due to limitations in the curriculum, lack of qualified teachers, and other factors, and re-enroll their children for high school. Interrogating TUSDstats enabled district personnel to better understand the circumstances and trends around the charter schools, and they now are trying to determine how to remediate the problems and stem the outflow of children from the district.

Reducing the Number of Underperforming Schools. Prior to NCLB, the only schools using the district's data systems for instructional decision making were schools with low student achievement. The district, concerned about these schools, focused its data efforts on them. When the first round of AYP results was released and Arizona LEARNS labeled each school, teachers began the data-investigation process. This occurred at the 26 schools labeled failing. Over the course of 3 years, the district was left with only one failing school. Administrators are convinced that focused interrogation of data to identify specific problem areas, to which resources and attention can be devoted, has, in part, improved AYP performance over time. Principals in the failing schools were urged to use data to help remediate the underperformance. Grade-level or subject-level teacher meetings were convened to work through existing data and to discuss potential instructional actions to help specific students. This approach seems to be working for many of the schools.

Building-Level Use of Data

District leadership believes that principals who use data for decision making will build more successful schools. For the past few years, the district has focused on providing professional development to principals on how to access TUSDstats and use the data residing there. District-wide principal meetings are held at computer labs where principals have the opportunity to practice using the warehouse. The district also hired a consultant to facilitate a workshop on how to use data specifically designed for building administrators.

Principals are strongly encouraged to use TUSDstats for instructional planning. Specially trained coaches work with principals to examine data and develop strategies and interventions for improving test scores. The district requires principals to complete and submit their school accountability plans electronically, using a template within TUSDstats. This plan prompts them to focus on goals based on their test data, professional development to support those goals, and how they are going to meet their goals. Recently TUSD incorporated a data exercise into the application process for new principals. To apply to become a principal, applicants take an online assessment that includes viewing data for a fictitious school. In 4 hours, they have to examine the data, identify three problems, and then write a school improvement plan, a memo to parents, or talking points for a meeting with their staff.

Building-level administrators reported that they were using data for conversations and presentations to their community and to identify student needs. Principals also are encouraging teachers to use data for instructional planning.

Using Data for Conversations and Presentations. Some of the principals we interviewed include data in presentations to faculty and parents. They present assessment results and discuss strategies for raising test scores. One principal noted that everything she presents to her faculty is backed by data or research. Another commented on how data add legitimacy to conversations and explanations of problems. Still another principal explained that before the data warehouse, when she met with teachers about their performance she would just say, "You're doing a good job." Now, she can show them data confirming their effectiveness and talk about specific areas and activities.

Identifying Student Needs. Principals look at aggregate student data to determine where to place individual students. Most mentioned looking at AIMS assessment scores to identify trends and examining demographic and achievement data to see how different groups of students are performing. TUSDstats makes such aggregation simple. High school principals also use the warehouse to examine dropout rates and demographics of dropouts to try to identify these students' needs.

Encouraging Teachers to Use Data for Instruction. Principals encourage their staff to use student data to inform instruction. Some principals ask teachers to select a few students and examine their data over a period of time to try to identify trends. They encourage teachers to log into TUSDstats to view individual student data. One principal said her goal was to help teachers respond effectively to students' needs by encouraging them to develop individual plans for students based on data.

Challenges in Building-Level Data Use. Despite the district's focus on improving principals' ability to use data, actual use of data by principals varies from building to building. District administrators recognized this as an issue, and one commented, "Some principals are very astute at using data while others do it superficially." District leaders were able to identify top data-using principals by name. Although supervisors are supposed to work with principals to make sure data use is part of their performance plan, district administrators were not certain this actually was happening. One principal told us she felt that while the message from the district on using data is clear, the accountability is not. Certainly there are holdouts and Luddites who refuse to use data, and for some, data use is confounded by a principal's refusal to use technology.

Classroom-Level Use of Data

Using data for instructional decisions and planning is new to some TUSD teachers who have received no formal professional development from the district on how to use data in the classroom. Most teachers are influenced by the value their principal places on using data. Some principals have provided their own training to teachers on how to use data for instructional planning, while others fail to communicate to their teachers the importance of using data. The building leader sets the tone. Some teachers, however, will use data despite having a less than supportive principal.

When describing how they use data, teachers discussed the importance of multiple sources rather than relying on a sole data point from which to make decisions. This issue is particularly salient when teachers examine standardized test scores in addition to classroom assessments because the former do not always align well with instructional practice. Teachers use aggregate class assessment data and individual student scores, grades, attendance, and contact information to supplement the data provided by the high-stakes assessments.

Differentiating Instruction. Teachers who use data to differentiate instruction refer to the quarterly writing assessments. Teachers score quarterly writing prompts using the Six Trait Writing Model (NWREL, n.d.), where each piece of writing receives six scores. Because teachers enter the scores into TUSDstats, they can view their class results immediately. With the visual organization of the data, teachers can see which students are falling below the standards for any writing trait. At one school, cadres of teachers discuss the data as a group and develop a plan for how to improve instruction and student performance. These teachers focus on students who are falling below the standards in a particular trait and separate children into small groups to provide mini-sessions for those needing help in a given writing skill. Teachers credit their ability to transform those data into actionable knowledge to the immediate aggregation of student scores that TUSDstats supports.

Assessment of Students. Some teachers use TUSDstats to examine assessment scores at the beginning of the year to gain an understanding of their students' level of academic performance. A few teachers develop assessments and curriculum based on their students' scores. Teachers also reported that examining assessment data for new students entering their class in the middle of the year is useful when trying to determine where new students are in relationship to their class.

Other Uses of Data. Sharing student information with parents was another use of data. During parent conferences teachers share children's attendance patterns, assessment scores, and grades, and these become points of conversation between teacher and parents.

Many teachers use the data warehouse to talk to students about their progress and how they are doing in other classes. Some middle and high school teachers log onto TUSDstats and view the data together with students. This process allows them to discuss test scores, attendance issues, and problems in other classes. In some cases, students ask to log onto TUSDstats to view their own data.

Teachers use the tool to look up student contact and background information. They credit the tool with helping them be more efficient since they no longer have to obtain student information from the office. As one teacher expressed, "It's like having a cum folder online."

Nonusage of the Data Warehouse. Not all teachers use the warehouse. Among the nonusers, some expressed skepticism about the purpose, use, and interpretation of formal, standardized test data, in contrast to more formative or local data sources, for instructional purposes. Teachers gave reasons for not using the data warehouse. Some nonusers were not familiar with TUSDstats. Most of these teachers were either middle or high school teachers, so they were not required to use TUSDstats to enter quarterly writing scores. Among the nonusers who were familiar with the tool, most said they use their professional judgment to assess where students are academically and don't feel the need to see test scores to confirm classroom sources of data. This is a common finding because teachers tend to rely more on data that can be linked directly to instruction than on standardized test data, which are considered too far removed from the classroom (Love, Stiles, Mundry, & DiRanna, in press). One teacher asserted that any good elementary school teacher knows where his or her students are within the first few weeks of a school year and doubted that looking at the data would reveal anything new. Another reason for not using TUSDstats is teachers' lack of expertise with data. These teachers emphasized that although they thought of themselves as technology-literate and had no problem accessing the tool, they didn't understand or know what to do with the assessment data. For example, a middle school math teacher felt that teachers at his school lacked the expertise to understand how to use data and feared that data might not be properly interpreted. Instead of using the standardized data, some of these teachers prefer to generate their own data to monitor student learning, usually through assessments they develop.

Next Steps

A number of different initiatives are under way that will give the TUSD community access to even more data. Principals and teachers believe that a student's mastery of performance objectives, measured by an annual state test, does not provide a clear picture of how to help the student. Differentiated instruction requires specific, frequent assessment to monitor learning. In the fall of 2006, the district implemented benchmark assessments in reading and math to complement the writing prompts. Included in this implementation are specific, structured interventions based on the data so that students are given the support they need immediately. The State of Arizona has passed a law requiring that reading assessments be administered to all students three times a year in Grades K–3. The district adopted the Dynamic Indicators of Basic Early Literacy Skills (DIBELS) as the measure of progress in early-reading strategies. Both of these data sets will be available on TUSDstats. TUSD is adopting the technology developed by Wireless Generation (see http://www.wirelessgeneration.com) to deliver the DIBELS on handheld computers (see Hupert, Heinze, Gunn, & Stewart, chapter 8). The handhelds enable the immediate administration, scoring, and analysis of the assessment, as well as offering web-based technology that facilitates flexible aggregation and examination of student-, class-, school-, and district-level data.

Teachers currently use a grade application at the middle and high schools to track their traditional grades. The district is moving to enable teachers to automatically load grades and grade-book assignments daily on the parental-access page of TUSDstats. The district also plans to give students access to data. Students will be issued an email address—sponsored, monitored, and organized by the district—with which to log onto TUSDstats and see the same information that parents can view.

IDEAL: **Arizona's State Data Warehouse**

Arizona has moved toward state involvement in data-driven decision making. The Arizona Department of Education has developed IDEAL (Integrated Data to Enhance Arizona's Learning; http://www.ideal.ade.az.gov), an online information system providing access to educational data, resources, and services, including combined statewide student data currently stored in distinct databases. Users are provided a customized screen with relevant information based on their access permissions. IDEAL also contains information and resources about state standards, formative assessments, AIMS, and instructional/tutoring resources focused on AIMS. The intent of IDEAL is to assist small districts in data collection, interrogation, and instructional interface. IDEAL's link to TUSD and how it will be implemented in the district remains to be determined. TUSD in fact may take a leadership role in its implementation, just as the district played a crucial role, through Mojave, in the development of the statewide attendance-reporting system.

SYSTEMS MAPPING OF TUSD'S DATA CULTURE

Our project has used systems thinking (Mandinach, 2005; Mandinach & Cline, 1994) as an analytical tool to examine the interconnections among components in complex systems such as school districts. Systems mapping allows us to depict the factors influencing the creation of a data culture in our six sites, how those factors interact, and their relative importance.

Figure 12.3 shows TUSD's data culture and leadership with its vision as a surround. Also depicted are external components that influence the district.

We began our research by examining the technology-based tools, the data warehouse, TUSDstats, and the student information system, Mojave. Both TUSDstats and Mojave were constructed with particular tool characteristics and functionalities, as described above. The data that reside in these tools themselves, in addition to the tool characteristics and the tools, influence how the data are used and ultimately the district's data culture. The state accountability measures help shape the data characteristics residing in Tucson's two systems, as do the district-level accountability measures, such as the quarterly benchmark assessments. TUSD has been at the forefront of developing systems and therefore has helped the Arizona State Department of Education construct and implement its information system. Thus, there is a reciprocal influence between the state and the district in terms of the technological infrastructure.

Leadership within the district consists of the typical three levels. The superintendent and central administration espouse the vision of a data-centered culture. It is at the building level, however, that leadership plays the most important role. Principals make things happen. If a principal is data

Figure 12.3. Systems Map of TUSD's Data Culture

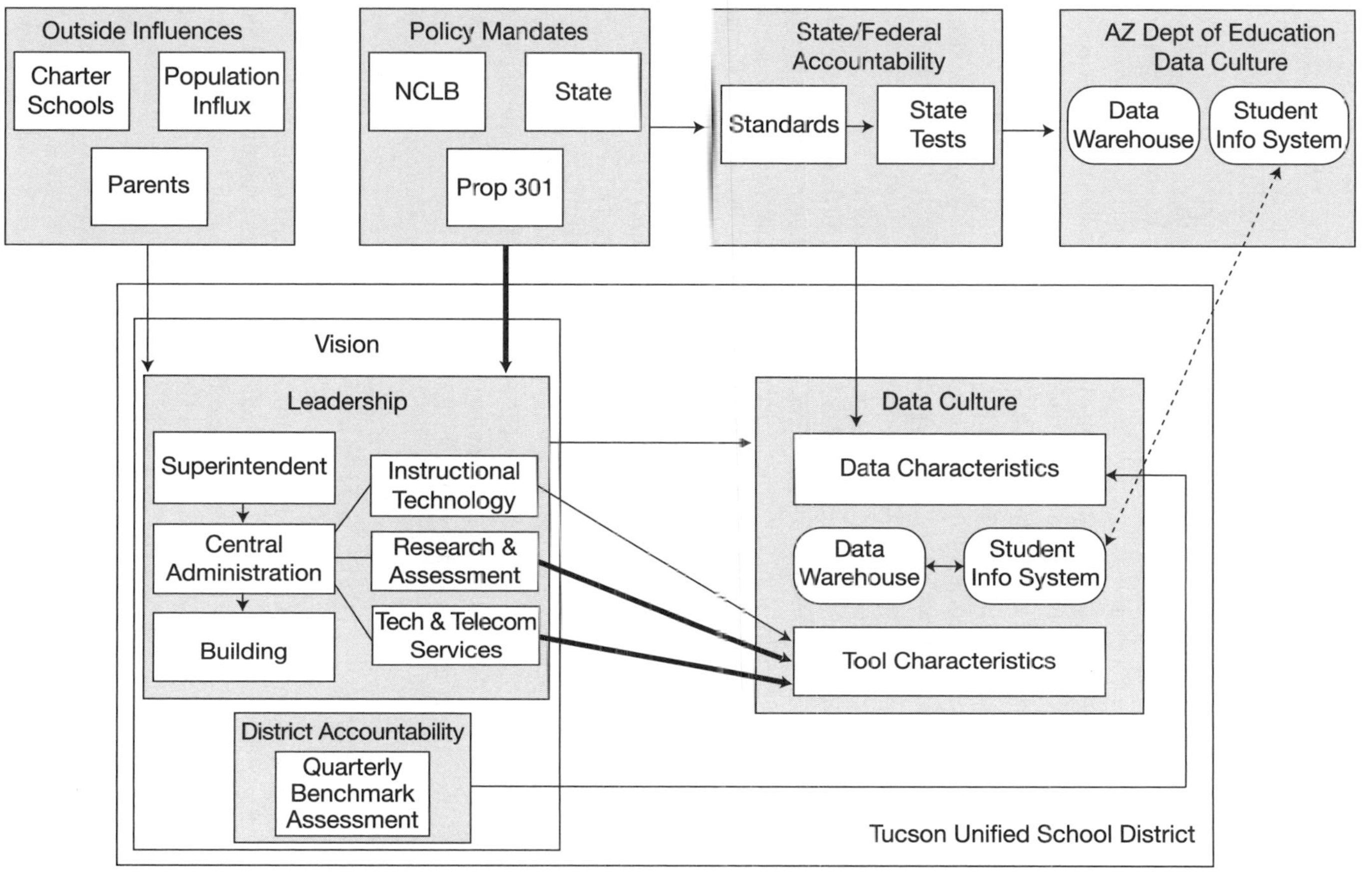

savvy and models the use of data in everyday activities, teachers in that school are more likely to appreciate the need for data and embrace the same philosophy. If a principal does not rely on data and is not data savvy, teachers and staff interpret that to mean that using data is of no importance. Principals set the tone and teachers take their cues accordingly.

Within Tucson's central administration reside three departments that have been tasked with the development, maintenance, and training around data-driven decision making and the technology-based tools. The Research and Assessment Department developed TUSDstats and its predecessor. Technology and Telecommunication Services developed and maintains Mojave. The Instructional Technology Department provides professional development and on-site assistance and training for both TUSDstats and Mojave. These three departments directly impact how the tool characteristics have been developed and deployed. Another component within the district that promotes data use is district accountability, a result of district leadership and vision.

Districts do not exist in isolation. We identified four types of external factors influencing TUSD: policy mandates, outside influences, federal and state accountability measures, and the Arizona Department of Education's data culture. Federal and state policy mandates strongly impact the district. TUSD must function within the guidelines of NCLB, Arizona LEARNS, and Proposition 301. Outside influences such as the charter school issue, the huge population influx to Tucson, parents, and other stakeholders also shape and impact the actions of district administration. State and federal accountability (e.g., the standards and tests) directly impact the types of data that are available and how they are accommodated in terms of the tools that support interrogation of the data. A final component is the Arizona State Department of Education's data culture. As mentioned above, the department launched IDEAL and also requires districts to upload attendance data to its student information system daily.

LINKING TUSD TO THE CONCEPTUAL FRAMEWORK

Our work in TUSD has helped us refine the conceptual framework for data-driven decision making that Mandinach and colleagues presented in chapter 2. Although the policy mandates cause educators to deal with data in an effective and efficient manner, TUSDstats and Mojave no doubt have had a huge impact on and facilitated the spread of a data culture throughout TUSD. Many teachers, staff, and administrators look to the technology-based tools as a vehicle for helping them interrogate data when seeking answers to questions and solutions to problems. Such data interrogation occurs at the classroom, building, and district level. Our observations of TUSD data use indicate that there is a progression and transformation from data to information, and ultimately to actionable knowledge, just as is depicted in the conceptual framework. Data are only as meaningful as the interpretation that arises from investigating them and the actions that result from connecting interpretation to a specific context.

To depict the link between our experiences in TUSD and the conceptual framework, we offer an explicit example of how TUSD personnel transformed data into actionable knowledge. This example focuses on TUSD's concern about losing students to local charter schools. As mentioned above, a large number of children leave TUSD annually to enroll in charters, significantly decreasing revenue to the district. The superintendent wanted to isolate where the outflow of students was occurring and try to understand the reasons.

A query was sent to the Assessment and Research Department to examine data on student transfers to charters. To run the cohort analyses, the researchers first had to *collect* the necessary data on transfers, enrollments, and re-enrollments over time and then *organize* the data into manageable entities. That was the first step in the conceptual framework, enabling the transformation of data into information. Researchers then *analyzed* the information resulting from each cohort run on transfers and enrollments. They then *summarized* that information. This process was followed by the production of *syntheses* of findings. Staff concatenated the accumulated information into a usable entity. The syntheses enabled staff to *prioritize* and transform the information into usable knowledge. In this case the results of this transformation of data into usable knowledge indicated that: (a) many students leave TUSD at the end of elementary school and transfer to charters; (b) the transfers disproportionately leave elementary schools and affect the middle schools those students would have attended; (c) middle schools in close proximity to the charters are more likely to be underenrolled than middle schools with no charters nearby; and (d) many of the students who transferred after elementary school returned to TUSD for high school, stating that the charters failed to provide the desired educational opportunities.

The answers extracted from the data interrogation led to a district-wide effort to help stem the outflow of students leaving for the charters. The district is working with the most severely affected elementary and middle schools to improve articulation and serve their parents and students more effectively. Further data are being collected to determine how the district can better serve its stakeholders, with the expectation that TUSD middle schools can be made more attractive to parents and students.

The original data interrogation identified some of the sources of student outflow, but additional data have enabled the district to isolate further causes and potential solutions that can be implemented. Thus, an iterative feedback loop has been established, beginning with data, initial findings, a decision about next steps, then actions and assessments of impacts, and it continues with additional data collection, decisions, and implementation. Such iterations are normal, rational ways to proceed. No complex decision is linear, but instead relies on feedback loops indicating where further data must be collected, information analyzed, or knowledge prioritized, before a decision can be made and implemented and the outcomes observed. In the case of TUSD's charter school problem, administrators will need to undertake several iterations through the data-driven, decision-making process before their desired outcome can be achieved.

CONCLUDING REMARKS: BENEFITS AND CHALLENGES OF A HOMEGROWN SYSTEM

Choosing homegrown technology enabled TUSD to customize the warehouse to the specific needs of the district and its stakeholders. The custom fitting continues to this day. The district has been able to respond to NCLB and state policies and to make changes to TUSDstats to reflect new assessment and reporting requirements. Users are encouraged to call the developers to ask questions, and they have praised the quality of the support provided by the developers. One principal remarked that principals have opportunities to give feedback and talk to the developers about their needs, and the developers respond by customizing the systems.

Despite the benefits, the two homegrown systems have created some challenges. The two systems were developed by two separate departments within the district. There has been some confusion among district personnel about the roles of the systems and the responsibilities of the departments that support and maintain the systems. Issues often in contention include: What data belong in which system, who is responsible for gathering the data, and what data need to be shared?

In terms of data use, administrators use TUSDstats much more than teachers. This is partly a professional development issue, as the district has concentrated on providing training and data-analysis support to administrators. Teachers are more familiar and comfortable with Mojave because of the state's attendance-reporting requirements. Although some teachers still do not fully grasp the instructional benefits of interrogating data through TUSDstats, their use of the quarterly writing scores sheds light on the type of data they find relevant to their practice. These data are collected, scored, and entered into TUSDstats by teachers and they jointly analyze the data. These data are linked to instruction; therefore, teachers see their immediate relevance to inform classroom practice. It will be interesting to trace the continuing evolution of system use as increasing accountability mandates pressure teachers to use data to make informed instructional decisions, and TUSD provides more benchmark assessments like the writing prompts in other subject areas.

Many lessons can be learned from the experiences of TUSD. First, the decision to develop a homegrown data warehouse is complex and requires the appropriate investments of financial and human resources. Few commercial options existed when the district chose to develop its warehouse. For TUSD, now a leader in the field, the decision has worked well. The district developed the internal capacity to maintain and improve its data systems while working on ways to educate and encourage users at all levels to use data appropriately. TUSD has recognized that in addition to having the right technologies in place, staff need to know how to access and interface with the warehouse and also need to be conversant with data-inquiry skills. Appropriately targeted professional development opportunities are necessary, and all staff need to recognize the importance of data use.

Today, many commercial warehouse options are available, and few districts may choose to undertake a large development process. However, we can appreciate the pioneering work Tucson and other districts like Broward have undertaken, and we can reap valuable lessons from their experiences as other districts consider the decision to build or to buy. In addition, Tucson has set an excellent example of how to provide professional development opportunities for administrators and to create a data culture in which administrators communicate the importance of data-driven decision making throughout the district. More targeted professional development for teachers is an important next step. Once teachers have the necessary data skills and recognize the connection to instructional practice, data-driven decision making should become an essential, integrated pedagogical tool.

NOTE

The research on which this paper is based has been funded by the National Science Foundation under Grant No. REC 03356653. Any opinions, findings, and conclusions or recommendations expressed in this material are those of the authors and do not necessarily reflect the views of the National Science Foundation.

REFERENCES

Ackley, D. (2001). Data analysis demystified. *Leadership, 31*(2), 28–29, 37–38.

Ackoff, R. L. (1989). From data to wisdom. *Journal of Applied Systems Analysis, 16*, 3–9.

Arnott, D. (1998). A framework for understanding decision support systems evolution. In B. Edmundson & D. Wilson (Eds.), *Proceedings of the ninth Australasian conference on information systems* (pp. 1–13). Sydney, Australia: University of New South Wales.

Consortium for School Networking. (2005). *From vision to action: How school districts use data to improve performance.* Washington, DC: Author.

Drucker, P. F. (1989). *The new realities: In government and politics/in economics and business/in society and world view.* New York: Harper & Row.

Feldman, M. S., & March, J. G. (1988). Information in organizations as signal and symbol. In J. G. March (Ed.), *Decision and organizations* (pp. 409–428). Oxford: Basil Blackwell.

Gorry, A., & Scott-Morton, M. (1971, Fall). A framework for information systems. *Sloan Management Review, 13,* 56–79.

Lehman, M. M. (1990). Uncertainty in computer application. *Communications of the Association of Computing Machinery, 33*(5), 584–586.

Light, D., Wexler, D. H., & Heinze, J. (2004, April). *Keeping teachers in the center: A framework of data-driven decision making.* Paper presented at the annual meeting of the American Educational Research Association, San Diego, CA.

Love, N., Stiles, K. E., Mundry, S., & DiRanna, K. (in press). *A data coach's guide to closing achievement gaps: Unleashing the power of collaborative inquiry.* Thousand Oaks, CA: Corwin Press.

Mandinach, E. B. (2005). The development of effective evaluation methods for e-learning: A concept paper and action plan. *Teachers College Record, 107*(8), 1814–1835.

Mandinach, E. B., & Cline, H. F. (1994). *Classroom dynamics: Implementing a technology based learning environment.* Hillsdale, NJ: Erlbaum.

Mandinach, E. B., Honey, M., Light, D., Heinze, J., & Rivas, L. (2005, November–December). *Technology-based tools that facilitate data-driven instructional decision making.* Paper presented at the ICCE Conference, Singapore.

Militello, M. (2005, April). *Too much information: A case study of assessment and accountability in an urban school district.* Paper presented at the annual meeting of the American Educational Research Association, Montreal.

No Child Left Behind Act of 2001. (2001). Retrieved September 13, 2005, from http://www.nclb.gov

NWREL. (n.d). *6+1 trait writing scoring guide.* Retrieved October 17, 2005, from http://www.nwrel.org/assessment/scoring.php

Sarmiento, J. (n.d.). *Technology tools for analysis of achievement data: An introductory guide for educational leaders.* Retrieved March 7, 2004, from http://www.temple.edu/lss

Spielvogel, R., & Pasnik, S. (1999). *From the school room to the state house: Data warehouse solutions for informed decision making in education.* New York: EDC Center for Children and Technology.

Stein, M. (2003). *Making sense of the data: Overview of the K–12 data management and analysis market.* Boston: Eduventures.

Stringfield, S., Wayman, J. C., & Yakimowski-Srebnick, M. (2005). Scaling up data use in classrooms, schools, and districts. In C. Dede, J. P. Honan, & L. C. Peters (Eds.), *Scaling up success: Lessons learned from technology-based educational improvement* (pp. 133–152). San Francisco: Jossey-Bass.

Wayman, J. C. (2005). Involving teachers in data-driven decision making: Using computer data systems to support teacher inquiry and reflection. *Journal of Education for Students Placed at Risk, 10*(3), 295–308.

Wayman, J. C., Stringfield, S., & Yakimowski, M. (2004). *Software enabling school improvement through analysis of student data* (CRESPAR Tech. Rep. No. 67). Baltimore: Johns Hopkins University.

CHAPTER 13

Models of Data-Based Decision Making: A Case Study of the Milwaukee Public Schools

Liane Moody & Chris Dede

The recent focus on accountability testing in public schools has driven increasing efforts to use assessment data for school decision making. The most basic claim made by all versions of data-based decision making (DBDM) is that collecting and analyzing education data—particularly at the classroom and school level—provide valuable information that can lead to educational improvement. However, all DBDM policies and tools are not alike in their implications for school-based educators. The nature of the benefits that accrue, the types of data considered fruitful, and the processes for collection and analysis are often very different across implementations. In addition to these structural differences, policies and tools can be grouped according to the levels of professional autonomy and freedom to make judgments each grants to teachers. Supporting the professional autonomy of teachers is an important, if underused, strategy for school improvement. As the frontline workers in education, teachers are an essential part of any successful school reform and bring a unique perspective to the interpretation of school data. DBDM policies and tools that allow teachers the freedom to interpret school data, and make their own judgments about changes in teaching practice, can encourage greater teacher buy-in to school improvement efforts.

By documenting and categorizing the ways in which data-based decision making is used for reform in one urban district, this case study contrasts competing models of DBDM to illustrate the tensions created when a focus on school data is used to address multiple, sometimes divergent purposes. We argue that the most useful function of DBDM is in providing teachers and school-based administrators with the tools and freedom to interpret school data. By engaging practitioners in an examination of teaching practice and its outcomes, DBDM has the potential to empower school staff to build a form of internal accountability that we believe is necessary to create and sustain school improvement.

Data for this case study were collected between 2002 and 2004 and include interviews and informal discussions with the Milwaukee Public School (MPS) District and school staff, as well as observations at schools and district offices. In addition, we examined 2 years of transcripts from online professional development courses on DBDM offered to Milwaukee practitioners, as well as any district or school documents we identified as related to these initiatives.

Our study found that the many tools and initiatives supporting DBDM in Milwaukee demonstrate a lack of shared understanding of data-based decision making as a reform at the district level. This lack of agreement has led to a fracturing of the district's efforts to support this type of work. Nonetheless, the work being done in Milwaukee suggests that DBDM holds great promise as a reform because it requires collaboration between departments that traditionally have been isolated in school districts. For Milwaukee, the remaining major challenge is not technical, because much of the technological infrastructure to support DBDM is already in place, but is the need to create understanding and buy-in among practitioners.

DBDM AND PRACTITIONER RELATIONSHIP
TO SCHOOL DATA

Schools today produce large amounts of information on student learning (e.g., standardized test scores, classroom-based assessments, student written work, teacher notes, etc.). It is these "data" that DBDM initiatives seek to harness to support school improvement. In some cases, the use of DBDM is a policy that is set at the district level. In other cases, individual schools or teachers use data independently to inform their decision making. In either case, the implementation of DBDM initiatives is always at the school site.

The use of data to support decision making requires that data be collected, analyzed, and interpreted. During interpretation, judgments are made about the meaning of the analyzed data and they become a form of knowledge that can guide action at the school site. DBDM initiatives differ from traditional uses of school data because school administrators and teachers, individuals who previously were excluded from data interpretation, are responsible for performing the interpretation of data to create usable knowledge.

Classroom teachers have a long history of estrangement from the knowledge generated by their work. Categorized as the "doers" rather than the "thinkers" in the educational professions, teachers traditionally have been assigned an inferior status to educational researchers when it comes to the production of educational knowledge (Lagemann, 2000). The lack of what

Lortie (2002) calls a "technical subculture" in the teaching profession has resulted in a form of "intellectual dependency" among teachers in which knowledge about effective teaching practice is codified primarily by researchers outside the school building. Indeed, researchers have so dominated the process of translating educational data into knowledge that any knowledge generated at the school site is considered inferior or lacking in objectivity. As Cochran-Smith and Lytle argue in their book *Inside/Outside: Teacher Research and Knowledge* (1993), "high-status" research produced in the academies has created barriers to legitimacy for knowledge generated by teachers about their own work.

We believe that DBDM in schools has the potential to redistribute the power inherent in knowledge production to those at the front lines of the educational profession (Cochran-Smith & Lytle, 1993; Kallick & Wilson, 2000). By engaging teachers in a process of interpretation by which data become meaningful, DBDM endorses the legitimacy of knowledge created by school practitioners and implies a level of autonomy in school decision making. Ensuring greater professional autonomy for teachers not only recognizes the unique skills and information teachers have about their students' learning, but helps teachers become invested as important actors in the process of school improvement.

Whether through training or practice with data over time, in our experience, teachers who are empowered in this way gain a firmer understanding of the practice and limits of research methods. This understanding helps practitioners turn a critical eye on their own and others' research. As teachers understand more about the limits of what data can tell us, they are able to make better judgments for their own classrooms.

In our work with public school districts implementing DBDM, we found that not all policies for DBDM support the growth of professional autonomy. Rather, various models of DBDM create very different experiences for school-based staff. In order to understand better the district's DBDM work and its effect on school practitioners, we developed a provisional framework of three models based on the different purposes to which DBDM is put: DBDM for Accountability, DBDM for School Improvement, and DBDM as Reflective Process. As a whole, these models represent a movement from standardization to uniqueness, from strict to loose definitions of data, and from external to internal accountability (see Table 13.1).

DBDM FOR ACCOUNTABILITY

DBDM for Accountability focuses on the importance of data as evidence or proof of responsible action on the part of school staff. Underlying this model of DBDM are notions of external accountability promoted in policies, such

Table 13.1. Three Models of DBDM

	Types of Data Valued	Purpose of DBDM	Effect on School Site
DBDM for Accountability	Standardized assessment data	Focus is on *products* that demonstrate accountable action (e.g., AYP calculations, school improvement plans).	Encourages standardized solutions to school improvement by emphasizing external forms of accountability; supports teaching to the test; creates a culture of blame focused on "weaknesses" uncovered in the data.
DBDM for School Improvement	Standardized assessment data, formative assessment data, and other "hard" data from the school site (such as demographic data)	Focus is on in-depth data *analysis* from which solutions will arise; emphasis on compiling lots of data and performing "deep" analysis to understand school problems (e.g., root-cause analysis, assessment-item analysis).	Encourages large amounts of data work focused on finding solutions to school problems; data work is often carried out by an individual or small group, and meanings and interpretations of data findings are often dictated to school staff.
DBDM as Reflective Process	All assessment data, demographic data, perception data, and all sources of information including "soft" data (such as teacher intuition)	Focus is on a *process* of reflection; data do not provide solutions, but serve as a way to ground meaningful discussions around practice.	Encourages schools to define their own problems and solutions leading to unique strategies and goals at school sites; conversation and reflection about practice are normal parts of an improvement process.

as the No Child Left Behind Act (NCLB), which dictate the type of data that matter. In the case of NCLB that means standardized assessments. By sanctioning schools that fail to demonstrate appropriate performance on that measure, NCLB also attempts implicitly to ensure that instructional and administrative decisions are made on the basis of those scores. Policies in the DBDM for Accountability model attempt to use data to hold schools and their staff accountable to outside authorities. Consequences tied to performance data represent an attempt by external sources to influence what goes on in the classroom.

DBDM for Accountability policies function to standardize schools more in the sense that all schools under their jurisdiction are expected to focus on the same measures of improvement and cannot create and respond to their own values. For example, NCLB pressures schools to concentrate on classroom subjects (reading and mathematics) that are the priority of the policymakers. Extra instructional time given to those areas often comes at the expense of untested areas. As a result, a school that traditionally has excelled in science may be forced to realign its resources to reflect a view of curricular priorities that it does not share.

This model of DBDM often leads to "teaching to the test" rather than teaching the broader curriculum that the test represents, because the policies giving rise to this perspective designate a single type of data as the measure of achievement and focus on compliance as opposed to formative feedback for instructional improvement. Far from promoting practitioner autonomy, such uses of DBDM function as watchdogs over schools and, therefore, often are met with resistance from teachers when promoted at the school level. Under this model, the emphasis is not on the *process* by which teachers and school administrators use data to support their decision making, but instead on the end product as embodied in test scores.

In the Milwaukee Public School District, this model of DBDM appears most strikingly in requirements for school improvement plans that, until recently, were not reviewed at the district level. Instead these documents were simply a product to demonstrate responsible action by the school, a fact not lost on school staff. District staff informed us that often the data analyses had no correspondence to the other parts of the plan. Far from being meaningful at the school site, school administrators regarded the compilation of data analyses as a burden grudgingly fulfilled and rarely revisited afterward.

Another example of DBDM for Accountability that we observed in MPS is a district-distributed data report on standardized test scores that specifically identifies "bubble kids" who are near the cutoff line for passing, encouraging schools to focus on those students to improve school performance on external accountability measures. Such district-created reports communicate that reaching a certain passing rate is the only important measure of school effectiveness. Rather than encouraging discussion about school goals and effectiveness, such representations of data suggest their own solutions and can lead to questionable school practices such as warehousing children who either have passed the test or are far below passing levels.

DBDM FOR SCHOOL IMPROVEMENT

DBDM for School Improvement is similar to the first type in its emphasis on accountability. However, this model is more school-centered, moving from an externally mandated focus on a particular set of high-stakes data to a school-based process by which schools themselves address challenges posed by external authorities. Data are seen not merely as evidence of responsible action by school staff, but also as a tool by which schools can diagnose problems that lead to poor performance. While school goals are still set externally, districts that embrace DBDM for School Improvement encourage schools to engage in data analysis to diagnose student learning problems. This model of DBDM is the most common and includes most initiatives where DBDM is mandated outside the school.

DBDM for School Improvement policies engage teachers and school administrators in the analysis and display of data to find answers to school problems. The focus on using data as diagnostic tools allows schools to explore other, school-generated data sources, often in the form of formative assessments aligned with curriculum standards and high-stakes tests. However, as with the previous model, politicians determine relatively narrow measures of quality. Such policies communicate to schools a preference for "hard" data and a disdain for teachers' intuitions about educational processes and outcomes that are harder to quantify. While not meeting the rigor of standardized data sources, such "soft" data contain valuable information on student learning that is not often brought to data discussions.

Widespread use of this model of DBDM can be seen in the many "cookbook"-type resources marketed to schools for using data. For example, Bernhardt describes the "power" of such data analysis in her book *Data Analysis for Comprehensive Schoolwide Improvement*.

> Data can help identify and uncover powerful solutions to schools' biggest problems. I believe that we have to look deeper than we are used to looking to get to analyses that make the difference. What I am professing is to take the data available to most schools and torture it until it confesses. (1998, p. xii)

As Bernhardt's statement exemplifies, this view endorses the idea that data will reveal the "solutions," and the right analyses will "make the difference." In this model, the data and their analysis are the source of value, and schools that dig deep enough will uncover comprehensive and workable solutions to problems of educational improvement. One principal we worked with explained that DBDM initiatives of this type often lead school staff to become "data happy." She described how teachers and administrators sometimes become convinced that collecting more and different types of data and performing multiple forms of analysis will solve school problems. The data and their analysis are overemphasized as the way to increase educational effectiveness at the expense of ideas and judgments of teachers and school administrators.

A concern raised by the DBDM for School Improvement model is whether those who participate in these initiatives in schools are properly skilled to carry out and interpret statistical analyses of educational data. Because analysis is the key to finding solutions, the skill level of teachers and school administrators becomes important if they are to be successful. Our work with schools using data has revealed some problematic practices. For example, small numbers of students in schools and classrooms can make attempts to disaggregate scores at the school level misleading if not inappropriate. Also, making inferences based on single items from standardized tests is difficult, despite its popularity in some districts, because of measurement error and the complexity of most items (Price & Koretz, 2005). If solutions to school problems reside in data analysis, as this model suggests, it is imperative that practitioners be trained well enough to find them.

Online discussions among Milwaukee practitioners who were new proponents of DBDM demonstrate this type of faith in data as the solution to school problems. Many schools and individuals that "buy into" data-based decision making initially hold this view, often searching out as many "hard" data sources (e.g., standardized test scores, school records, etc.) as possible in the belief that the route to school improvement can be found in the analysis of data. While school staff retain some autonomy, external sources such as district administration or even politicians define "valid" data and "meaningful" questions, and teachers and school administrators involved in analyzing data often lose confidence in their ability to interpret data correctly.

DBDM AS REFLECTIVE PROCESS

The third model, DBDM as Reflective Process, calls for the creation of internal accountability focused on the professional capacity of school staff. In this model, DBDM is a reflective process by which teachers work collaboratively to examine their practice. Reflection in this context includes the interpretation of data to create knowledge, but emphasizes the importance of teacher perspectives and intuitions in the process. In DBDM as Reflective Process, what counts as "data" is expanded to include any "soft" information that can serve to start conversations about teaching practice.

Unlike DBDM for School Improvement, in this model the process of collaboration and reflection is more important than the data and their analysis. Data analysis itself does not provide final solutions, but the process of looking at the data is inherently valuable in creating a reflective school culture (Boudett, City, & Murnane, 2005). This model would include protocols of looking at student assignments used in some districts in which teachers gather in small groups to look at samples of their students' work. The quality of the assignments considered "data" in these protocols is not as important as the reflection that they promote. Because collaboration and reflection—rather than the "right" analysis—are the goal of these policies and initiatives, teacher training in research methods is less critical. When "hard" and "soft" data sources are seen simply as information to guide conversations, there is less danger of any one source of data being given too much importance.

For schools using DBDM as Reflective Process, external mandates like NCLB do not determine actions; instead, accountability policies become challenges that inspire internal reflection and modification. This model opens up interpretation of data to the school and empowers staff not only to respond to problems defined by those exterior to the school, but also to redefine their own priorities. For example, a school practicing this type of DBDM may decide that the state standardized test does not address the type of critical-thinking skills it values most. Rather than simply being dictated to by an external policy, such schools could create and analyze their own assessments (or student portfolios) to ensure that a focus on standardized tests does not detract from their school goals. This ability to define their own priorities is important in order for school practitioners to see data as useful tools rather than instruments of blame. When the analysis of data serves goals that teachers and school administrators have set for themselves, it is more readily accepted as a useful process.

As the decision-making process becomes wholly located in and dictated by the school, each school uses its unique local understandings to meet the challenges it faces. For example, while one school may determine from its analysis of data that more after-school tutoring is needed to address student learning needs, another with similar data might institute a new type of professional development for teachers to accomplish the same goal. In this model, DBDM leads to less standardization and more local ownership of school-improvement work. Such lack of standardization implies that some schools will find and employ better solutions than others. This represents a dilemma for districts that embrace local ownership of DBDM processes.

WHICH FORM OF DBDM IS MOST EFFECTIVE?

We believe that DBDM as Reflective Process is the model of data-based decision making that holds the most promise. In *The Reflective Practitioner* (1983), Schon demonstrated the importance of reflection on practice as a means of dealing with the uncertain environment in classrooms. He and other educational scholars have supported the idea of "teacher as researcher" as a powerful means of professional development for teachers as well as a source of school improvement (see Blase & Blase, 1994; Cochran-Smith & Lytle, 1993; Kallick & Wilson, 2000; Stoll, 1992; York-Barr, Sommers, Ghere, & Montie, 2001).

In their development of a "practice-based" theory of teacher education, Ball and Cohen (1999) support an inquiry stance into practice that involves "continuing thoughtful discussion" among teachers. As Ball and Cohen point out, this work of critical reflection is important in empowering teachers to make meaning of their own practice in order to make their instruction more effective.

> The more teachers developed methods of professional inquiry, articulated ways of knowing, and determined standards for knowledge in practice, the more teachers would have interpretive power, which could contribute to improving both their own teaching and their own and others' learning. (1999, p. 16)

The focus on the teacher as researcher emphasizes the role of teachers as interpreters of data within an ongoing discussion around practice. While an increase in statistical skills remains important for practitioners, the real developmental task that this model of DBDM promotes is a changing relationship to knowledge production. Such a change is perhaps most visible in the increased confidence level and engagement of teachers in data-based discussions.

While the literature more often discusses the role of teachers in this work, school administrators also can be empowered through participation in reflective process. In his work on school leadership, *Cultivating Leadership in Schools* (2001), Donaldson explains the role that school administrators play in these thoughtful discussions, both as participants whose different perspectives add to the discussion, and as facilitators who ask probing questions about practice and provide the time and support for those conversations to occur. A model of DBDM that is grounded in promoting such reflection supports professional autonomy throughout the school building by granting teachers and administrators the role of meaning makers for their profession.

These ideas about reflective process seldom are discussed in conjunction with DBDM. Typically, public understandings of data-based decision making are consistent with the models we've called DBDM for Accountability and DBDM for School Improvement, both of which endorse a theory of technical rationality that emphasizes solutions and rational planning over reflection. However, the technological gains we have made in collecting and distributing formative data in real time enable school staff to engage in a process of reflection and interpretation of data that was previously the exclusive province of outside officials (politicians or district administrators) or researchers. By moving the power to interpret from outside to inside the school, DBDM can help develop a type of internal accountability that builds ownership of school-improvement work. In their work on "inquiry-minded" schools, Rallis and MacMullen (2000) discuss how educators who engage in ongoing collaborative questioning of their effectiveness develop an internal accountability that enables them both to respond to measures of accountability imposed externally and to meet their own needs for growth. For example, internal accountability is demonstrated when a school, not satisfied with success as defined by the state accountability policy, carries out an inquiry process aimed at achieving student learning goals that exceed those dictated by the state. This is the type of empowerment that DBDM as Reflective Process seeks to achieve.

While much of the DBDM use we've observed in schools corresponds to the other models identified (DBDM for Accountability and DBDM for School Improvement), our examination of current work in the Milwaukee Public Schools shows an evolution in the use of data in schools and programs that is moving toward a more collaborative, reflective reform strategy. Below, we examine the conditions that make the MPS a promising site for the development of DBDM as a model of collaborative practice, and discuss the challenges this district faces in aligning its resources to support this work.

What separates the MPS from other school districts is the extensive technological infrastructure and impressive array of technological tools available to support DBDM. Whereas in recent years other districts have found themselves struggling to address the technology and data needs generated by policies like NCLB, in MPS the technological infrastructure was already in place.

Like many urban districts, MPS has changed leadership frequently and suffered the instability arising from changing priorities and agendas. Public education in Milwaukee was notably politicized by heated debate over the issue of vouchers and school choice (see Hess, 2002). Despite the subsequent political turmoil, a succession of superintendents starting in 1991 (with the appointment of Howard Fuller) up through the tenure of Spence Korte (who left the position in 2002) supported strategic investments in technology and partnerships with local businesses. These investments resulted in a sophisticated, reliable technological infrastructure that is just now being put to extensive use (Dede & Nelson, 2005).

In their case study of the evolution of technology usage in MPS, Dede and Nelson document how Superintendent Howard Fuller (1991–1995) and his successor Robert Jasna (1995–1999) created important relationships with local corporations and benefited from their advice in implementing technology to support MPS's business processes. In addition, Jasna instituted a new Department of Technology at MPS, which won grants to support technology investment, leading to the creation of district-level technology tools, investment in a data warehouse, and construction of an extensive network infrastructure connecting all the schools in the district.

With the latest change in the superintendency, in 2002, the focus on building a technological infrastructure shifted to putting that infrastructure to work. William Andrekopoulos, who began his tenure as superintendent in 2002, has publicly stressed the need for all schools to develop an effective educational plan that includes a "needs assessment" (Andrekopoulos, 2003). As described by the district-wide educational plan, a needs assessment requires analyzing district-wide assessment data, school-based data, and other data, including attendance, retentions, suspensions, and truancy rates (Milwaukee Public Schools, 2003–2004). In addition, schools are asked to analyze perception and demographic data for parents, students, and staff. The needs assessment is intended to inform a strategic planning process articulated in both action plans and a professional development plan submitted to the district. The district's tools and technology infrastructure, created earlier, allow schools to conduct the type of in-depth data analysis envisioned for the needs assessment. Further, funding sources, such as Enhancing Education Through Technology (E2T2) grants, are beginning to provide professional development in DBDM to Milwaukee school-based staff.

TECHNOLOGICAL TOOLS FOR DBDM IN THE MILWAUKEE PUBLIC SCHOOLS

This is an exciting time to be teaching in MPS because, unlike ever before, MPS teachers can see data—both standardized test data and previous teachers' classroom assessment data—on the computer screen in their classroom for the students that they are *currently* teaching. Reports like the MPA and SPS give teachers a much higher level of access than they have ever had.

Anne Knackert, MPS School Technology Support

Using technology, MPS has created four distinct tools—the MPA, Brio, the Student Promotion System, and the School Climate Survey—that make data accessible to staff at all levels in the classroom, the school, and the district, and assist staff in displaying those data. This supportive infrastructure set the stage for DBDM to be conducted in a meaningful way.

The MPA

The most basic MPS DBDM tool, the MPA, was created by the Milwaukee Partnership Academy (MPA), a partnership between the MPS and a number of community organizations. This tool is an online application that creates printable reports of standardized assessment data specifically designed for three sets of users: schools, teachers, and parents. These reports break down student performance on standardized tests into skill areas to help pinpoint student strengths and weaknesses. In addition to assessment information, the Parent Report contains strategies and resources for parents based on their child's demonstrated weaknesses, as well as a general set of remarks from the principal.

The School and Class Reports summarize standardized assessment data at their respective aggregate levels. District staff reported that the School

Report was designed to help schools determine whether their educational plan was on track. The Class Report was intended to help teachers identify "bubble kids"—students very close to passing sections of the test. For many in the research community, the latter use of DBDM is controversial. Nonetheless, the type of information conveyed in these reports is understandably of great interest to schools for which the cutoff line for passing holds consequences. Understanding the intention behind the design of these reports and tools reveals a particular model of DBDM—in this case, DBDM for Accountability—at work in the district and communicated through the technology itself. The E2T2 grant encourages teachers to move from information on "bubble kids" to looking more closely at the individual reports, called the Student Score Profile (see Figure 13.1). In addition, a potentially inappropriate focus on "bubble kids"

Figure 13.1. MPA Sample Student Score Profile

Student Score Profile for Jamie Goodwin

Pupil Number: 0000007

Address: 2222 Main Street
                    Milwaukee, WI 53218

School: Sunnydale School
Grade: 07

Scale Scores

Test Date	Subject	Grade	Test Type	Score
Nov 01, 2002	Reading	06	Terra Nova	670
Nov 01, 2002	Language Arts	06	Terra Nova	696
Nov 01, 2002	Math	06	Terra Nova	640
Feb 01, 2002	Reading	04	WKCE	659
Feb 01, 2002	Language Arts	04	WKCE	669
Feb 01, 2002	Math	04	WKCE	672
Feb 01, 2002	Science	04	WKCE	626
Feb 01, 2002	Social Studies	04	WKCE	659
Mar 01, 2002	Reading	03	WRCT	63
Feb 01, 2002	Reading	03	Terra Nova	673
Feb 01, 2002	Language Arts	03	Terra Nova	665
Feb 01, 2002	Math	03	Terra Nova	631

OPI Scores

Test Date	Subject	Grade	OPI	OPI Description	Score
Nov 01, 2002	Reading	06	02	Basic Understanding	89
Nov 01, 2002	Reading	06	03	Analyze Text	84
Nov 01, 2002	Reading	06	04	Evaluate & Extend Meaning	63
Nov 01, 2002	Reading	06	05	Identify Reading Strategies	68
Nov 01, 2002	Language Arts	06	07	Sentence Structure	91
Nov 01, 2002	Language Arts	06	08	Writing Strategies	89
Nov 01, 2002	Language Arts	06	09	Editing Skills	86
Nov 01, 2002	Math	06	10	Number & Number Relations	63

is countered by lessons that teach teachers to use all of the proficiency levels reported on the state standardized test to create heterogeneous groups for cooperative learning. Cooperative-learning groups place students who score in higher performance categories with those whose performance is weaker in order to encourage peer tutoring. District staff we spoke to felt that these strategies helped prevent teachers from focusing their teaching on a select group of students in order to improve the school's performance.

The MPA tool is particularly important to Milwaukee's efforts at DBDM because it connects to the MPS student information system, thereby always depicting the current students in the building. While each school receives paper printouts of standardized test results from the state, those results are for students from the previous year. Given high student mobility in Milwaukee, the ability to retrieve data on students currently in the classroom allows teachers to address the specific needs of those students.

Brio

The second major tool for DBDM in Milwaukee is Brio, a program that gives school staff access to the district's data warehouse containing standardized test, enrollment, and behavioral data organized around the child from every school in the district. This online tool offers canned reports and also allows users to create interactive "pivot tables." Pivot tables summarize and reorganize data so that new and different relationships can be found and recognized. The pivot table in Figure 13.2 displays the number of students in each proficiency category on one of Milwaukee's performance assessments, but

Figure 13.2. Brio Sample Pivot Table

				2003				
				WKCE				
				1-Minimal	2-Basic	3-Proficient	4-Advanced	No Score
				Sdnt Count	Sdnt Count	Sdnt Count	Sdnt Count	Sdnt Count
0094	Language Arts	04	M			1		
		05	F	5	6	10	7	
			M	7	9	10	4	
	Mathematics	04	M	1				
		05	F	13	2	12	2	
			M	19	3	6	2	
	Reading	04	M	1				
		05	F	6	2	14	6	
			M	8	9	7	6	
	Science	04	M	1				
		05	F	8	11	10		
			M	6	11	11	2	
	Social Studies	04	M	1				
		05	F	7	4	11	7	
			M	7	4	12	7	
	Writing-Narrative/Descriptive	04	M					1
		05	F					28
			M					29

also breaks down those counts by grade, subject, and sex. Virtually all of the demographic variables (e.g., sex, race, free or reduced-price lunch status, etc.) captured by the MPS information systems can be used to organize data in Brio. Brio training shows school staff how to use pivot tables to engage in open-ended "data discovery"—approaching the data without searching for answers to particular questions, but letting the data lead their inquiry.

The Brio tool embraces an understanding that schools becoming engaged in a process of self-reflection need access to many types of data, from student assessment scores to student demographic data. The ability to access and use data flexibly is critical once inquiry moves beyond simple questions about meeting high-stakes cutoffs toward an ongoing process of reflection. The availability of this tool throughout the MPS district makes the implementation of DBDM as a Reflective Process possible for all staff members in all Milwaukee schools.

Brio serves more advanced data users by allowing great flexibility in manipulating data. When we conducted our study, district technology staff described the use of the MPS data warehouse as limited, and its development as a district technology project as relatively "immature." Only a small subset of school staff had been trained to use the technology, and district technology staff envisioned that the tool would be improved over time.

The SPS

The third MPS technology tool is an online system called the Student Promotion System (SPS), designed to capture school-based assessment data for the elementary and middle grades. In all MPS elementary and middle grades, classroom assessments are administered and scored twice a year. The scores, which range from 0 to 4, are recorded in the SPS system for informational purposes, and in Grades 4 and 8, they are used to determine a student's promotion to the next grade level. Like the MPA, the SPS tool is connected to the district's student information system and thus reflects current student enrollment, allowing the classroom teacher or school administrator to see current students' assessment scores throughout their primary school years (see Figure 13.3).

Unlike the other tools that distribute district-level data to schools, the SPS collects school-site data and links them to the student so that they follow the learner anywhere in the district. The ability to access this type of school-based data enables teachers and school administrators to look beyond high-stakes test scores to understand student learning. However, because classroom-based assessments in Milwaukee are not standardized across schools, school staff play out the tension between standardization and local meaning making as they struggle to determine the meaning of scores for students not assessed in their buildings. For a district with significant mobility,

Figure 13.3. SPS Screen Shot

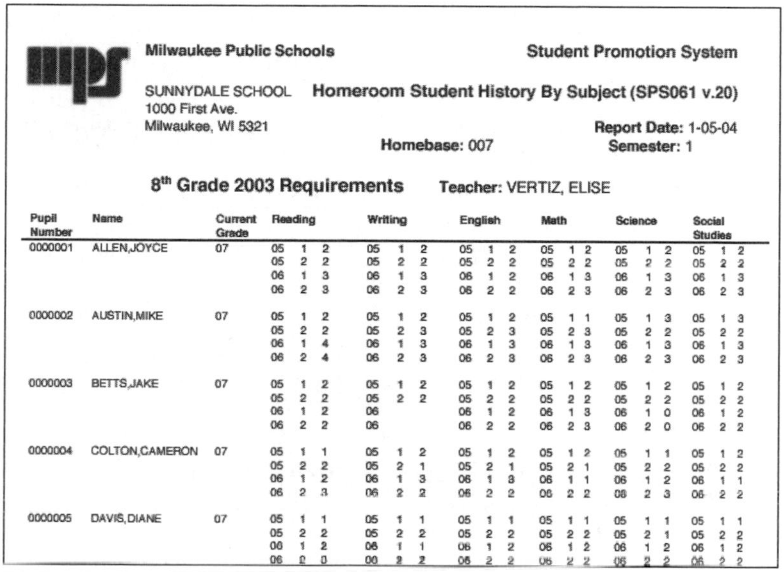

mps Milwaukee Public Schools   Student Promotion System

SUNNYDALE SCHOOL Homeroom Student History By Subject (SPS061 v.20)
1000 First Ave.
Milwaukee, WI 5321
                                              Report Date: 1-05-04
                        Homebase: 007   Semester: 1

8th Grade 2003 Requirements   Teacher: VERTIZ, ELISE

Pupil Number	Name	Current Grade	Reading			Writing			English			Math			Science			Social Studies		
0000001	ALLEN,JOYCE	07	05	1	2	05	1	2	05	1	2	05	1	2	05	1	2	05	1	2
			05	2	2	05	2	2	05	2	2	05	2	2	05	2	2	05	2	2
			06	1	3	06	1	3	06	1	2	06	1	3	06	1	3	06	1	3
			06	2	3	06	2	3	06	2	2	06	2	3	06	2	3	06	2	3
0000002	AUSTIN,MIKE	07	05	1	2	05	1	2	05	1	2	05	1	1	05	1	3	05	1	3
			05	2	2	05	2	3	05	2	3	05	2	3	05	2	2	05	2	2
			06	1	4	06	1	3	06	1	3	06	1	3	06	1	3	06	1	3
			06	2	4	06	2	3	06	2	3	06	2	3	06	2	3	06	2	3
0000003	BETTS,JAKE	07	05	1	2	05	1	2	05	1	2	05	1	2	05	1	2	05	1	2
			05	2	2	05	2	2	05	2	2	05	2	2	05	2	2	05	2	2
			06	1	2	06			06	1	2	06	1	3	06	1	0	06	1	2
			06	2	2	06			06	2	2	06	2	3	06	2	0	06	2	2
0000004	COLTON,CAMERON	07	05	1	1	05	1	2	05	1	2	05	1	2	05	1	1	05	1	2
			05	2	2	05	2	1	05	2	1	05	2	1	05	2	2	05	2	2
			06	1	2	06	1	3	06	1	3	06	1	1	06	1	2	06	1	1
			06	2	3	06	2	2	06	2	2	06	2	2	08	2	3	06	2	2
0000005	DAVIS,DIANE	07	05	1	1	05	1	1	05	1	1	05	1	1	05	1	1	05	1	1
			05	2	2	05	2	2	05	2	2	05	2	2	05	2	1	05	2	2
			06	1	2	06	1	1	06	1	2	06	1	2	06	1	2	06	1	2
			06	2	0	06	2	2	06	2	2	06	2	2	06	2	2	06	2	2

the trade-offs between standardization versus the creation of local assessments meaningful to the school are an issue that DBDM brings to the fore.

School Climate Survey

The assessment, demographic, and behavioral data available to schools have been supplemented by the results of a School Climate Survey, first conducted by MPS in 2002–03 with the support of a local public policy research organization, the Public Policy Forum. Surveys were distributed to parents, staff, and students in Grades 4 and above to gauge each group's perception of their school climate. This type of data is useful as schools take a larger view of how the environment of the school affects student learning. The results, which schools are expected to use to inform their educational plans, are available for the entire district as well as by school.

Starting in 2003–04, all MPS surveys have been conducted online, and the district can provide each school with data about the perceptions of stakeholders in its own building. The focus that MPS has placed on demographic information in addition to assessment data expands the types of knowledge the district considers important to school staffs.

These four data resources, in addition to public data sources like Wisconsin's Information Network for Successful Schools (WINSS) site (http:

//www.dpi.state.wi.us/sig/) and the Milwaukee Public Schools site (http:
//www2.milwaukee.k12.wi.us/acctrep/Schools.html), make up an impressive set of technological tools available to all MPS schools. Each tool was
created with a particular purpose in mind, which reflects different models of
DBDM. The MPA Class Report, for example, was developed specifically to
help teachers identify "bubble kids." This aim reflects a commitment to standardized assessments as the measure of success and a role for teachers in
ensuring that success by focusing on "bubble kids," which many researchers
consider controversial. In contrast, the data warehouse, designed to facilitate "data discovery," arises from a model of DBDM that allows the school
to explore its own needs, although this exploration ultimately is shaped by
the data that the district chooses to include in the tool. The different models
represented by these tools demonstrate a lack of a common definition at the
district level of what DBDM means and what its goals should be.

THE MILWAUKEE PUBLIC SCHOOL DISTRICT
AND THE E2T2 GRANT

> It seems that the more people in a school we get used to looking at
> and applying data to their decisions, the better that school will be at
> meeting their students' needs.
>   Anne Knackert, MPS School Technology Support

Anne Knackert, a School Technology Support Specialist for the Milwaukee Public Schools, works with Milwaukee schools every day to help them
understand the role that DBDM can play in facilitating teaching and learning. Knackert, previously a classroom teacher, left her role as a middle school
technology coordinator in 2003 to coordinate the district's Enhancing Education Through Technology grant. The E2T2 grants were established as part
of NCLB with the goal of improving academic achievement through the use
of technology.

Milwaukee has used its E2T2 grant to provide professional development
on the use of DBDM in schools. In 2003–04, 30 Milwaukee Public Schools
and three nonpublic schools participated in the project. Each participating
school designated a School Site Coordinator, whose role included attending
meetings once a month as a member of the E2T2 Leadership Team, applying for mini-grants based on school needs related to data or technology, and
participating in staff development offered centrally in order to transfer the
skills learned to the rest of the school's staff.

The professional development provided to the School Site Coordinators
has so far consisted of two online courses designed by Milwaukee district
staff in collaboration with the Education Development Center (EDC). Using

EDC's EdTech Leaders Online model, a Web-based professional development program, Milwaukee district staff first were trained in creating content and facilitating online professional development courses. Those staff then created two online courses on data-based decision making. The first, titled "Data-Based School Reform," was offered twice, during the spring and fall of 2003 to School Site Coordinators and other teachers and school administrators. A follow-up course, "Applications of Data-Driven School Reform," was offered during the spring of 2004.

The first course was an introduction to DBDM. Participants read articles and participated in online and face-to-face discussions about the role of DBDM in schools. They helped their schools download state, district, and school data from the WINSS Web site and created an action plan based on static graphs or simple manipulations of the data in a spreadsheet. Participants were encouraged to integrate their action plans with school improvement plans and were expected to find ways to transfer their skills to their school staffs.

The second course focused specifically on how to use the technology tools available in Milwaukee to analyze data in order to complete the educational plans. Students in this course, including School Site Coordinators, teachers, and school administrators, were taught to use the Self-Directed Improvement System (SDIS), a data-driven planning process developed by the Efficacy Institute, a national nonprofit agency, in collaboration with Milwaukee Public Schools. The process relies on three core steps—Data, Feedback, and Strategy—to improve decision making. Course participants were expected to train school teams as well as individual classroom teachers to use this system when conducting the data analysis necessary to complete the educational plan. The Milwaukee district required schools use the SDIS approach or some other school-improvement process during their analysis and planning.

Transcripts of online discussions in both classes show that many participants started out resisting the use of data. Identifying the push for teachers to use data with the model of DBDM as Accountability, the reluctant teachers or school administrators conceived of using data as a way for district administration to blame school staff for student failure. Over time, many participants embraced the second model—DBDM for School Improvement—and became enthusiastic about the power of data to help them "solve" their schools' problems. While some participants continued to suspect that the use of data was motivated by a reform strategy focused on externally imposed accountability mandates, most evolved toward a more instrumental view of the work. While this was not an explicit goal of the courses, this evolution demonstrated that the courses facilitated a new understanding of DBDM as a reform that holds promise for schools.

Throughout both classes, participants were frustrated by their inability to transfer their learning to others in their schools. The frustration arose in part because many of the School Site Coordinators were chosen because of their technology background and were not necessarily a part of the instructional decision making in the school. While classroom teachers who participated in the online classes were able to examine their own practice, they too were frustrated by their isolation as the only members of their faculty who understood the importance of data. These ongoing tensions indicate the importance of making data use part of a collaborative process involving instructional as well as technology-proficient staff. While the E2T2 project has succeeded in moving most participants from a resistant stance to one more receptive to DBDM, much work remains to be done to ensure that schools will make use of data as part of their everyday culture.

FINDINGS ABOUT DBDM IN MPS

All the tools and initiatives (see Table 13.2) available to support DBDM in MPS combine to create a comprehensive set of resources for data use in schools. However, based on our observations, the links between these initiatives and district goals are tenuous and for the most part unfulfilled by the majority of schools in the district. Our case study produced three major findings on the implementation of DBDM in Milwaukee.

Lack of Coordination at District Level

The various tools and initiatives supporting DBDM in Milwaukee demonstrate a lack of shared vision of DBDM as a reform at the district level. By embracing several models of DBDM, these resources support conflicting purposes that ultimately fracture the district's efforts. In addition, the lack of coordination within the district in providing these resources to schools has further disrupted efforts to promote school participation. The best example of the waste stemming from the lack of district coordination can be seen in its Problem Solvers initiative. Part of a national program aimed at stemming the number of children referred to special education, the Problem Solvers initiative employs a data-based, problem-solving system that works to diagnose student difficulties early in their education before special education referrals are necessary. Schools that participate in the initiative administer frequent diagnostic assessments to all children and monitor their progress.

The Problem Solvers initiative developed in relative isolation out of the Special Education Department. The Problem Solvers group in the Special Education Department created its own online data management tool, linked to the district servers, that, like MPS tools, facilitates DBDM by allowing schools to enter assessment information and produce graphs and reports. The Problem Solvers initiative involves administering frequent formative assessments and analyzing the results. Any Milwaukee school requesting services

Table 13.2. Milwaukee Data-Based, Decision-Making Initiative Map

Initiative	Type	Key Players in District	Availability	Purpose
MPA Reports and Tool	Reports and tool	Research and Assessment Department, Technology Department	Whole district access	Communication with parents Help teachers identify "bubble kids" Help schools check up on progress toward Educational Plan
SPS Reports and Tool	Reports and tool	Research and Assessment Department, Technology Department	Whole district access	Gather information of children's promotion requirements Provide schools with performance assessment information from previous schools
Data Warehouse	Reports and tool	Research and Assessment Department, Technology Department	Whole district access after training	Allow schools to generate and investigate their own questions about their school data
E2T2/EDC Online Classes	Training and support	Anne Knackert, MPS School Technology Support and E2T2 Grant Coordinator	Schools chosen by application	Train coordinators in each school to use data to inform instruction and decision making and have them train other staff in their schools
Problem Solvers Initiative	Tool, training, and support	SPED Department	~30 schools Whole district access	Stem the number of referrals to SPED by monitoring and diagnosing student difficulties early using frequent formative assessment and direct intervention
Efficacy Institute Training	Training and support	Professional development	Whole district access	Teach school staff a framework for making decisions based on data
School Climate Surveys	Reports	Research and Assessment Department	Whole district access	Provide reports to each school, parents, and the community on student, staff, and parent perceptions about their school

from this initiative receives training and support from a member of the Problem Solvers group who commits to spending a half day per week in the school. The availability of ongoing data support in the schools represents a significant resource not available with other district tools. However, perhaps due to its genesis in the Special Education Department, this initiative has remained relatively disconnected from other efforts at DBDM in the district. Discussions among the Research and Assessment Department and the Special Education Department are now under way to find ways to forge connections between the Problem Solvers initiative and other data-based work throughout the district (Table 13.2 lists the data-based initiatives identified in Milwaukee as of June 2004).

DBDM Challenges to the Traditional Silo Structure of School Districts

We believe DBDM holds great promise for school reform because it requires the collaboration of different actors in the school to interpret data and make them meaningful in terms of everyday practice. At the district level, a commitment to DBDM similarly requires collaboration between departments that traditionally have been isolated. If the district is to implement a coherent strategy to serve schools that use data as part of a reflective-planning process, the alignment of administration responsible for curriculum, assessments, evaluation, technology, and school-improvement planning is necessary. Encouraging examples are appearing in the Milwaukee Public School District of the collaboration necessary to make such efforts a success.

The district has made several conscious attempts to forge connections across district departments. One was the inclusion of the SDIS reform-planning process within the second E2T2 class—run through the Technology Department. This represented an effort to combine information about school planning with technology training in a thoughtful way that would facilitate schools' use of data to complete their educational plans. Another effort was an unusually popular training session, offered in the spring of 2003, that was advertised as a way for schools to use available technology tools to complete the needs assessment in their educational plan. The response was far greater for this training than for other technology tool trainings because this course offered schools an opportunity to employ district-provided tools to complete a required part of their work. The connections between the district departments responsible for technology and for school planning in these two examples represent the type of collaboration—that meant to integrate technology and data use into required school work—that is needed to overcome school staff's initial resistance and provide meaningful support to schools' efforts in DBDM.

This type of collaboration is increasing in Milwaukee. A successful partnership between the Technology Department and the Assessment and Accountability Department led to the creation of the MPA, Brio, and the SPS tools. The close ties forged between these two departments have facilitated and will continue to facilitate the ongoing creation and support of tools that meet the needs of schools in the district. Such collaboration is essential in bringing together the fragmented efforts that characterize the work around DBDM now in place.

The Need to "Move People"

The understanding and use of DBDM in MPS are in the beginning stages—with some early-adopter schools leading the way and others slowly becoming aware of the resources available. The process of reaching all schools is complicated by Milwaukee's decentralized school policy, which mandates that schools control their own budgets and make their own professional development decisions. Therefore, the district cannot mandate training, but instead must find ways to persuade schools that using district resources is in their best interests.

Schools that have made early strides in DBDM often have someone on staff who belongs to a small group (e.g., the E2T2 Leadership Team or the Problem Solvers group) that encourages and provides training and support for using data to influence school and classroom decision making. Other schools involved in DBDM may have principals or other staff members who understand the importance of data for decision making and who pursue data use on their own. Challenges remaining for all those involved in promoting DBDM include reaching schools and individuals that are not part of these smaller efforts. As one administrator described it, the challenge for Milwaukee is not on the technical side, but rather in the need to "move people."

CONCLUSION

As exemplified by the Milwaukee Public School District, effective DBDM requires collaboration across district departments. If the district continues to treat DBDM as a priority, then cross-departmental collaborations presumably will continue to evolve and will find ways to reach all of Milwaukee's 161 schools. The pockets of implementation in Milwaukee are a promising start to institutionalizing a process of data use in all schools, and the district's provision of suitable technological tools is an important prerequisite. MPS now needs to embed a reflective process of DBDM at all levels of district functioning. This will require rethinking the tools and initiatives for DBDM so that both district- and school-based staff incorporate these strategies into their everyday practice.

REFERENCES

Andrekopoulos, W. G. (2003, December 2). *Address to Milwaukee public school administrators*. Milwaukee, WI.

Ball, D., & Cohen, D. (1999). Developing practice, developing practitioners. In L. Darling-Hammond & G. Sykes (Eds.), *Teaching as the learning profession* (pp. 3–32). San Francisco: Jossey-Bass.

Bernhardt, V. L. (1998). *Data analysis for comprehensive schoolwide improvement*. Larchmont, NY: Eye On Education.

Blase, J., & Blase, J. R. (1994). *Empowering teachers: What successful principals do*. Thousand Oaks, CA: Corwin Press.

Boudett, K. P., City, E. A., & Murnane, R. J. (Eds.). (2005). *Data wise: A step-by-step guide to using assessment results to improve teaching and learning*. Cambridge, MA: Harvard Education Press.

Cochran-Smith, M., & Lytle, S. L. (1993). *Inside/outside: Teacher research and knowledge*. New York: Teachers College Press.

Dede, C., & Nelson, R. (2005). Technology as Proteus: Digital infrastructures that empower scaling up. In C. Dede, J. P. Honan, & L. Peters (Eds.), *Scaling up success: Lessons learned from technology-based educational improvement* (pp. 110–132). San Francisco: Jossey-Bass.

Donaldson, G. (2001). *Cultivating leadership in schools: Connecting people, purpose, and practice*. New York: Teachers College Press.

Hess, F. M. (2002). *Revolution at the margins: The impact of competition on urban school systems*. Washington, DC: Brookings Institution Press.

Kallick, B., & Wilson, J. M. (2000). *Information technology for schools: Creating practical knowledge to improve student performance*. San Francisco: Jossey-Bass.

Lagemann, E. C. (2000). *An elusive science: The troubling history of education research*. Chicago: University of Chicago Press.

Lortie, D. C. (2002). *Schoolteacher: A sociological study*. Chicago: University of Chicago Press.

Milwaukee Public Schools. (2003–2004). *Milwaukee public schools educational plan 2003–2004*. Milwaukee, WI: Author.

Price, J., & Koretz, D. M. (2005). Building assessment literacy. In K. P. Boudett, E. A. City, & R. J. Murnane (Eds.), *Data wise: A step-by-step guide to using assessment results to improve teaching and learning* (pp. 29–55). Cambridge, MA: Harvard Education Press.

Rallis, S. F., & MacMullen, M. M. (2000). Inquiry-minded schools: Opening doors for accountability. *Phi Beta Kappan, 81*(10), 766–773.

Schon, D. (1983). *The reflective practitioner: How professionals think in action*. New York: Basic Books.

Stoll, L. (1992). Teacher growth in the effective school. In M. Fullan & A. Hargreaves (Eds.), *Teacher development and educational change* (pp. 104–122). Washington, DC: Falmer Press.

York-Barr, J., Sommers, W., Ghere, G., & Montie, J. (2001). *Reflective practice to improve schools: An action guide for educators*. Thousand Oaks, CA: Corwin Press.

PART V

Data-Driven Decision Making and Education Reform

A Functionality Framework for Educational Organizations: Achieving Accountability at Scale

David V. Abbott

The term "standards-based" has become common in education reform but rarely is applied to educational systems or organizations. Every level of educational organizations—classroom, school, district, and state—needs a clearer understanding of what is expected. How well educational organizations operate within and across these levels is far more important than the content of the programs they implement. The primary role of education support systems is to build and maintain capacity to deliver and improve instruction. Capacity to perform precedes performance. Focusing accountability efforts solely on performance, or outputs, tells us little about how our educational systems must adapt to build requisite capacity to perform at high levels. Sustained improvement of teaching and learning requires a coherent representation of how individuals within educational organizations interact, as well as a detailed description of the specific functions we expect to see at each level of an integrated educational system.

INTRODUCTION

In the early 1990s, the Rhode Island Board of Regents established a statewide agenda to ensure that all students meet high expectations of academic proficiency and personal growth. Working with the Rhode Island Department of Education (**ride**), the Governor and the General Assembly adopted the state Comprehensive Education Strategy (CES) in 1992. As set forth in

---

the CES, there are three sequential components to an inquiry-based, evidence-dependent system of improving school and student performance:

- Setting high standards and clear expectations for student achievement;
- Measuring school and student progress toward the shared standards; and
- Ensuring accountability for results in terms of achievement.

An effective accountability system is dependent on all three components, which must be reflected in both peer-driven "internal" accountability and hierarchical "external" accountability.

Standardized expectations for instructional practice and education support systems, provided they are meaningfully linked to building and maintaining capacity, are as important as expectations for student achievement. Capacity to change performance is the key to sustainable improvement, yet it often is just assumed to exist. If we do not know how classroom, school, district, and state efforts need to work together to build and maintain capacity within individuals, we can be sure that they will not do so. Accountability requires an understanding of the complex and overlapping systems at work in schools and school districts. We no longer can view each piece of the puzzle in isolation, hoping it will trigger a sustainable system in the aggregate.

Evidence-based inquiry requires standards against which current performance can be measured and evaluated. In order to improve teaching and learning, we first must improve the educational systems that support effective instructional practice. Clarity of expectations provides the context to make information about current practice relevant. Measuring school and district progress toward established standards requires corresponding information systems. Effective leadership is the applied use of informed professional judgment to address gaps in the capacity of individuals to perform to predetermined, shared expectations.

MAKING EDUCATIONAL ORGANIZATIONS
ACCOUNTABLE FOR TEACHING AND LEARNING

The typical approach to accountability relies heavily on *external* bureaucratic controls. At a minimum, these external controls consist of standards for student performance as mandated by the No Child Left Behind Act. However, focusing solely on outcomes does little to help adjust inputs and processes to achieve those outcomes, given the context of the situation (Abbott, 2005). Educational organizations are comprised of many levels—classroom, school, district, and state education agency—each of which is accountable to the adjoining levels, both above and below. When viewed in a typical organization pyramid, these external forces can be seen to exist on a vertical axis.

Sustainable improvement requires that these external influences be matched by *internal* expectations within each level of the organization. The manner in which peers interact and hold one another accountable is as important as the clarity of external expectations, if not more so. Schools as "professional learning communities" is certainly an idea whose time has come (Dufour, Eaker, & Dufour, 2005), but we are still experimenting with the role that district oversight and capacity building plays in their development. Understanding how vertical articulation of purpose and horizontal efforts at collaboration need to mesh, in order to achieve commonly held goals of improved student achievement, is the key to sustained improvement of instructional practice.

Although it may be obvious, it is worth restating that changes in learning will not occur without changes in instruction. Organizational changes must be geared toward, and measured against, actual changes in instructional practices in individual classrooms. Attempts to change instructional practice without regard to the organizational structures and belief systems that support the classroom will be ineffectual at best. As Dewey (1938) noted 70 years ago, "Attempt to deal with [institutions and customs] simply on the basis of what is obvious in the present is bound to result in adoption of superficial measures which in the end will only render existing problems more acute and more difficult to solve" (p. 77).

We therefore are tackling the task of improving the professionalism of educational practice at scale. This is less a question of pedagogy than of understanding how human beings learn to do things differently (Elmore, 2004b). The influence of internal controls, as exercised through peer relationships, has proven to be far more effective in generating sustained change than the isolated influence of external controls operating alone (Bolman & Deal, 1991). The dynamics of positive change are inherently bound up with both the internal organization of the group and the external environment, or organization, within which that group operates. Organizational structure must not only focus on expected changes in behavior, but also support change in the causes of unwanted behaviors and attitudes in order to accomplish sustained, comprehensive changes in behavior by every member in the targeted group (Argyris, 1990). Meaningful and sustained change will not occur solely by bringing external controls, expressed as standards, to a group of education professionals accustomed to operating as free agents.

This, then, is the goal of educational leadership—to build shared ownership of both the end goals of effective instructional systems and the manner in which such systems are built. Shared ownership requires shared responsibility. "Professional educators should not be held acountable for their ability to impact student learning unless and until they have been provided with the opportunity to acquire the knowledge and skills necessary to produce the desired level of performance" (Elmore, 2004a, p. 281). This notion of reciprocal accountability should exist within each level of every educational organization, as well as between each level from classroom practice to district, state, and federal policy creation.

The hierarchical, or vertical, articulation of policy and accountability formulation is therefore no more important than the lateral, or horizontal, reality of how education professionals interact. The vertical structure of systems hierarchy must support the ability of each horizontal element of the system to operate at its highest possible level (Homans, 1950). To be effective, capacity building from one level of the organization to the next must be informed by accurate information about current levels of performance. The three components of evidence-based practice exemplified by the CES therefore must be aligned across both the vertical and horizontal planes of organizational structure.

An accurate model of an effective statewide educational system, one that stimulates a clear understanding of both purpose and design from state agency to classroom, requires several distinct elements. First, we must understand the basics of human interaction within each level of the organization—that is, how individuals relate as peers within an internal system at the classroom, school, district, and state levels. Second, we must understand how different levels of an overall systemic hierarchy interact to achieve mutual goals, as well as how policy initiatives from the top of the hierarchy become shared goals across other levels of the system. This is the key to migrating capacity from one level to the next, which in turn illustrates the need for leadership and capacity building to be fully integrated throughout the system. Third, we must formulate the role of information gathering, analysis, and dissemination in creating common goals and accountability measures in order to ensure full functionality at every level of the organization as measured against commonly held expectations.

School Improvement as Evidence-Based Practice

The single purpose underlying this linking of vertical and horizontal accountability is the improvement of teaching and learning in the classroom. The mission statement of the Board of Regents and Department of Education exemplifies this underlying purpose:

> To ensure that all Rhode Island public school students have equal access to a rigorous, consistent curriculum designed to prepare them for life beyond secondary school, not just in core academics, but in civic education, technological skills, health and fitness, and artistic awareness and appreciation. (Rhode Island Department of Elementary and Secondary Education, 1999, online)

When we are truly committed to ensuring the success of every student, inputs, rather than expectations, will be variable. Students with more difficult paths to high achievement, such as students with disabilities, students living in poverty, and children with limited English proficiency, will require more individualized instruction, more time in the educational environment, more support, and more resources. The ability to differentiate these inputs is dependent on the underlying ability to provide the services and resources at all.

There is an inherent disconnect between what we expect as learner/teacher outcomes and the realities of the educational systems that support instruction. Over the years, we have created a system of inputs that do not sufficiently impact the many layers of complexity that exist in public education. We continuously implement new strategic directions without an adequate understanding of either the interplay among diverse reform impulses or the hard reality of the predicative work necessary to prepare individuals to embrace the changes in behavior that such reforms require.

Demanding improvement of student achievement outcomes without addressing learning environments, access to educational opportunities, sufficiency of instructional resources, consistency of access to educational rigor, teacher training, the role of administration and accountability, and dozens of other variables—will not result in a more effective or equitable system of education. A fully functional school or district is able to be effective regardless of the particular programs or initiatives it relies upon. Conversely, even the most promising or research-based approach will have little lasting impact if implemented in a dysfunctional educational system.

Internal Accountability

Evidence-based practice requires clear expectations, responsive information systems, and two-way accountability. Application of evidence-based practice to education reform within each level of the overall system should result in a continuum of improvement efforts. In Rhode Island, this continuum at the school level is known as School Accountability for Learning and Teaching (SALT). It is an expression of the ideals of internal, or horizontal, accountability in which peers interact and collaborate to pursue commonly held goals. SALT's four sequential stages of internal accountability for change are expressed in the familiar cycle of continuous improvement (see Figure 14.1).

We first measure our current performance against a pre-established set of clear expectations. This "gap analysis" of the distance between where we are and where we want to be is *needs assessment*. Accurate needs assessment requires clarity of expectations and relevance of available information.

Needs assessment precedes *planning*, the second step of evidence-based improvement. Just as needs assessment is impossible without relevant infor-

Figure 14.1. SALT Cycle of Continuous Improvement

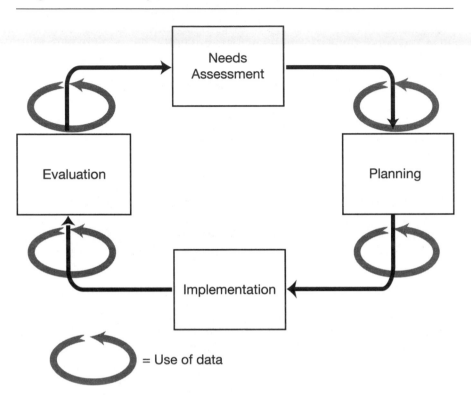

mation, effective planning requires access to accurate information regarding both current practice and expected outcomes. Well-intentioned planning to use "research-based" strategies and programs is meaningless without effective *implementation*. Finally, evidence-based practice requires *evaluation* of the effectiveness of what has been implemented. Evaluation in turn provides new information for the next round of *needs assessment*.

The four stages of evidence-based improvement—needs assessment, planning, implementation, and evaluation—form a cycle informed by data. Being sequential, these stages also can be expressed as a four-step linear process (see Figure 14.2).

Seen in this way, the question is how to ensure that an educational organization is ready to engage in a meaningful effort to improve. The level of collective skill and mutual drive required to sustain improvement is often overlooked.

Figure 14.2. Four-Step Linear Process of Evidence-Based Improvements

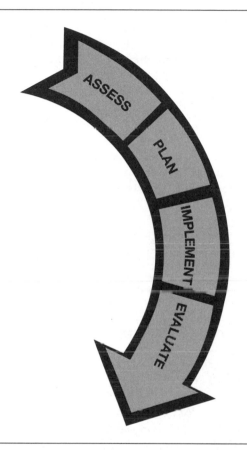

Readiness

Educational organizations consist of individuals, each with a set of discrete tasks. The purpose of such organizations is to enable individuals to work together to achieve common purposes or functions. We need a better understanding of how educational organizations operate in order to design programs that meet the behavioral, systemic, and organizational needs that must be met if we are to improve the educational opportunities provided to students. Too often we attempt to measure the performance of individuals within the educational system without also taking into account whether those individuals have the capacity to perform to our expectations. Capacity to perform precedes performance.

Performance evaluation, while necessary, is insufficient. When an individual does not perform as desired, we need to know that, but we also need to know why. Was it that the person was unready, unwilling—or unable? Capacity building should ensure that people are first *ready* to perform, before trying to make them *able* to perform. Recognition of the need to develop readiness skills is crucial to effective implementation of new programs or initiatives. Accordingly, it should be the goal of every level of educational organizations to build the capacity of both individuals and the system to improve. The use of relevant data to inform those individuals of the gaps between expectations and current performance is a crucial element to developing organizational readiness.

Readiness occurs in two stages (see Figure 14.3). *Internalization* comes first, when a single individual is ready to change his or her practice. An important element of internalization is awareness. Too often individuals are not able to change simply because they do not understand what is expected of them or how to get there. Ignorance of the need or lack of the ability to change will be the primary stumbling block to internalization, which is more a measure of knowledge than of belief.

Collective readiness to work together to improve a system is *collaboration*, the second and external stage of readiness. The existence of a collective readiness to collaborate to achieve a common goal often is referred to as the "culture" of an organization. Collaboration involves a collective appreciation of the need to change, a willingness to work together, an understanding of the work ahead, and a tolerance for risk taking and potential failure. These internal variables are essential to sustained change (Elmore, 2004a). However, collaboration goes beyond culture; the organization also must provide the opportunity for individuals to collaborate through infrastructural support, including time and facilitation to foster collaborative efforts.

Leadership is the engine that moves an educational organization to readiness and then through the four stages of evidence-based improvement (see Figure 14.4). Readiness and ability to change precede improvement. It is the building of individual and collective capacity to improve that moves a school or district from awareness to internalization to collaboration to improvement. Although there is a sequence to this process, it is clearly cyclical, with internalization and collaboration needing to be developed for each successive round of improvements. When fully operational, leadership operates to keep the cycle moving, ready to adapt to new external forces and reform agendas.

Every step must be informed by relevant information and evaluated against clear expectations. Leadership and effective management skills are necessary to guide the use of relevant evidence of current practices throughout this cycle of readiness and improvement. As individuals become more adept in their reliance on evidence to guide their individual choices, the more sustained the improvement will become.

Figure 14.3. Readiness

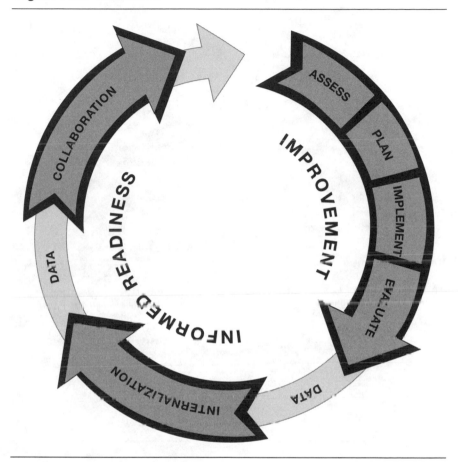

Capacity Building and External Accountability

So far, we have focused on the internal workings within any one level of an educational organization. Classrooms, schools, and districts do not exist independent of one another. Each is part of a larger, interdependent system. Individual classrooms are, hopefully, supported by an effective school structure, which in turn is supported by a responsive district structure, which in turn is supported by the state. The vertical relationships between these levels are as important as what occurs within each horizontal layer of the overall system.

Each layer of the overall organizational structure is responsible for building the capacity of the next level down in the system. Thus, it is the respon-

Figure 14.4. Leadership

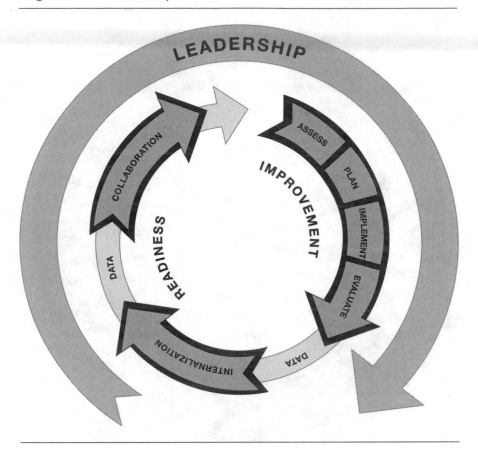

sibility of the state education agency to build the capacity of school districts, so that they in turn can build the capacities for leadership, readiness, and improvement in their schools. Just as collaboration within each level of the organization is required for sustainability, alignment through the vertical axis of the overall structure is equally important to ensure that such collaborations work toward common goals.

Only by providing the appropriate degree of training, resources, opportunity, and organizational climate can we ever hope to hold individuals accountable for their lack of production or performance. This emphasis on capacity building and readiness, which is the essence of two-way accountability, rather than on content alone, has profound implications for how we approach and implement our educational accountability systems. We must be willing to hold ourselves accountable for the presence or absence of capacity of the individuals whose performance we intend to measure and then hold them accountable.

Building capacity for readiness and improvement requires input across four dimensions, the most important of which is *leadership*, simply because it controls the application of the other three relevant inputs as dictated by the context presented (see Figure 14.5). *Personal supports* constitute the second element of capacity building. Common aspects of support efforts include professional development, mentoring, technical assistance, peer observation, formative evaluation, and exposure to modeled effective practices.

The third element of capacity building is *infrastructure*. Infrastructure includes organizational structure, process and facilitation, access to technol-

Figure 14.5. Dimensions of Capacity Building

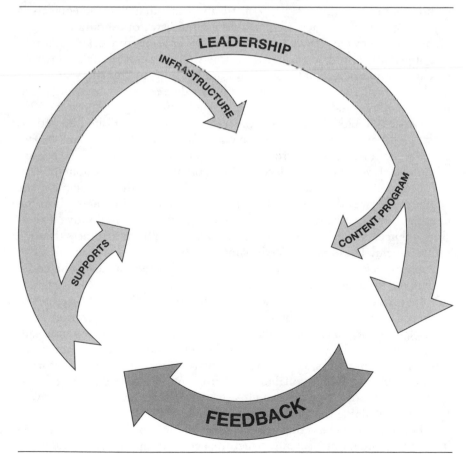

ogy, appropriate resources and materials, and, most important, opportunity, which typically is quantified as time. For example, joint review of student work is a key element of developing a professional learning community, but teachers must have the time, that is, the opportunity, to meet to accomplish that task. The fourth aspect of capacity building, and the one most often emphasized to the exclusion of the others, is the actual *content* of the program, practice, or initiative to be implemented. Leadership informs and guides the appropriate application of supports, infrastructure, and content as circumstances and individual needs dictate.

These four aspects of capacity—leadership, personal supports, infrastructure, and programmatic content—*must* be present to effect sustainable change. The presence or absence of capacity building between hierarchical levels of the organization structure—from state to district, from district to school, and from school to classroom—determines the success or failure of improvement efforts. All education professionals within the organization must frame their responsibilities in terms of their contribution to enhancing someone else's capacity and performance. Central office administrators should be judged on how well they contribute to school leaders' capacity to work with teachers; principals should be evaluated by how well they contribute to teachers; teachers should be evaluated by their contributions to students—and each level of performance should be gauged by the degree to which the organization has built the individuals' capacity to perform as expected.

Capacity building, including leadership, fuels the requisite interactions between theory and practice, between planning and implementation (see Figure 14.6). It must be present from one level to the next, and it must be present within each layer of the overall educational organization, classroom to state.

Leadership from one level of the organization to the one below is the engine that drives the specific elements of capacity building needed for the next level of the system to adapt to external demands. Distributive leadership within each level moves that part of the system from readiness through improvement. These two leadership impulses must work in concert in order to apply capacity to stimulate needed behaviors—thereby achieving functionality in the targeted area.

Reform efforts that focus solely on the content of a new program or approach at the expense of building the readiness of the organization to assess, plan, implement, and evaluate that initiative will fail to become self-sustaining. They simply will fade away, become incorporated ad hoc into a few teachers' practices, or be pushed out by the next round of reforms. Sustainability requires a collaborative effort, individualized to the context presented, supported and led by effective leadership, and at all times welcoming of available feedback on effectiveness.

Educational systems that provide this combination of concerted capacity building, organizational infrastructure, personal supports, and leadership

Figure 14.6. The Full Model

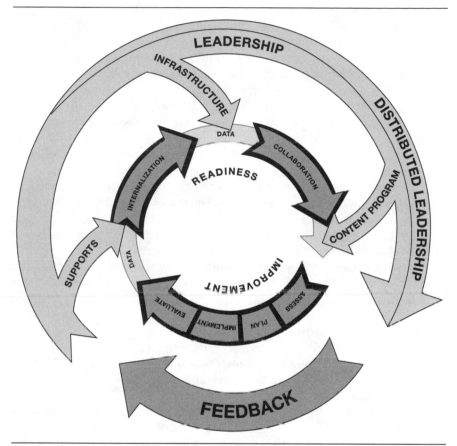

demonstrate incredible results (Education Trust, 2005). Those that do not will be unable to incorporate or sustain new and effective practices with any measure of consistency or coherence.

Defining Expectations for Functionality at Each Level of the Organization

Understanding *how* educational organizations function is of little use if we have no agreement on *what* we expect those functions to accomplish. Common understanding is the cornerstone of effective leadership. It is also the essential first stage of evidence-based practice as set forth in the Comprehensive Education Strategy:[1] Set high standards and clear expectations for student (and organizational) achievement. Continuous and sustained improvement is a series of activities, not a single event. These activities can best be described as *functions* specific to each level of educational organizations—classroom, school, district, and state.

An integrated framework of functions, expressed as expectations, would build a common language regarding the specific individual behaviors required to improve learning for both students and instructional professionals, and serve as a common point of reference for school, district, and state agency operations and improvement efforts. Focusing on function, rather than on program or performance alone, would enable education leaders to move from reflection to action across a greater number of areas that demand improvement.

There are, therefore, two aspects of an effective framework of functionality for our educational system: a description of how individuals within educational organizations interact in pursuit of their professional goals; and a description of the functions an educational organization accomplishes at each level in order for the entire system to be effective.

It is convenient to think of systemic education functions as part of a hierarchical pyramid, where the hierarchy reflects levels of relevance rather than levels of authority (see Figure 14.7). In such a system, the student, not the state Department of Education, would be at the apex. Functions build upon one another, starting with the needs and expected outcomes for the student. "The student" in this context is *every* student, not *a* student. Everything builds from the student. The interaction between teacher and learner is, of course, the heart of education. Everything else, while vitally important to that relationship, is part of an education support system. The farther away from the interaction between teacher and learner, the more attenuated the connection.

By the time you get to the state education agency, you are looking for evidence that the state effectively builds district capacity through the provision of leadership, content, personal supports, and infrastructure. If present, we can then move to the district and gauge the provision of leadership, content, personal supports, and infrastructure to the schools in that district. Evaluation of the same four measures at the school level is next. Behaviors of every individual within each level provide feedback both within that level, as well as to those further removed from instructional practice as one moves away from the student at the apex. This feedback is essential to the provision of capacity-building efforts from leadership at every level of the overall organizational structure (Homans, 1950).

A picture begins to emerge of the core functions we need to identify in order to measure the effectiveness of a classroom, school, district, or state agency. First, core functions need to be established at each level of the overall system, shown in Figure 14.7. The further away from the educational

Figure 14.7. Systemic Functions of Education: A Hierarchical Pyramid

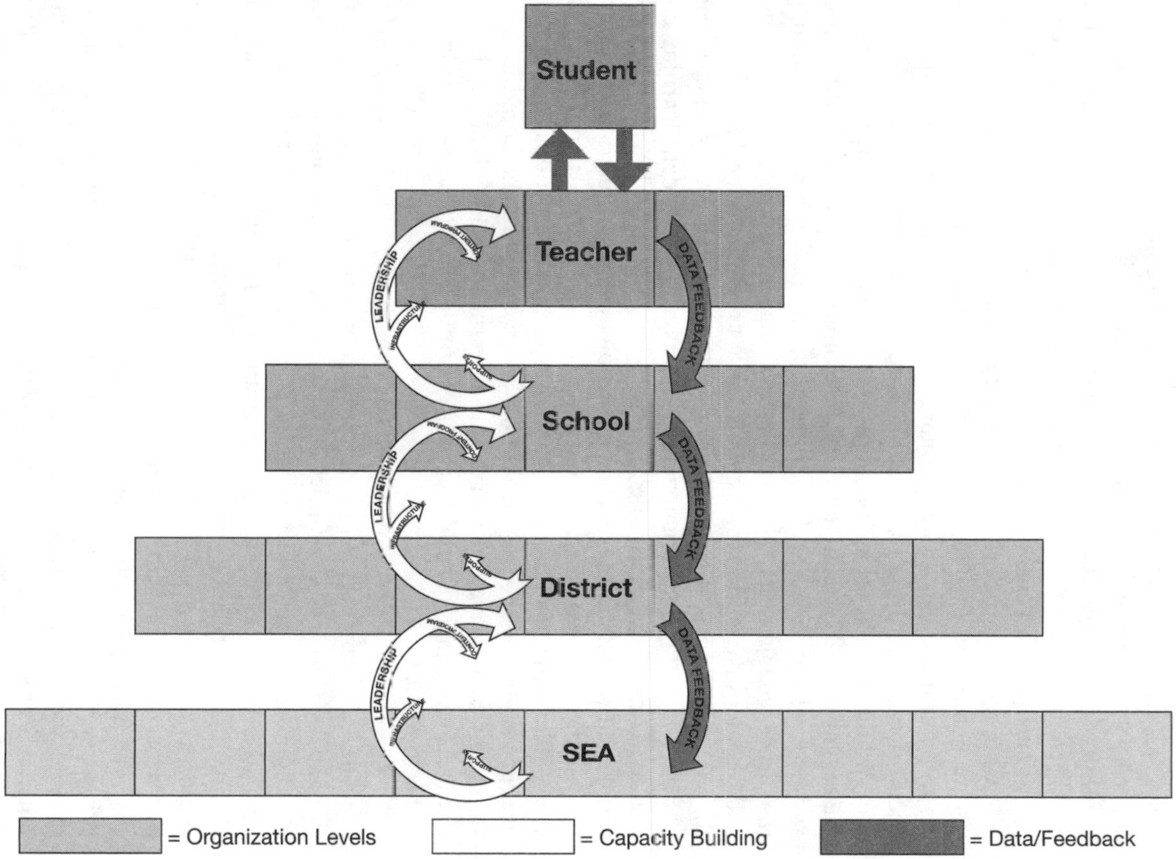

Student
Teacher
School
District
SEA
DATA FEEDBACK
DATA FEEDBACK
DATA FEEDBACK
LEADERSHIP
LEADERSHIP
LEADERSHIP
= Organization Levels
= Capacity Building
= Data/Feedback

relationship of teacher and learner, the more attenuated and diffuse the work will become. A greater number of functions should not be confused with greater importance. In this model of organization, the student has only one function—to grow and learn as the recipient of a collective effort from every other level of the educational system supporting him or her. However, the concept of instruction as a tool for building students' capacity to learn is a highly complex endeavor far beyond the scope of this chapter, but one worthy of much further discussion.

Conversely, at the other end of the continuum, a state education agency has many functions. Foremost, it supports school districts that are next closest to the learner. Two-way accountability requires the state to build districts' capacity for every function the state asks districts to fulfill. There are also two functions the state must provide that districts do not: advocacy with the executive and legislative branches around policy issues and resources, and oversight of state and federal funding and policy mandates. Similarly, the district engages in levels of policy making, infrastructure development, and resource distribution that schools are not required to perform. However, the school takes on different functions due to its dual role as a key element of a larger educational organization and as an independent learning community. For example, school employees are both the authors of school-improvement action plans as well as the implementers of district strategies.

This model, therefore, consists of a series of levels, each of which contains several boxes, or functions. The all-important interactions between levels are represented by the four areas of capacity building, anchored in leadership, which are delivered from one level to the next. Finally, there is an active system of providing and receiving continuous feedback on current levels of performance.

Capacity plus performance equals functionality. Capacity to perform precedes performance. What we ultimately want to measure is the functionality of instructional practice. At present, we evaluate only performance. An individual's capacity to perform is usually not measured adequately, nor is leadership typically held accountable for building that capacity. Evaluating performance without evaluating capacity will never reveal what the organization must do in order to generate the desired performance behavior, or level of functionality.

The world of public education is complex. Each *core function* comprises several *component functions*. Fulfilling every component function within a core area results in the core function being fully implemented. Functions at every level of the organization are a combination of capacity and performance. Therefore, it makes sense to define both the capacity required to generate the desired performance for each component function, as well as the actual performance or behavior desired. This level of detail is absolutely necessary for the meaningful design of the information and evaluation systems we will need in order to gauge the effectiveness of each systemic function (Elmore, 2000).

Some aspects of capacity building can be directly observed as behaviors; others cannot. Indicators constituting a data-collection and -analysis system must be designed to measure those capacities that cannot be directly observed as distinct behaviors. School and district visitation structures need to focus on direct observations of desired behaviors and interactions. These two different information systems need to complement each other, each operating to create an accurate picture of the current functionality at every level of the organizational structure.

Correspondent information systems then can be developed to gauge the effectiveness of both performance and capacity. When observation reveals performance to be lacking or nonexistent, information about relevant capacity should alert leadership of the need for future allocation of resources. That is the essence of effective needs assessment and planning. Changes in measures of capacity and performance then must inform the question of effectiveness of implementation. That is the role of evaluation.

Despite the value of specifying various functions for the purpose of information gathering and evaluation, functionality appears to operate only in the aggregate. In other words, if correctly identified, *all* of the functions, expressed through capacity building and leadership, for each level of the educational organization must be present in order to sustain improvements in instructional practice (Duffy, Rogerson, & Blick, 2000). It does not appear that linear support of specific initiatives or programs has any lasting effect without attention to capacity building and leadership—specifically targeted for those initiatives or programs. Achieving functionality at scale requires systems for all three phases of the CES: setting high standards and clear expectations; measuring progress toward predetermined expectations; and ensuring accountability for results in terms of achievement.

Embedding the Functionality Framework into Practice

A framework of functionality could serve as a common base for the many tools we use to organize improvement efforts. To be truly effective, this framework must incorporate both an awareness of how individuals interact within an organization, as well as a means of anchoring expectations for specific functions across levels. Consensus regarding the construct and content of such a framework would provide educators with the opportunity to create a system of supports and accountability in which information systems, improvement planning, budgeting, professional development, leadership expectations, and evaluation efforts are tied together in a seamless structure—both within each level, and from one level of the overall system to the next.

Continuous and sustained improvement of student achievement requires an organizational construct that:

- Ensures commonality of purpose at every level of the organization to build trust among educational professionals;
- Makes information systems relevant to the decisions facing instructional leaders at each level of the education organization;
- Maintains a system of hierarchical organization that supports professional learning and collaboration within each level of the organization; and
- Anchors needs assessment, planning, and evaluation in clear expectations.

There is a need to build readiness within each level of the educational structure through the progressive process of internalization and collaboration. Effective improvement efforts rely on both internal (horizontal) and external (vertical) accountability within an overall system of organization from the classroom to the state agency. These two concepts are readily adapted into practice if we simply adopt the presumption that accounting for capacity building, including the development of individual and collective readiness, is as important as the content of what we are trying to implement in the name of reform.

In order to achieve sustained results, every initiative or program that a state, district, or school implements should account for the necessary four elements of capacity building: leadership, personal supports, infrastructure, and specific content or program. For example, in order to implement a new student advisory program within a school, it is not enough for the principal to attend training designed for teachers. There also must be training designed specifically to build the principal's capacity to oversee and monitor the implementation of the new program. Likewise, infrastructural adjustments may be needed to ensure that teachers have *structured* opportunities to engage in the desired activities. Only then will the training and supports necessary to deliver the content of the advisory continue to be effective over time.

Continuing with the example of implementing student advisories, this framework also could provide a base for use of relevant data to inform efforts to monitor or evaluate program effectiveness. Measurable indicators, drawn from these data, then could be mapped against the specific functions contained in the framework. For example, the presence of a professional learning community can be measured by the degree to which teachers actually meet to examine student work on a periodic basis, and the degree to which those teachers express a belief that such opportunities favorably impact their instructional practice. Mapping a new initiative, such as the provision of common planning time in a school schedule, against a longitudinal measure of that aspect of functionality would allow predetermined indicators to measure levels of impact in a pre/post fashion. Going a step further, aligning school and district improvement plans with their respective functions would allow such indicators to ensure alignment of both strategic direction and effective measurement across levels within the organization. The concept of measuring both the level of capacity and efficacy of targeted performance allows for more accurate measures of the effectiveness of implementation of a specific intervention or action plan.

Finally, comparing current levels of performance with desired levels of functionality would provide an opportunity to respond to low levels of performance by addressing capacity gaps of both individuals and the system itself. Requiring each tier of the organization to focus on its own functionality, with the knowledge that there would be meaningful assistance in the form of capacity building to address gaps in performance, would go a very long way to ensuring that implementation of proven practices would generate positive results over time. Capacity to perform precedes performance. The attention that must be paid to preparing individuals to perform, prior to holding them accountable for a specific level of performance, may be the most important message of education reform, but it is one that largely has been lost in the effort to improve educational organizations.

NOTES

I would like to thank Ellamae Gurney and Patricia McGee of the Education Alliance at Brown University for their work turning my crayon drawings into graphic art. My thanks also go to Dr. Arnold Shore of Boston College and Margaret Votta of the Rhode Island Department of Elementary and Secondary Education for their invaluable editing assistance.

1. The Comprehensive Education Strategy (CES) is Rhode Island's action plan for preparing all the state's children to be lifelong learners, productive workers, and responsible citizens. Governor Lincoln C. Almond charged the Rhode Island Goals 2000 Panel, with the active collaboration of the Board of Regents, to develop this critical policy document. Completed in 1996, its clear agenda of high educational standards, meaningful student assessments, and accountability for school improvement continues to serve as a guide for all of the state's education efforts (Rhode Island Department of Elementary and Secondary Education, 1996).

REFERENCES

Abbott, D. V. (2005, Winter). Bringing measurement to district-based accountability: The challenge for state education departments. *Voices in Urban Education, 6*, 14–21.

Argyris, C. (1990). *Organizational defenses: Facilitating organizational learning.* Needham, MA: Allyn & Bacon.

Bolman, L. G., & Deal, T. E. (1991). *Reframing organizations: Artistry, choice, and leadership.* San Francisco: Jossey-Bass.

Dewey, J. (1938). *Experience and education.* New York: Collier Books.

Duffy, F., Rogerson, L., & Blick, C. (2000). *Redesigning America's schools: A systems approach to improvement.* Norwood, MA: Christopher-Gordon.

Dufour, R., Eaker, R. L., & Dufour, R. (Eds.). (2005). *On common ground: The power of professional learning communities.* Bloomington, IN: National Education Service.

Education Trust. (2005). *Gaining traction, gaining ground: How some high schools accelerate learning for struggling students.* Washington, DC: Author.

Elmore, R. F. (2000). *Building a new structure for school leadership.* Washington, DC: Albert Shanker Institute.

Elmore, R. F. (2004a). Conclusion: The problem of stakes in performance-based accountability systems. In S. H. Fuhrman & R. F. Elmore (Eds.), *Redesigning accountability systems for education* (pp. 274–296). New York: Teachers College Press.

Elmore, R. F. (2004b). *School reform from the inside out: Policy, practice, and performance.* Cambridge, MA: Harvard University Press.

Homans, G. C. (1950). *The human group.* New York: Harcourt, Brace.

Rhode Island Department of Elementary and Secondary Education. (1999, August). *Rhode Island Board of Regents for Elementary and Secondary Education mission statement.* Retrieved March 12, 2007, from www.ride.ri.gov

Rhode Island Department of Elementary and Secondary Education. (1996, June). *Education Policy.* Retrieved February 26, 2007, from www.ride.ri.gov

About the Editors and Contributors

David V. Abbott has been serving as Deputy Commissioner at the Rhode Island Department of Elementary and Secondary Education (RIDE) since December 2001. Mr. Abbott oversees the Department's Division of Systems Support, including the Offices of Progressive Support & Intervention, Educator Quality and Certification, Network and Information Systems, and Finance. Mr. Abbott became General Counsel to the Department in January 2007. Prior to joining RIDE, Mr. Abbott was a partner in the law firm of Asquith, Mahoney & Robinson, where he represented several Rhode Island school districts in the areas of public policy, special education, civil rights, and labor law. He holds an M.Ed. in Educational Policy and is a former public school teacher and Outward Bound course director.

Carrie Amon has "lived" education for 25 years. She began as a New York City elementary school teacher and later became a staff developer specializing in teaching literacy through the content areas. Eager to apply her new professional knowledge, she joined the Mamaroneck Schools 12 years ago, putting into classroom practice the innovative ideas and philosophies she had acquired. Seven years ago she became an administrator at Mamaroneck Avenue School, where she continues her learning and leadership today. She considers herself fortunate to work with a supportive community that is open to change, a faculty willing to continuously reflect together on their practice, and eager students with open minds.

Jonathan Bertfield has been developing educational technology products since the early 1990s. In the role of Producer or Executive Producer, he has led the development of more than 20 titles for the consumer and school markets. His credits include Reader Rabbit from the Learning Company, National Geographic archives from Broderbund, and Scholastic's Read 180. At the time of contributing to this project, he was a product management consultant at SchoolNet. He is a founder and currently VP of Product Development at Readio Network, developing a groundbreaking reading product for the consumer market.

Cornelia Brunner, Interim Director of the EDC's Center for Children and Technology, has been involved in the research, production, and teaching of educational technology in a variety of subject areas for 40 years. In addition to conducting research projects about the relationship between learning, teaching, and technology, she has designed and implemented educational materials incorporating technologies to support inquiry-based learning and teaching in science, social studies, media literacy, and the arts. During the past 40 years, Dr. Brunner also has been an industry consultant for the design of educational and entertainment products for children of all ages. She holds a Ph.D. in developmental psychology from Columbia University.

Fred Carrigg is a Special Assistant to the Commissioner for Literacy in the New Jersey Department of Education. His responsibilities include oversight of the Abbott-mandated Intensive Early Literacy program in Grades Pre-K–3, and the Literacy is Essential to Adolescent Development and Success (LEADS) middle-grades initiative for Grades 4–8. He is also in charge of the new IDEAL K–4 literacy initiative in the non-Abbott districts. From 2002 until December 2003, he was the New Jersey Director of Reading First. From 1989 to 2002, Fred was the Executive Director for Academic Programs in Union City, New Jersey. Fred has a B.A. in foreign languages from Montclair State and an Ed.M. in Intercultural Education from Rutgers University.

Jere Confrey is the Joseph D. Moore Distinguished Professor in Mathematics Education at North Carolina State University. She was formerly a Professor of Mathematics Education at Washington University in St. Louis. She was Vice Chairman of the Mathematics Sciences Education Board, National Academy of Sciences (1998-2004). She chaired the NRC Committee, which produced *On Evaluating Curricular Effectiveness*, and was a co-author on the NRC's *Scientific Research in Education*. She was a co-founder of the UTEACH program for secondary math and science teacher preparation at the University of Texas in Austin, and was the founder of the SummerMath program for young women at Mount Holyoke College and co-founder of SummerMath for Teachers. She co-authored the software Function Probe, Graph N Glyphs, and sets of interactive diagrams. She has served as vice-president of the International Group for the Psychology of Mathematics Education, chair of the SIG-Research in Mathematics Education. Dr. Confrey has taught school at the elementary, secondary, and post-secondary levels. She received a Ph.D. in mathematics education from Cornell University.

Katherine Conoly was born in Tibu, Colombia, South America, and earned her Doctorate of Education in Bilingual Education at Texas A&M University–Kingsville. Dr. Conoly has taught at the elementary and secondary school level and as an adjunct professor at Texas A&M University in Corpus Christi, Texas. She served as an elementary and middle school principal for 13 years, during which her schools received numerous state and national recognitions. Currently, Dr. Conoly is the Executive Director for Instructional Support for the Corpus Christi Independent School District and oversees the offices of special education, guidance and counseling, student support services, student health services, and grant program management. She also has served as the District's Executive Director for Technology Services and Research and Executive Director for Curriculum and Instruction.

Valerie M. Crawford is a senior scientist at the Center for Technology in Learning at SRI International. Her research investigates the design and effectiveness of technology-based learning environments to enhance learning, the use of handheld computer devices in learning and performance support, and learning in immersive virtual environments. She also conducts research on adaptive expertise in professional practice. She holds a Ph.D. in developmental psychology from Clark University.

Chris Dede is the Timothy E. Wirth Professor of Learning Technologies at Harvard's Graduate School of Education. His fields of scholarship include emerging technologies, policy, and leadership. His funded research includes a grant from the National Science Foundation to aid middle school students learning science via shared virtual environments and a Star Schools grant from the U.S. Department of Education to help high school students improve their math and literacy skills using wireless mobile devices to create augmented reality simulations. Chris has served as a member of the National Academy of Sciences Committee on Foundations of Educational and Psychological Assessment, a member of the U.S. Department of Education's Expert Panel on Technology, and International Steering Committee member for the Second International Technology in Education Study. He serves on advisory boards and commissions for PBS TeacherLine, the Partnership for 21st Century Skills, the Pittsburgh Science of Learning Center, and several federal research grants.

John Gasko is a second-year doctoral student in Educational Policy and Planning at the University of Texas at Austin. He is a former teacher and administrator in the Edgewood school district in San Antonio, Texas. His research interests include data-informed inquiry and capacity-building in schools, the impact of globalization on educational systems, organizational learning, and various facets of Pre-K–16 educational policy, from school readiness to high school-to-college transitions. He presently serves as the Director of Research and Public Policy for the Children's Defense Fund/Texas Early Childhood Education Coalition in Austin.

Greg Gunn is Chief Scientist and Co-Founder of Wireless Generation, a leading provider of assessment and data solutions to K–12 schools nationwide. He currently leads the company's efforts in data mining and data analytics to help customers achieve the greatest instructional impact using student achievement data. Prior to founding Wireless Generation, Greg was Product Manager for InterDimensions, a Web solution firm. Greg has extensive experience teaching mathematics, physics, and computer science to all ages from Grade 4 through postgraduate. Greg received his MBA and Masters of Electrical Engineering at the Massachusetts Institute of Technology. He also attended Oxford University as a Rhodes Scholar.

Juliette Heinze has worked in the field of education for 10 years as an educator, a researcher, and a writer. Ms. Heinze taught elementary school in Costa Rica with the WorldTeach program, and second-grade bilingual students in the Los Angeles Unified School District. She received her Masters in Education and Sociology from Teachers College, Columbia University. For the past 4 years Ms. Heinze has worked on a variety of research and evaluation projects at EDC's Center for Children and Technology, with a particular specialization in projects that focus on literacy and data-based decision making. For the past 3 years she has worked on the New Mexico Reading First evaluation.

Margaret Honey is Senior Vice President for Strategic Initiatives and Research for Wireless Generation, a Brooklyn-based software development company that has pioneered the use of handheld-to-Web technology for formative assessment in Pre-K–6 classrooms. Her career in education research spans 25 years during which time she has published scores of papers; overseen numerous large multiyear projects and initiatives developing, implementing, and evaluating creative applications of digital technology and media to K–12 school environments; and testified before Congress, state legislatures, and federal panels on education technology policy. Prior to joining Wireless Generation she was a Vice President at the Education Development Center and Director of the Center for Children and Technology. Her work at EDC also involved co-directing the Northeast and Islands Regional Education Laboratory.

Naomi Hupert has worked at the EDC's Center for Children and Technology for 13 years. Her current work focuses on literacy, addressing the needs of students who struggle to meet grade-level benchmarks in literacy, and supporting teachers to provide high-quality instruction to their students. She is the co-director of two evaluation projects: the formative and summative evaluation of the 3-year New Mexico Reading First program and the IBM Reinventing Education 3 national evaluation. She holds a Masters of Science in Education, with a specialization in literacy and language-related learning disabilities, from Bank Street College of Education.

Sherry P. King is Director of Field Services at America's Choice, Inc., a subsidiary of the National Center on Education and the Economy. Prior to that she served as Superintendent of the Mamaroneck (New York) and Croton-Harmon (Croton-on-Hudson, New York) school systems, as well as a high school principal, assistant principal, and English teacher. She was a senior researcher on Great Strides: A Study of New Small Schools in Chicago (Bank Street College, 2000). She has published a number of articles and book chapters, including "A Science Experiment That Shows All 8th Graders Can Reach Higher Standards" (Educational Leadership, November 2004), "Tracking Data on Student Achievement: Questions and Lessons" (Information Technology for Schools, Jossey-Bass, 2001), and Leadership in the 21st Century: Using Feedback to Maintain Focus and Direction (*ASCD Yearbook*, 1999).

Mary Jane Kurabinski currently serves as Language Arts Supervisor, Pre-K–5, for the Elizabeth Public Schools in New Jersey, with responsibility for 19 elementary schools. She served briefly as a Vice Principal, opening a 750-student Pre-K–8 building, and just prior to that as Coordinator–Urban Literacy for the New Jersey Department of Education. Her experience includes coaching and teaching in urban districts in New Jersey. She holds a Masters in Urban Education, Administration and Supervision from New Jersey City University.

Daniel Light, a Senior Researcher at EDC's Center for Children and Technology, has a background in qualitative and quantitative sociological research methodologies. His work focuses on the social issues of school reform and technology integration across school systems both in the United States and internationally. He is currently project manager for the evaluation of an international professional development program supporting the introduction of technology and project-based approaches into teaching and learning. Dr. Light received his Ph.D. in Sociology from the New School for Social Research. He was an invited researcher for a year at the Universidad Autónoma de Madrid, Spain. Daniel also received an M.A. in International Affairs from Carleton University, Canada, and an M.A. in Sociology and Historical Studies from the New School for Social Research.

Lisa Long is currently Director of Curriculum, Instruction and Technology Integration for the Tucson Unified School District in Arizona. In this position she is responsible for all curriculum and technology initiatives throughout this K–12 district. Prior to this role, Ms. Long was Coordinator of Educational Technology, a technology trainer, and a primary teacher.

Ellen B. Mandinach is a Senior Project Director at the CNA Corporation in Alexandria, VA. She formerly was a Principal Research Scientist and Associate Director for Research at the Education Development Center's Center for Children and Technology. She was the co-organizer of the Wingspread Conference on which this book is based. She received her Ph.D. in Educational Psychology from Stanford University in 1984. Dr. Mandinach has done extensive work in the field of educational technology and has a background in research methodology and measurement. Dr. Mandinach's research has focused on the implementation and impact on learning of computer environments and the measurement of individual differences in cognitive and affective processes. She serves on several editorial boards, is a frequent reviewer for IES and NSF, has been a program chair for AERA, and was the program chair for APA's Division of Educational Psychology for the 2007 conference. She is the division's president-elect.

Michael Merrill has taught American literature at UCLA and Georgia Tech. He has helped develop educational products for Turner Learning, Pearson Learning, and SchoolNet.

Liane Moody is a doctoral student at the Harvard Graduate School of Education. She previously worked for the Boston Plan for Excellence where she helped design and implement MyBPS Assessment, an online assessment data analysis tool for the Boston Public Schools. Liane also taught a course on data-based decision making in the Leadership and Education Department at the University of Massachusetts, Boston. Her research investigates the role of adult development in professional life.

William R. Penuel is Director of Evaluation Research at the Center for Technology in Learning at SRI International. His research focuses on the ways that technology can support the improvement of teaching and learning in science and mathematics reform initiatives in schools and community settings. He is the author, with Barbara Means and Chris Padilla, of *The Connected School: Technology and Learning in High School* (2001). He holds a Ph.D. in Developmental Psychology from Clark University and an Ed.M. in Human Development and Psychology from Harvard University.

Luz M. Rivas is currently a program manager at the California Institute of Technology where she manages an outreach program for high school students interested in science and engineering. Prior to the position at Caltech, Luz was a research associate at the EDC's Center for Children and Technology where she worked on a project focusing on creating an evaluation framework for data-driven instructional decision making. Before that, Luz was a research associate at the American Museum of Natural History. Luz holds a

Bachelor of Science in Electrical Engineering from the Massachusetts Institute of Technology and a Masters in Technology in Education from Harvard University.

Mark S. Schlager is Associate Director of Learning Communities at the Center for Technology in Learning at SRI International. Dr. Schlager's research focuses on the application of cognitive and social learning theories to the development of online strategies and technologies for teaching, teacher education, and professional development. He also consults for commercial firms and nonprofit organizations on the design and implementation of online learning. Dr. Schlager earned a Ph.D. in Cognitive Psychology from the University of Colorado, Boulder.

John Stewart is a technical executive at Wireless Generation, where he heads the technology infrastructure group and is a founding member of the analytics group. Prior to his position at Wireless Generation, he ran a boutique software consulting company in New York that serviced clients mostly in the media and publishing industries. John is also a Ph.D. student in Linguistics at the CUNY Graduate Center and holds a B.A. from Yale.

Sam Stringfield is a Distinguished University Scholar and Director of the Nystrand Center for Excellence in Education in the College of Education and Human Development at the University of Louisville. He is a founding editor of the *Journal of Education for Students Placed At Risk (JESPAR)* and is currently serving as the acting chair of the Educational and Psychological Counseling Department. His research focuses on designs for improving programs within schools, for improving whole schools, for improving systemic supports for schools serving disadvantaged students, and international comparisons of school effects. Prior to coming to the University of Louisville, Dr. Stringfield directed the systemic supports for school reform program of the Center for Research on the Education of Students Placed at Risk at Johns Hopkins University.

Ronald Thorpe is Vice President and Director of Education at Thirteen/WNET, the nation's flagship public broadcasting station. Throughout his career as a teacher, administrator, and foundation executive, and in public television, he has focused on issues related to professional development of teachers. The author of numerous articles and the editor of *The First Year as Principal* (Heinemann, 1995), he is a graduate of Harvard College and has a masters degree and doctorate from the Harvard Graduate School of Education.

Yukie Toyama is an educational researcher at the Center for Technology in Learning at SRI International. She has conducted research and evaluation focused on technologies for improving learning and teaching, teacher education, and professional development for more than 7 years. Together with Valerie Crawford, she is investigating adaptive expertise in professional practice. She holds an M.A. in Education from Stanford University.

Jeffrey C. Wayman is an Assistant Professor in the Department of Educational Administration at the University of Texas at Austin. His research focuses on the effective use of student data to provide information and inform practice at all levels of the educational system. Recent work in this area surrounds teacher use of data, policy influences on school data use, and technological supports for school data use. Other research interests include school dropout and research methodology.

Viki M. Young is a researcher in SRI International's Center for Education Policy. Her work focuses on district and school reform, teacher development, and teachers' use of data using mixed methods, and applies organizational and policy approaches to research problems. She holds a Ph.D. in Education Policy from Stanford University.

Index

285